Guarded

by Angels

Guarded by Angels

| HOW MY FATHER AND UNCLE SURVIVED HITLER AND CHEATED STALIN |

by ALAN ELSNER

with a foreword by DAVID CESARANI

YAD VASHEM AND
THE HOLOCAUST SURVIVORS' MEMOIRS PROJECT
New York • Jerusalem

This book is published by Yad Vashem, the Holocaust Martyrs' and Heroes' Remembrance Authority, c/o American Society for Yad Vashem, 500 Fifth Avenue, 42nd floor, New York, New York 10110-4299, and P.O.B. 3477, Jerusalem 91034, Israel

www.yadvashem.org

and

The Holocaust Survivors' Memoirs Project of the World Jewish Congress, 501 Madison Avenue, New York, New York 10022

in association with the World Federation of Bergen-Belsen Associations, Inc.

The Holocaust Survivors' Memoirs Project, an initiative of Nobel Peace Prize laureate Elie Wiesel, was launched through a generous grant from Random House Inc., New York, New York.

Cover photos and all other photographs courtesy of Alan Elsner.

Library of Congress Cataloging-in-Publication Data
Elsner, Alan.
    Guarded by angels : how my father and uncle survived Hitler and cheated Stalin / by Alan Elsner.
        p. cm.
    ISBN 0-9760739-1-9 (pbk.)
1. Olesiuk, Eugene. 2. Olesiuk, Mark, 1923- 3. Jews–Poland–Nowy Sącz–Biography. 4. World War, 1939-1945–Biography. 5. World War, 1939-1945–Prisoners and prisons, Soviet. 6. Nowy Sącz (Poland)–Biography. I. Title.
    DS135.P63A1366 2005
    940.54´7247´0922438–dc22

2004065646

Printed in Jerusalem, Israel.

DEDICATION

For Micha and Noam, the next generation

Try to remember some details. For the world
is filled with people who were torn from their sleep
with no one to mend the tear.

Yehuda Amichai

CONTENTS

FOREWORD

by Professor David Cesarani

Every story of Jewish survival to have emerged from the years of Nazi persecution and mass murder is unique and most contain episodes that cause the jaw to drop in amazement. Tragedy, loss, resistance, lucky escapes, cunning, quick thinking and resilience are the characteristic elements of survivor memoirs. But few have the quality of adventure that distinguishes the odyssey of Gene and Mark Elsner. As described in this valuable new book, these young brothers from Nowy Sącz endured and outwitted not one but two vile, totalitarian regimes.

First they were seized by the Russians and deported to the Gulag where they overcame incredible hardship in arctic conditions. Despite efforts to separate them they stuck together. After the German invasion of the Soviet Union, in June 1941, they were miraculously released so that they could join other Polish internees who were being set free on Stalin's command to join a new Polish army fighting the Nazis. Gene and Mark and their cousin Henek took months to work their way southwards on an epic journey that took them through Tashkent, Samarkand, and Bukhara. The description of that odyssey provides us with an invaluable snapshot of what life was like deep within the Soviet heartland during wartime. Eventually the brothers reached the Caucasus where they found a haven of relative tranquility.

However, in the summer of 1942 the German army burst into the Caucasus and the youngsters were again plunged into peril. And, once again, they were saved by their quick wittedness. In one of the most astonishing chapters in any survivor narrative, Gene became a translator for the occupying German army. From this vantage point he was able to observe an endless string of atrocities. But he had to stay silent and remain focused on keeping himself and his brother alive. Amidst this maelstrom Gene enjoyed romance and the unlikely friendship of a

German commandant. This story is as much about family and brotherhood, and a boy growing to manhood, as it is a testimony to the cruelty of the Soviet and Nazi regimes. But it also gives us a precious historical insight into the Nazi occupation of the Caucusus.

Gene and Mark also personify the Jewish will to resist Nazi oppression under the most adverse circumstances. During the German occupation of the Caucasus Gene made contact with the resistance and actively aided them. After the Germans pulled out in 1943, following the debacle at Stalingrad, he and his brother enrolled in a Polish brigade fighting alongside the Red Army. Gene then fought his way across Europe and was about to take part in the final push against the Third Reich when he was wounded in action.

This story underlines the difficulty that Polish Jews faced in organizing any kind of resistance against not one but two tyrannies that, one after another, pulverized their communities. It shows how the ties of family could both empower and imperil. Gene and Mark were unusually resourceful but their hair-raising escapes tested the limits of willpower, intelligence and physical strength. How much harder it was for the very young, the old, the sick or families determined to stay intact, to survive—let alone contemplate escape or resistance.

Most of Gene's family perished. It is another mark of his resilience that he was determined to start a new life in Britain, but never to forget where he came from. He passed on to his children a keen appreciation of the past and a determination to remember. This book, written by his son who went on to build a distinguished international journalistic career, also chronicles the process by which memory is transmitted from generation to generation.

In the past twenty years, countless memoirs by survivors have appeared. This one stands out as one of the best, not only because of the amazing story it tells but also thanks to the vivid writing that grabs the reader's interest and never lets go.

After his retirement Gene and his brother settled in Israel in adjacent houses in Zichron Ya'acov. They remained side by side, as once they had been brothers united against adversity. I have been privileged to meet Gene Elsner on several occasions, in Britain as well as in Israel, and his story has both humbled and inspired me every time I heard it. Now through this engaging and powerful book it will become a source of inspiration to readers around the world.

Royal Holloway, University of London, January 2005.

CHAPTER 1

Ambush

My father was killed on my birthday.

More precisely, I was born on the ninth anniversary of his presumed death. He has his obituary to prove it. For him, my arrival that day was more than a coincidence. It was nothing less than a symbol of his personal victory over Hitler, over Stalin, over fate. As my delivery approached, it seemed not only natural but also inevitable that my birth would occur on the fateful anniversary. It closed the circle. On that date, death had brushed my father with its wings and held him in its talons. For years, my father had avoided those memories. But as he paced the hospital corridor, smoking furiously, he found himself back in the forests of northern Germany, reliving the ambush. As he listened for the first cry of the newborn, he heard the shouts of dying comrades. He sat down, overcome by memories. Suddenly he was a Polish officer again, about to embark on a desperate mission.

It was February 1945, and the snow that carpeted the borderlands of Poland and Germany was beginning to melt, baring a dismal, dripping forest landscape. It was a thinly populated area of boundless woods bisected by narrow, mud-churned lanes choked by military traffic. After a whirlwind advance through western Poland, the Red Army under Marshal Zhukov had crossed the old German frontier a week earlier. But the offensive had run out of steam in the face of stiff opposition, and the Soviets were regrouping. Command cars and motorcycles skidded down slushy roads, weaving their way past an endless column of trucks and requisitioned vehicles crawling toward the front. Tanks rumbled slowly forward; heavy artillery drawn by tractors lurched into position for the next offensive. The Russian steamroller was about to move again, this time with Berlin in its sights.

For tired Soviet troops, it had been a relentless two-year trek from the heart of their violated homeland. That winter, they had battled their way through ruined Poland, liberating flattened cities and blackened remains of deserted villages. Now, they were encamped on German soil, eager to give the enemy a taste of his own medicine.

Lieutenant Eugene Olesiuk—Gene to his friends—shared that desire. He was lucky to be alive. There had been many times in the past six years when he thought he might not make it. Of course, Olesiuk was not his real name. Two years earlier he had shed that and his Jewish identity to stay alive under Nazi occupation in a far away Cossack village in the Caucasus. Hardened beyond his 26 years, he was an artillery battery commander in the Tadeusz Kościuszko brigade. Though its soldiers wore Polish uniforms, they were under the firm operational and political control of the Red Army. Most of the top commanders were Russians of Polish ancestry or simply Russians who happened to have Polish-sounding names. Lt. Olesiuk was in charge of 70 officers and men, assorted armaments, and a number of 152 mm cannons—some of the heaviest guns in the Soviet armory.

A few photographs survive from that time. One shows him staring at the camera with hard eyes, wearing a military cap. His steely determination comes through even in the faded black-and-white print. It was tough face; experience had made it so.

That evening, Gene attended a briefing about the next morning's operation. Emerging into the cold, he sniffed the air, and then began crossing the camp in search of his younger brother. The light was fading; low clouds pressed down, dark and heavy. Sidestepping puddles, Gene's attention was drawn by the sound of a violin. He grinned. That had to be Mark. The music came to him muffled by the damp, as if through a closed door.

Gene stretched out his arms as if to hug Mark, and then drew back. He tended to play the big brother and constantly had to remind himself that Mark was a battle-hardened soldier and veteran of several campaigns. Five years younger than Gene, he bore only a slight resemblance to his brother in appearance and almost none in temperament. Somewhat smaller in stature, he was more cautious and conciliatory. Gene watched him immersed in the violin, as if the war was continents away.

"I'd wrap your fiddle well in this damp weather," he said after a while. "There won't be much time to play in the next few days."

"I know. The camp is full of rumors," Mark said. Everyone knew the next big push could be only a short time away.

"Word has finally come down. We move out tomorrow morning, your battery and mine," Gene said.

"Where are we going?" asked Mark.

Gene unfolded a map and pointed to a spot about seven miles to the north. "We're setting up an observation point here," he said. "I suppose you'll get your own detailed briefing later."

Mark frowned at the map. "Where are the Germans supposed to be?" he asked.

Gene shrugged. Since the army had crossed the German border, the front had been so fluid that it was impossible to pinpoint all the enemy's positions. Intelligence provided only rough estimates and guesses. The Germans had set up their main line well to the west along the Oder River, but had left numerous detachments behind for delaying actions. "Intelligence thinks the Germans are here," Gene said, pointing to some positions along the shores of three small lakes to the south. "But nobody knows exactly. And this map we were issued at the briefing doesn't tell us much. We just have to be careful. This is perfect ambush country."

Mark disliked uncertainty, especially when it came to maps. As an officer in charge of a reconnaissance and communications platoon, maps and topography were his business. "It's getting chilly," he muttered, reaching for the violin case. "I'd better put the violin away before the cold wrecks it."

Both he and Gene were acutely aware that the war had grown much fiercer since they had entered Germany territory. Until recently, they had been operating in Poland among a population that hailed them as liberators. Now, the Germans were defending their own soil and a terrain they knew intimately. Their resistance had stiffened noticeably since the Red Army had crossed the border. Hitler, still ranting in his Berlin bunker, had ordered his troops to sell their lives dearly by inflicting maximum casualties. And even now there was no shortage of Germans ready to follow their Führer.

Mark closed the violin case. "So we move forward tomorrow," he said.

"Right. I'll be taking 25 men in the truck to set up the forward position, somewhere around here," Gene said, indicating an area on the map. "I'll dump the telephone cables by the side of the road along the way. You'll be following on foot and laying the lines to the batteries."

"You'd better take some of my gear in the truck, and take the violin. Just be careful with it," Mark said.

"Yes, yes, don't worry, your treasure will be safe with me."

"I'll see you tomorrow afternoon then," Mark said.

"Right, tomorrow afternoon."

"I'll play you that piece I was practicing then."

"I can't wait. I'll send an orderly over for your gear. Get a good night's sleep," said Gene. He picked up the precious violin and was swallowed by the night.

Mark watched him disappear before turning to his own quarters. Later, reflecting on their conversation, he wished he had said something more significant. One said good-bye too easily. There had been many partings—with his parents, his girlfriend, his cousin, and now his brother. "See you tomorrow, see you next week, see you soon," one would say. Lightly uttered words, they floated into the air and evaporated. Only in retrospect did they acquire unbearable weight.

The next day, February 7, dawned cheerless as only a north European winter day can be. The temperature had risen a degree or two overnight, but it still felt cold. The damp worked its way under the soldiers' greatcoats. The snow was wet and slushy under a leaden sky; trucks had mashed parts of the road into a stew. There were still some patches of ice about, and the tractors pulling the big guns slithered from side to side. Officers yelled at the drivers to be careful; if one of the cannons overturned, operations would be held up for hours.

Gene's troops gathered early. "Keep your eyes open out there," he heard someone shout as he swung himself into the truck next to the driver. "Reports of snipers ahead." He stowed the violin under his seat and tossed Mark's other things into the back.

For the first mile or two, the road was clogged with trucks moving as slowly as a funeral procession. Gene's men dozed in the back. At prearranged intervals he ordered them to drop a roll of telephone cable for Mark and his men to pick up. Otherwise there was little conversation. There was a bottleneck across a narrow bridge, and it took an hour to get across. There were fewer vehicles on the other side. Almost immediately, Gene heard shots. "Snipers," several men shouted nervously, ducking. Gene swore but stayed upright. "Go faster," he ordered the driver.

Another mile down the road more shots came from the woods.

A bullet whined overhead, sounding ominously close. The countryside was flat, crisscrossed by shallow gullies. The trees were as bare as skeletons, their branches gnarled and twisted. Ditches lined the road on either side. They came to a junction. Gene glanced down at the map. "Here, turn right here," he ordered the driver.

Three miles down the road they reached another intersection, where an old German hunting lodge stood beside a stream. A soldier in a Polish uniform was waiting. Gene recognized him as a member of Mark's battery. "What's happening?" he called out.

"You've got to go straight on here, sir," the man replied.

Gene consulted the map. "But we're supposed to turn right," he objected.

"There are snipers that way. I've been sent here to warn you. There's another road you can take a mile or so to the right. I've just come from there," the soldier replied.

"Shouldn't there be warning signs on the road?"

"They haven't had time to put them up yet."

"Very well." Gene ordered his men to drop a roll of cable at the crossroads for Mark's men to collect. Then he motioned to the driver, and they rolled slowly down the road.

Gene was uneasy as soon as they pulled away from the hunting lodge. There was no traffic at all on the new road. "This can't be right," he muttered. He took another look at the map, trying to figure it out. Could the solider at the crossroads have been mistaken? It seemed unlikely, but still.... The road was unnaturally quiet. He had an empty feeling in his stomach. "Slow down a bit," he told the driver. "I want to see if there are telephone wires about." There weren't any. He was about to order the driver to turn around when he saw two soldiers in Polish uniforms walking down the road in his direction. "This must be the right way," he thought with relief. They drove on.

In the back of the truck, the soldiers had come to life. They knew they would soon arrive at the observation point. Someone made a joke, raising a general laugh. They went round the corner. Gene propped the map up against the windscreen and leaned forward, looking for the turn that was supposed to be ahead. Suddenly the woods on either side erupted. "Go full speed, pass them," he yelled at the driver.

Too late! A bullet grazed the back of Gene's head, hitting the driver in the ear. He heard the thud, blood showered over him. The driver slumped forward; the truck stopped. They were immobile, sitting ducks in a shooting gallery. What do you think about in the moment of your death? Nothing, there isn't time. He heard shouting and screams. It was faint, unreal. Soldiers reached for weapons and began firing back. Gene managed to wrench out his revolver and get off one shot at the unseen enemy. But that was all. A bullet thudded into him with tremendous force, then another. He was thrown sideways and forward. He dropped his revolver. He was falling, sinking into blackness. Another bullet hit him somewhere, and yet another, he could not tell where. He slumped to the floor of the cabin. He was drowning. The shots were fading; he could not hear them.

CHAPTER 2

Origins

How did Gene and Mark come to find themselves in that godforsaken German forest in 1945? That story begins with the Nazi invasion of Poland in September 1939. Their story begins some 20 years earlier, at the close of World War I.

Gene and Mark grew up in Nowy Sącz, a small town in southern Poland. But Gene was actually born in Russia. His birth could be called one of the lesser, unintended consequences of World War I. Before the war, there had been no Poland, and Nowy Sącz was ruled from Vienna as part of the Austro-Hungarian Empire. Gene's father, Adolf, had fought in the Austrian army on the eastern front and was captured by the Russians. As the war ended, Adolf washed up in a town near Odessa, where he met a young girl named Bertha and fell in love. Soon, Eugene arrived.

When the war ended, Adolf brought his young family home. Within weeks of their return, he was called to war again, this time to fight for Poland against the invading armies of the Soviet Union. Gene's earliest memory is of seeing his father off at the station. There was a dizzy glimpse of a gyrating world from an impossible height as he was lifted onto Adolf's shoulders and a blur of sensations: smoke, soldiers, train whistles, shouts, tears, all mixed in a confusing jumble. Then he was rubbing against his father's rough mustache, brushing his lips, falling back to earth, set down on rickety legs. Adolf returned a few months later, a hero. The Russian advance was halted just before Warsaw, and Polish independence was preserved.

Nowy Sącz was a fairly typical Polish town. Its population was about 35,000; about one-third were Jews. Life revolved around the bustling market square with its neo-baroque town hall. Nearby was the Jewish quarter, a labyrinth of cobbled lanes, muddy alleyways, and culs-de-sac where beggars pleaded for alms and Hasidim with beards and twisted sidelocks congregated in black coats. Relations between Christians and Jews were usually calm. They led largely separate lives, meeting only on the weekly battlefield of the market to haggle over goods. But antisemitism was pervasive and accepted. It was preached from the pulpits; it was in the air they breathed.

Adolf was easygoing. Prematurely gray with a bristling mustache, he liked to meet old army cronies to drink, play cards, and tell war stories. He was already moving away from Orthodox Judaism before the war, but his drift was confirmed when he married Bertha. The marriage led to a rift with the rest of his family. They resented the young woman from Russia and referred to her disdainfully as "the Muscovite." She spoke no Yiddish, and when a whisper went around that she might not be Jewish, Adolf found himself cut out of his inheritance.

Adolf opened a butcher shop in a single-story house on the outskirts of town. The house belonged to his brother-in-law, Jacob Klafter, who lived in the back of the building with his family. Adolf's family occupied the front section next to the shop. Mark was born in 1923, and a third son, Nunek, followed two years later. It was a happy, boisterous household. The three boys were often joined by Klafter's eldest son, Henek. He was a year older than Mark, and the two became as close as brothers. In fact, Mark was much closer to Henek than to Gene. It was the war that brought Gene and Mark together. Even then it required much adversity and shared danger to forge a relationship of equals. Nearly five years older than Mark, Gene was intent on playing the role of mentor. It took a while for him to appreciate Mark's qualities, his inherent toughness.

Gene took after his mother. From her he inherited those remarkable blue eyes and a persistence that occasionally spilled over into pigheadedness. She was very young, wide-eyed, and bewildered when she encountered hostility and ridicule in a strange country. But Bertha would not be subdued for long. She soon won respect where love and affection were denied her. It was Bertha who decreed that her sons would not go to Jewish schools. Instead, they would receive the best available secular Polish education. Though Jews had lived in Poland for centuries, the majority spoke Yiddish as their mother tongue; many neither spoke nor understood Polish. In Gene's family, it was the other way around. The boys grew up among Poles, having little contact with Orthodox Judaism.

Nowy Sącz lay in a valley, surrounded by undulating foothills of the Carpathian Mountains. Gene developed a lifelong passion for those mountains. He explored their slopes, dotted in late summer with hundreds of haystacks. He scaled peaks and roamed valleys blanketed by a patchwork of wheat fields. He fished the fast mountain river that flowed through the town. On warm summer days, he often plunged into its frigid waters and emerged, his heart racing with exhilaration, his body shivering with the cold joy of being alive.

While Gene spent his youth outdoors, Mark began his love affair with the violin and learned that achieving beauty requires dogged perseverance. He discovered a talent for drawing, acquiring respect for straight lines and precise lengths and angles. His diary charted his progress in handwriting so microscopic that it required a magnifying glass to decipher.

There were only a few Jews in the high school that Gene and Mark attended. Many Poles at that time claimed to be able to recognize a Jew just by looking at him or at least by his Yiddish accent. But the brothers did not fit the stereotype. They spoke the Polish of educated Poles. They were both excellent athletes, confounding the popular wisdom that Jews were no good at sports. They were also fluent in German. Gene had a pen pal in Germany, a girl his own age. They exchanged long letters about culture and philosophy. Suddenly, in 1934 or 1935, the tone of her letters changed. She started preaching about German racial superiority and the evil effects of Jews on society. The correspondence lost its charm.

At 15, Gene joined Akiba, a Zionist youth movement. Within a year, he was elected troop leader. Even at that age, he had a flair for leadership. He was not tall. Full grown, he stood about five feet eight inches. But people were drawn to him; he enjoyed authority and they were happy to follow his lead. With his black wavy hair and easy smile, he seemed to have everything going for him.

Nusia Chanales, a fellow Zionist from another town, certainly thought so when she met Gene in 1935. Nusia was bright and vivacious; an innocent romance soon developed. Her home in Sanok was about 100 miles to the east, so the two met only on school holidays. But they wrote each other every week.

In 1936, when he was 18, Gene left home to attend the Jagiellonian University in Kraków. Founded in the fourteenth century, it was Poland's most prestigious university and one of the oldest in Europe. It was also fervently nationalistic, rigidly conservative, and resolutely Catholic. Antisemitism was endemic. There were serious brawls between Jews and Poles at the beginning of each academic year, when the antisemites would try to prevent Jews from registering for courses.

Gene studied hard but he also found time for Zionist activity. Akiba had a farm just outside the city where they trained youngsters who wanted to settle in Palestine as agricultural workers. Gene organized a physical fitness and self-defense program. He pushed himself and his trainees hard. They needed to be tough for what awaited them if they ever got to Palestine.

Nusia came to Kraków to be with Gene in his second year of university. She lived with her uncle, only a few blocks from his dormitory, and the two were together almost every day. Dark-eyed, uninhibited, full of pluck and mischief, Nusia was in love and did not care who knew it. The two of them often wandered, hand in hand, around Kraków, down tree-lined paths surrounding the old city walls. One of their favorite places was the great hill of the Wawel, where the medieval castle and cathedral stood. Nusia and Gene would sit on a ledge overlooking the Vistula River, which flowed in a wide bend beneath them, dreamy and unhurried. Gene would pretend to study and steal kisses.

That year, Europe headed for the brink. Hitler occupied Austria in March 1938, and began the dismemberment of Czechoslovakia six months later. A sense of doom hung over Poland. Gene reached some important decisions. He quit philosophy and took up chemistry. He planned to emigrate to Palestine as soon as he graduated and wanted to arrive there with a useful profession. He began drifting apart from Nusia. If they stayed together, they would have probably married, but Gene was not sure he wanted that. He felt too young. They had several anguished conversations about their future, but it was clear they were heading nowhere. The relationship finally ended one bright spring morning on top of the Wawel, the river glistening in the background. Nusia bowed her head so that Gene would not see her tears.

"But why?" she finally asked, her voice catching.

"We've been over this again and again, Nusia. We're too young to marry." Behind them, the great bell of the cathedral began to strike the hour. All over Kraków, a host of lesser bells joined the chorus.

"But I love you. I always will," she lamented as the last echo of the last chime faded and died.

"It's not just us, it's the whole situation. The whole of Europe is going to hell," he replied, his voice strained but under control.

"That's just nonsense. If you really loved me, you wouldn't care." Gene pursed his lips obstinately. Nusia knew that expression. It meant he was unmovable. "I'll always love you," she said again hopelessly, turning away from him.

"We'll be friends, we'll stay in touch. I do care about you. We'll always be friends," he said. His words sounded banal but were destined to come true.

Summer 1939: Mark was trying to earn next year's school fees by working in the office of a graphic artist. Gene finished his exams and left for the Akiba farm to help with the harvest. August was hot and sunny as Europe waited. Then, a stunned world learned that Hitler had signed a non-aggression pact with his archenemy, Stalin. Poland's fate was sealed. On the morning of September 1, without a declaration of war, German troops invaded Poland. World War II had begun.

CHAPTER 3

First Encounter with the German Army

That morning, Gene was up before dawn to pick tomatoes. He was lifting a full basket when a jagged rock came whistling over the wall straight at him. That was not unusual; the peasants on the next farm often threw stones at them. The Poles made no secret of their hatred of their young Jewish neighbors. Most of the rocks landed harmlessly, but this one struck Gene just below his knee, tearing a deep gash in his leg. He crumpled to the ground in agony, clutching his leg as it spurted blood. His friends rushed up to help. One bent down to take a closer look. "This is deep," he muttered with concern. "What happened?" "It's that bastard next door," Gene gasped.

In the house, someone switched on the wireless. It was playing Chopin's *Polonaise,* a symbol of Polish national resistance. No one paid attention. One of the young men came back with water and a bandage and started cleaning the wound. Gene stifled a cry as the hot water touched him.

"This should be seen by a doctor," his friend said. "I'll put a bandage on for now to stop the bleeding." He tied it tight. "Lie still for a few minutes," he ordered.

"No, I'm fine; it's nothing," said Gene, grimacing with pain. He tried to get to his feet but found that he could not stand. Cursing, he lay down again, biting his lip, gazing up at the sky with watery, half-focused eyes. Suddenly he caught his breath. "What the hell is that?" he yelled. The others looked up. Warplanes were circling high above Kraków. Silver in the sunlight, they wheeled over the city. As they turned away, silent puffs of smoke rose from below. "They're bombing Kraków," somebody shouted in disbelief.

Gene could hardly move. They took him to the station by cart and bundled him onto a train to send him home. There was total confusion; the train kept starting and stopping. People rushed in and out of the carriages, shouting hysterically and cursing the Germans. Everyone wanted to know what was happening, but there were only wild rumors. Occasionally, planes flew overhead. People leaned out the windows to see if they were German or Polish. Gene's leg was throbbing; he was slightly feverish, and angry and frustrated. Eventually, evening fell. Peopled huddled, talking in muted anxious tones. The train kept up its stop-go progress; the drone of planes continued overhead.

The German blitzkrieg was in full spate. Much of the Polish air force had already been destroyed. Now the Germans had begun targeting rail lines and road transport, anything that moved. Fortunately for Gene, his train was not attacked. It pulled into Nowy Sącz by the middle of the next day. The station was crowded with men waiting to board. Wives and sweethearts stood crying on the platforms. Two soldiers helped Gene out of the railcar. There was more delay while he waited for a cart to take him home. He arrived to find his mother crying, her hair in disarray, and the house in an uproar.

"What's happening?" he asked.

"Oh Gene," she wailed, rushing to hug him. "Thank God you're here. It's Mark. But what have you done to your leg?"

"Never mind about my leg," he replied. "What's happened to Mark?"

His father answered, his face white and drawn. "He's been evacuated to the east," he said heavily. "They took around 50 teenagers, all the members of the high school military training squad. There's nothing to worry about. He's together with cousin Henek. They'll be fine." But his voice sounded weak and uncertain.

For the next few days, the town was in turmoil. Peopled huddled around radios. It was clear that the Germans were winning the war. Many townspeople, the Jews especially, were near panic, trying to decide whether to flee. With the border of Nazi-controlled Czechoslovakia only 20 miles away, it could be only days before the Germans arrived. But it was hard to leave one's home, one's friends, one's possessions, one's livelihood. How bad could the Germans be?

On the fifth day of the war, the radio broadcast an urgent appeal for all able-bodied men to report for military duty in Przemyśl, a town in eastern Poland. Gene sat upright. Adolf banged his fist on the table and jumped to his feet, his mustache bristling with excitement. "At last," he exclaimed. A second later, Henek's father Jacob burst into the room.

"Did you hear that? They're calling anybody who can fight," he said. He was a domineering man, blond and bull-like with the muscular shoulders of a wrestler.

"Right," said Adolf. "That means us. We must go."

"There's no time to lose. You prepare some food for the journey while I hitch up the horse and cart," Jacob said. He owned a small farm behind the house and several horses.

"Give me an hour, then we can be on our way," said Adolf.

"On your way where?" asked Bertha, coming into the room. Fourteen-year-old Nunek trailed behind her.

"To the east," said Adolf. "The radio just said. We're being called up."

"Called up? A couple of old men like you?" Bertha snorted, wiping her hands on her apron and placing them on her hips. "Your fighting days are over. What would you be needed for?"

"We're both experienced soldiers," Adolf said, drawing himself up to his full height. "We've seen a few things. Don't forget, I helped save Poland in 1920. Even if we don't fight, we can be useful in other ways. Poland needs veterans like us, especially at a time like this."

Bertha sat down heavily, suddenly realizing that he was serious. She had taken Mark's absence hard; she could not sleep at night and there were purple circles under her eyes. Usually so strong, she was powerless against this wartime madness. "What makes you think your presence is so important?" she asked skeptically. "As if two more or less will make a difference."

"Three more," Gene put in from his place on the couch. "I'm going too." Bertha turned to him open-mouthed.

"You can't even walk and you want to go fight the Germans," she said. "It is true, Gene," Adolf interjected. "You do have a chipped bone in your leg. The doctor said you should rest. Besides, I counted on you to look after Mama and Nunek."

"The leg will be fine in a week," Gene said, his mouth set. "I can't stay behind." Bertha looked at him, then at her husband, and sighed.

"Please understand Mama," Gene pleaded. "All my friends will go. I'd feel like a deserter if I stayed behind."

"Well maybe it's best if you do go. Maybe it will be better if you aren't here when the Germans come. So now let's talk about what needs to be done."

His mother was a wise and altogether remarkable woman, Gene thought, not for the first time.

They left that afternoon. Gene lay in the back of the cart; Adolf sat up front with Jacob. The road was clogged with refugees. Some were walking. Some drove rickety carts piled with suitcases and trunks, bags of clothes, carpets, tools, books, silver candlesticks, scrawny chickens in cages, and wailing children. A few automobiles crawled along as slow as oxen, their drivers honking in frustration. After a few hours they reached the village of Grybów. As they drove through, a crowd of Orthodox Jews rushed to join the procession. Some were carrying sacred Torah scrolls wrapped in richly embroidered velvet coverings. Their wives followed, some carrying babies, others clucking at their frightened children not to fall behind.

Suddenly, someone shouted a warning: "Strafing ahead, strafing ahead." The rumor scattered the crowd. Panic-stricken refugees rushed to take cover at the side of the road. Frightened horses neighed and whinnied, some of them trying to bolt with their heavy loads. Jacob's horse, an unusually placid creature, stood amid the commotion calmly cropping roadside grass. Eventually, everyone realized that it was a false alarm. It there was any strafing, it was out of sight and earshot. After a few minutes, people emerged, hastening to calm their horses. The column reformed and began to inch forward again.

"This is hopeless," said Jacob. "We'll never get anywhere at this pace, and it's dangerous as well."

"I know another way," Gene called out from the back. "I've been walking in these hills before. We can go on side roads and paths used by peasants. It's longer, but it will be quicker and safer."

"Right, then, what are we waiting for?" said Jacob. Soon they found a dirt track leading off the road. Away from the crowd, Adolf and Jacob's mood lightened. Usually, relations between them were frigid. Because Adolf had been cut out of his father's will, Jacob owned most of what would have been Adolf's inheritance. But that was forgotten in the excitement of the adventure. They sat side by side, joking and laughing like schoolboys.

The road climbed steeply, and Adolf clambered off the trap to walk. Finally they reached the summit and stopped to admire the view while the horse rested. To the west, the sun was sinking in the horizon like a smoldering orange ball. Dusk was lapping at their feet, silencing the birds, sucking the color from the trees and hills. They found a sheltered spot on the edge of the woods and settled down for the night.

Next day, they started early. Mist clung to the valleys with wispy white fingers until the sun stripped them away, laying bare the shades of early morning. As the day warmed, the colors deepened; the greens and tawny browns of beech forests and the tans and yellows of humped haystacks. Directed by Gene, they slowly progressed on winding dirt tracks, passing an occasional peasant shack.

"Are you sure you know where we are?" Jacob asked after a couple of hours.

"Don't worry, we're going the right way. In another mile or two, the track dips down to cross a stream," Gene replied from the back of the cart. His leg hurt, but he was enjoying the journey, breathing the golden autumnal light. The war seemed far away. Soon, they reached the stream.

"What now?" asked Jacob.

"We cross it and keep going. It'll be quite shallow at this time of the year," said Gene. Jacob clicked his tongue and the horse plodded forward, down the bank and into the gurgling water. Suddenly Gene heard a hum in the sky. Screwing up his eyes against the sun, he looked in the direction of the noise. "German plane," he yelled. "Quick, take cover. Hide in the bushes." Jacob sprang out of the cart, splashed through the water, and threw himself into the vegetation, but Adolf hung back. "What about you?" he screamed.

"I can't move," Gene shouted. "For God's sake, take cover." By now the plane was almost upon them. Adolf scrambled awkwardly out of the cart and dived under a bush. The plane swooped low over the horse and cart standing in the middle of the stream. There was a rush of air and a hot blast of sound. Gene clearly saw the German markings on the side of the plane. He even thought he caught a glimpse of the sun reflecting on the pilot's goggles. The plane wheeled in a narrow circle as the pilot surveyed the scene. Time seemed to stop. The horse stood motionless. Then the aircraft began to climb and was lost to sight behind a hill. The metallic screech of its engines slowly faded; the trees stopped vibrating. Somewhere nearby a bird sang. Gene lay on his back quite still, listening to the bubbling stream and the bird, watching a thick puffy cloud sail slowly over the pure morning sky.

"Gene, Gene, are you all right?" his father shouted.

Gene snapped out of his reverie. "I'm fine," he said.

"That was close," said Adolf.

"Not really," said Gene. "It wasn't worth his while wasting ammunition on two old men and a cripple."

The next evening, they trotted slowly into the small town of Jasło. There Gene had a friend from his Zionist organization, a girl named Sarah, who lived with her family near the town square.

"Gene," she cried when she saw him at the door standing on one leg, leaning against his father for support. "What are you doing here? And what's the matter with your leg?" He explained the situation. She and her mother were glad to welcome them.

"My father and brother have gone east to get away from the Germans," she said.

"We're going east ourselves. We'll only stay the night," said Gene. "We need to get an early start."

But they were not early enough. The next day, they awoke to the sound of marching boots and orders shouted in German. While they slept, a German infantry unit had taken possession of the town.

"Now what do we do?" asked Jacob when they gathered at Gene's bedside to discuss the situation.

"Go home," said Gene, who was still unable to take a step unsupported. "There's no chance we can get to Polish lines any more." Jacob looked across at Adolf. He nodded slowly, his face downcast.

"Right then," said Jacob. "I'll get the horse and cart." Before he could leave the room, Sarah and her mother burst in. "Quick, come with me," Sarah cried. "The Germans are going around town arresting Jewish men."

"This way, quickly," said her mother. "I'll show you where to hide."

"But what about Gene?" asked Adolf. Gene tried to stand but it was hopeless.

"Go with her," he urged, pushing his father toward the door. "It will take too long to get me downstairs."

"I can't leave you," Adolf cried.

"You must," Gene insisted. "Don't worry about me. They won't take me anywhere in this state." Adolf gave his son a stricken look but allowed himself to be hustled out the door by the two women. Gene lay back on his bed, cursing the peasant who had injured his leg. He glanced out the window and saw a young Polish boy pointing out the house to two German soldiers, who started crossing the street. Soon, there was a crash as they kicked in the front door.

Gene heard them searching the rooms downstairs. They found the two women and started shouting. Next came muffled, frightened replies in Polish. Then boots clattered up the stairs. The soldiers burst into his room. "Here's one," the first shouted excitedly. He advanced on Gene. "Get up, you're coming with us," he yelled in German.

"I have an injured leg. I can't walk," Gene answered. Facing them, he suddenly felt calm. He slipped into German quite naturally.

"Come on, none of your Jewish trickery, hurry up," the second German shouted.

"I can't walk. It's my leg. You'll have to carry me." This made the Germans pause. The first one looked him up and down, his eyes resting for a moment on Gene's bandaged leg, his lips curling with contempt.

"Are you a soldier?"

"No."

"Are you a Jew?"

"Yes." There was no point in lying. The Germans knew they were in a Jewish household.

"Then you must come with us immediately," the first solider barked again, gesturing toward the door with his weapon.

"I told you, I can't move. My leg is injured."

The Germans went into a huddle. Gene could hear their muffled discourse.

"Should we drag him out?"

"Do you want to haul him all over town? I don't."

"Why don't we just shoot him?"

"Those weren't our orders."

"Are you sure we should just leave him? It doesn't feel right to me."

"What's one Jew more or less? We can always come back and get him later if we need to. If he is injured, he won't be going anywhere."

One of the soldiers poked his head through the door again and spat in Gene's direction. "*Auf Wiedersehen Jude* (good-bye Jew)," he said. Then they were gone.

Gene lay back, allowing himself the luxury of breathing, as a wave of dizziness and nausea passed over him. His heart thumped like a metronome. Sarah crept quietly into the room and picked up his shaking hands. He jumped. "Oh, it's only you," he whispered through lips as dry as parchment. She placed his hand gently against her cheek.

"Your father and uncle are safe in the cellar. They didn't find them," she said.

"You'd better tell them to stay there."

"What about you?"

"I have to stay here. If the Germans come back and find me gone, they might search the place more carefully and find all three of us," Gene said.

All that day, Jasło was in shock. Nothing had prepared its helpless citizens for the wave of brutality that descended on them. Germans strutted around town terrorizing people, especially Jews. From his window, Gene could see soldiers leading elderly Jews away, pulling their side curls, beating them with guns if they did not walk fast enough. Each time the Germans passed his window, Gene stiffened. But they did not come back to the house. In the afternoon, Sarah ventured outside. She returned shaking with anger and fear.

"What's happening out there?" Gene asked.

"It's terrible," she sobbed. "Beatings, robberies, abusing helpless old people. What's to become of us?"

"Things will probably settle down after a few days. You've got to expect them to go a little wild on the first day," said Gene, trying to reassure her. Apparently, all of the town's leading Jewish citizens had been arrested. Jewish shops in the main square were being looted. There was a rumor that the German commandant had demanded that the Jewish community pay a ransom of 40,000 złotys within a single hour. It was an absolute fortune; a family could live for a long time on 100 złotys. Some of the men who had attempted to escape town had been forced to turn back and returned with horrific tales of Jews being stopped on the road and murdered in cold blood.

That evening, Sarah and her mother came to sit with Gene. The mood was somber; they did not even dare turn on the light. Sarah kept poking her head out the window to see if there were Germans on the street. Then they heard shots from the direction of the town square.

"Something's on fire," Sarah cried out. She pointed at a red glow over the rooftops. As she spoke, a flame reached up to lick the night. They watched in silence. "I think that's the direction of the synagogue," said Sarah. There were more shots.

"Gene, you must leave tomorrow and go back to your own family. The Germans must be there as well," she said.

"I know," he replied.

Next morning, the town buzzed with rumors. One was that the Germans had locked 50 Jews inside the synagogue and set it on fire. Anyone trying to escape had been shot.* Adolf and Jacob did not linger to find out if it was true. They brought Gene downstairs to where the cart was waiting. The air was acrid. They felt as if they were inhaling pellets of fear. Adolf berated himself as they trotted onto the main road. "This was all a big mistake," he said bitterly. "We ought to have stayed at home with our families. Pray God they're alright."

The road west was empty. Occasionally they passed German military convoys speeding in the other direction, but they were not stopped. So they returned to Nowy Sącz.

---

* The events of that night in Jasło remain unclear. According to the Jasło Memorial Book, the synagogue was set on fire. However, some eyewitnesses reported that Jews were not burned to death inside. What is certain, according to the Memorial Book written by survivors after the war, is that there were many other atrocities that day. For example, a group of Jewish youngsters was stopped on the road from town and searched for weapons. One carried a cartoon of Hitler in his pocket. The Germans shot the entire group on the spot. As for the synagogue fire, the local Polish fire brigade extinguished it before the entire building was destroyed. When the Nazi commandant found out, he became furious and ordered the fire brigade itself to burn down the building on the night of Yom Kippur, the holiest day of the year. His orders were carried out.

CHAPTER 4

The Bridge

The three men came home to find the Germans well entrenched in Nowy Sącz. To their relief, their families were safe. The Germans had confined their early outrages to the Jewish quarter, taking young men for forced labor, expropriating property, and soldiers entertained themselves by humiliating religious Jews. Some prominent Jewish businessmen were arrested as hostages until a special "contribution" could be handed over for their release. The money was collected, but the men were not freed. Within days, the first Nazi proclamations were issued: Jewish lawyers were forbidden to practice, Jewish doctors could treat only Jewish patients, and Jewish teachers were barred from teaching in non-Jewish schools.

On the outskirts of town, where Gene's family lived, things stayed quiet. Bertha was sick in bed with stomach pains. She did not complain, but her eyes were dull with worry. The entire family was worried. There had been no word from Mark since his departure. To add to their despair, on September 17 the Soviet Union invaded and occupied eastern Poland. The family had no idea whether Mark was in the Soviet zone, had escaped abroad, had been taken prisoner, or even if he was still alive.

Gene spent much of the time lying on a couch. His leg healed slowly and he felt fretful and restless. His body ached for physical activity. He was in touch with school friends, and there was vague talk of organizing resistance to the Germans. Nothing came of it; the feeling of defeat was too overwhelming.

After two weeks, Gene finally felt fit enough to take his first steps outside. It was a pleasant day and he savored the autumn breeze straggling through his hair. It was so pleasant that Gene did not notice the Germany orderly, whom everyone already knew by sight, walking down the street until he almost bumped into him. The orderly was a little man. In civilian life, he might have been an anxious-to-please clerk. Now he was a conqueror, ready to crush inferiors under his Aryan heel.

"Get out of the way. Don't you know the rules? Poles and other inferior breeds are to vacate the sidewalk for Germans. Step into the street and let me pass!"

Gene was too startled to move, and too enraged. "What? This is my town." Fists clenched, he glared icily at the German.

Taken aback, the orderly flinched. This was not how "inferior breeds" were supposed to behave. Flustered, he wriggled past Gene and scuttled away. Gene grinned to himself. He felt good. Later he realized he had behaved like a fool. The German could have had him shot.

Three weeks later, a letter from Mark finally arrived. It had been mailed from Lwów, which was in the part of eastern Poland now under Soviet occupation. Mark and Henek had been briefly captured by the Soviets, then released. They had made their way to Lwów, where Henek had an uncle, but the man was unwilling to help them. He had separated from his wife and had a new woman in the house. Two teenagers were the last thing he wanted on his hands. Mark and Henek were almost out of money and did not know what to do. Mark sounded miserable—hungry, bewildered, homesick. But he was safe; that was the main thing.

The relief in the house was palpable as the family sat around Bertha's sickbed discussing the letter. "What should we tell him? Maybe we can apply to the authorities for permission to let him come home. Then we could be a complete family again," said Adolf. But Bertha disagreed.

"No," she said vehemently, sitting up in bed. "He mustn't come home. It isn't safe here. He must stay where he is."

"Not come home?" Adolf said, surprised.

"I would give anything for him to come home and for things to be as they were," Bertha said. "But he can't, not yet. He must stay there, at least for the time being."

"But he sounds so depressed in the letter, and winter's coming. How will he survive alone in Lwów?" Adolf argued. "I know he's got Henek with him, but neither one of them is much more than a boy."

"Gene must go to him," said Bertha firmly. "Gene will go and look after him and not come home until it's safe. Don't argue with me, Adolf, I've thought about it!"

So it was determined. Two days later, Gene was ready to leave. They decided he would take Nunek's bicycle. It was a long journey to Lwów, more than 200 miles. Bertha got out of bed to pack winter clothes for Gene and Mark while Henek's stepmother prepared some things for him. Adolf gave Gene as much money as he could spare.

The two stood looking at one another, thinking of things to say, not finding the words. Finally, they simply embraced. Gene felt his father's rough face, the bristles of his mustache, the slight tremor in his arms. "Go and say good-bye to your mother," Adolf said.

Bertha was crying softly when he entered the bedroom. Lost in the big bed, she looked pale and defenseless. He had never seen her as she was the last few days. True, her illness had taken its toll, but now Gene, who knew his mother well, could read worry and despair in her eyes. He took her in his arms and held her tight.

"Take care of Mark," she said.

"I will," he replied softly. "But you must get well too. We all need you."

"Yes, yes, soon I will get up. We must all be strong. Remember what I told you —you can do anything you set out to do if your mind and your will are strong."

"I'll remember."

"I know you will. You're like me. Of all of them, you're the most like me." She clasped him to her, and he felt her tears on his cheek.

"May God guard you," she whispered.

"It'll just be for a few months," said Gene.

"I hope so." She held onto him for a few more moments, and then he felt her push him gently away.

Sitting on the bike's crossbar, Nunek rode with Gene to the edge of town. The bike was almost new, a splendid red machine with three gears, the latest innovation. The brothers parted on a bridge at the eastern end of town.

"I want you to stop being wild and headstrong from now on," Gene told Nunek sternly. "You have to look after your mother and father."

"Don't worry, I will," said Nunek. He was a strong, sturdy boy with intense eyes.

"Don't be too impulsive," Gene continued.

"Don't worry about me."

"And stay out of trouble."

"All right, all right, I get the message," laughed Nunek.

"All right then. And thanks for the loan of the bike. I'll return it to you when this is all over."

"You'd better." They looked at each other for a moment. There was nothing else to say. Gene pulled his younger brother to him and gave him a bear hug. Then he took a long look back at the town, its warm yellow bricks fringed by a canopy of trees, its skyline of hospitable red-tiled roofs as familiar as an old friend.

"We'll be back before long," he said, mounting the bike.

"Write often," called Nunek.

"I will. You write too."

"I promise."

For the first mile or two, Gene pedaled tentatively, testing his leg for the effects of his injury. Then, the road began rising steeply, and he forgot all about the leg in the joy of the climb. At the top of the hill, he stopped to look back. Nowy Sącz was no more than a dark smudge in the uncertain light, its church spires poking through the haze. The air was warm, suffused with the cloying smell of fallen apples. Gene shook off his melancholy and gave his mind to the journey ahead. It was time to push on. He mounted the bike and pointed it down the other side of the hill, his lungs and mind emptying with the exhilarating descent.

He reached Jasło that evening and made straight for Sarah's house. The streets were empty; the town lay in terror. The Jews stayed cooped up indoors while Nazis prowled outside. Nothing remained of the synagogue but blackened foundations. Its collection of holy books had been reduced to ashes. Gene spent the night at Sarah's and left at daybreak.

After Jasło, the countryside flattened. There was little traffic, only the occasional truckload of German troops. Gene proceeded cautiously, avoiding military convoys and hiding at the approach of German patrols. The haystacks in the fields lining the road had always reminded Gene of soldiers. Now they stood stiffly at attention as if no one had told them that the war was over and they had lost. He passed little shrines every mile or two, statues of saints with their arms outstretched or Virgins holding doll-like figures of the infant Jesus. The sun dropped slowly toward the horizon. Gene spent the second night in the open.

The following day he headed for Sanok, the last town in German-occupied Poland. It stood on the banks of a wide river, the San. The Soviet zone was on the other side. He rode into town in the late afternoon and went straight to the home of Nusia, his former girlfriend. The house was shuttered; no one seemed to be at home. Fortunately, Gene knew two other girls from his Zionist organization who lived in Sanok—sisters Elizabeth and Renata. He found them in their father's shop, selling cloth for men's suits to a group of Nazi officers.

The younger sister, Renata, saw him first. "Gene, what are you doing here?" she squealed, causing the Germans to turn around and stare at him. "Er, nothing," he said nervously, not wanting to draw attention to himself. "Just visiting. I'll explain it all later." He could not believe the relaxed manner in which the girls were talking to the Germans. Elizabeth saw his embarrassment and came up to hug him. "We're closing the shop soon anyway. Why don't you take a walk around the square for 15 minutes, and then we'll take you home."

"Are those Germans really paying for the stuff they buy?" Gene asked in disbelief.

"Oh yes," said Elizabeth, "and with good currency."

Later, over dinner, he told them that he needed to cross the river to the Soviet zone. Elizabeth looked serious. "It's not so easy," she said. "A lot of people are trying to get across."

"Well, how do you do it?" asked Gene.

"The best way is to hire a local guide. They know the places where the river is shallow enough to wade across. But if the Germans see you, they will shoot. And if the Russians see you on the other side, they might shoot as well."

"And you can't trust all the guides," interrupted Renata. "They can take your money and leave you in the middle of the river or just turn you in to the Germans."

"What about crossing without a guide?"

"That's very dangerous," said Elizabeth. "The river is very cold and quite deep in some places."

"Isn't there a bridge you can cross?"

"There's only one bridge, and it's heavily guarded by both the Germans and the Russians."

"I have an idea," said Renata. "I can ask one of those German officers who was in the store, that Lieutenant Fromm who's always making eyes at me."

"Can you really trust him?" asked Gene, bewildered.

"Oh yes," said Renata. "He's a nice Nazi."

Next morning, Gene decided to do his own investigating. He asked around town for a guide and was directed to a weather-beaten man sitting in a tavern. Gene approached him diffidently. "I hear you take people across the river," he said.

"I might. Depends on the conditions," the man said.

"What conditions?"

"Maximum of 15 people in a group and not too many old people. No more than five of 'em at a time. Old people are slow. How many were you thinking of taking across?"

"It's just me," said Gene.

"In that case, you'll have to join a group. Not worth my while taking singles across. It will cost you 150 złotys," the man declared.

"You must be joking. That's a fortune."

"That's the price, take it or leave it."

Gene did not have 150 złotys. In any case, he did not trust the guide. People around town had told him that one recent group had been fired on while crossing, and eight people had been killed. He decided to see what he could learn from Renata's friendly Nazi.

The man seemed surprisingly affable, especially when he learned that Gene had traveled nearly 100 miles by bicycle. "What a wonderful trip," he bleated enthusiastically, "I envy you. I'd like to explore some of these hills by bike. Best wait 'til the war's over though." Gene did not know what to make of the man. "Is he playing me for a fool or is he a moron?"

"Anyway," the officer told him, "I promised young Renata that I'd answer your questions. Charming girl, pity she's Jewish. What do you want to know?"

"Is it possible to get across the river?" Gene asked.

"Well, officially the border is closed to all unauthorized traffic. But there are two places where Jews are getting across. Sometimes, we shoot them. Sometimes we close our eyes to it and let them go."

"What about the bridge? Can you tell me what the situation is there?"

"Glad to. After all, it's not a military secret. There are two guards. If they catch you, they're supposed to ask you to stop. If you don't stop, they shoot. Of course, they might shoot anyway if they think you are a Jew."

Gene decided to take a look for himself. The bridge was outside of town, about three-quarters of a mile to the south. The light was fading as he arrived. He hid in some bushes and watched.

A road led to a barrier guarded by a German soldier. Beyond the barrier, the road sloped steeply toward the bridge, about 200 yards away. The bridge, about 80 yards long by Gene's reckoning, lay low and narrow across the water. In the middle, a solid iron gate marked the dividing point between the German and Soviet zones. Gene settled in for further observation.

At about 8:30 p.m., the Germans closed the barrier. Two guards took up positions by the bridge. Each patrolled a stretch of river about 250 yards long. They would meet by the bridge, exchange a few words, and then begin a slow march in opposite directions. Gene timed them. It took them several minutes to complete their round; they were never more than 400 yards apart.

There was a small dirt track running down toward the bridge that bypassed the barrier. Gene figured it might take him about a minute to ride the bike down the track and up to the iron gate in the middle of the bridge. He shivered. A minute sounded like a very long time to expose himself to the Germans. But there was no sense trying to ride flat out. It would be dark when he made his attempt, and the track was quite steep and bumpy. A fall would be fatal.

Gene stayed and watched the Germans for several hours. The guard changed shortly after midnight, but the routine remained the same. Occasionally, as the hours lengthened, the soldiers would stop in front of the bridge for a chat or to smoke. Apart from that, their movements never varied.

Next morning, Gene borrowed a pair of opera glasses from the girls and went back to observe the bridge by daylight. There was a barrier on the Soviet side of the river as well and a large group of soldiers around it. He tried to see where the Russians were positioned. Were they in the middle of the bridge by the gate or on the banks, like the Germans? He could not tell. Finally he decided there was little point in further observation. "Either I'm going to do this thing or I'm not," he told himself. Even as he thought it, he knew he was going to test his luck.

Next evening, he parted from his friends. Soon he was hiding in the bushes, his bike beside him, waiting for the right moment. It was chilly, but he hardly noticed. He watched intently as the German guards slowly paced. Visibility was almost too good. It was a bright, moonlit night with few clouds. The river looked very wide.

Midnight passed with Gene in an agony of indecision. Twice, he almost set off, but stopped at the last moment because one of the Germans turned around. The minutes flicked by. "I'll go nearer dawn when the guards are tired and less alert," he thought.

Still he watched, timing the guards as they paced. "I wonder what it feels like getting shot," he thought. But that was no way to think. Of course he was going to make it. The Germans would not be expecting anything. He would be on the bridge before they even noticed. It would take an extraordinary shot to hit him. Unless he fell. But he would not fall. There was an unfamiliar feeling in the pit of his stomach. His muscles were stretched tight. "It's just cold," he thought. He looked at his watch; it was already 3 a.m. He had to do it soon. "I'll go if that cloud covers the moon," he thought, gazing up.

Slowly, the cloud drifted towards the moon. Gene checked the guards' positions. He could see one but not the other. No matter, it had to be now. Trembling, he jumped on the bike and hurled himself down the slope before he could change his mind. He careened down the path without being seen. Now he was in the open. Had the Germans spotted him yet? He sped past the barrier. Where were the Germans? No time to check. To present the smallest possible target, he leaned over the handlebars. Now he was on the road. He vaguely heard shouts behind him but ignored them as he reached the smoother surface and accelerated. With a bump, he was on the bridge, working his legs, wheels rattling over the wooden slats, his breath coming shorter.

He started yelling in his prepared Russian. "Don't shoot! Friend! Don't shoot!

Friend!" Hearing him, Russians on the other side began running toward the iron gate in the middle. Gene reached the gate first, clasping it with both hands, gasping. A bare light bulb hung from it. In its glare, he saw two Soviet guards run up, weapons drawn. He caught a glimpse of tense Asiatic faces, and then lifted both hands in the air.

"Friend," he panted. "Friend." An officer came trotting up, waving a revolver and yelling something. He opened the gate and gestured Gene in. "Friend, friend," Gene kept saying, not understanding the officer's Russian. A soldier grabbed his bag off his shoulders, another his bike. A third prodded Gene with his weapon. He stumbled forward, his hands in the air.

Soon, he was surrounded by more Russians, all very excited, chattering loudly. Eventually a truck arrived and took him to a building about a mile away. They gave him back his bicycle and rucksack and ushered him into a schoolroom. It was full of people, evidently all Poles who had been arrested trying to cross at different points, some still wet from the river. Suddenly Gene was very tired. His legs ached as if he had ridden 100 miles instead of 300 yards. His hands were quivering. He found a corner and lay down to sleep.

Gene was awakened by a loud shout. "Let me go," someone was screaming. "I'm a Communist; you ask anyone." Gene looked up and saw it was morning. Four Soviet soldiers were shoving a man into the room. "I shouldn't be held with this riffraff," the man shrieked, hanging onto the door. "I went to jail for the Soviet Union. I suffered for Russia."

"Oh shut your face," a man lying next to Gene shouted. "You can wait with the rest of us." The soldiers finally pried the screamer's hands from the door, wrestled him inside, and slammed it shut.

"What's the situation here?" Gene asked his neighbor.

"Who knows? They hold you for a few days, and then march you off in a group. What happens after that, nobody knows. It's roughest on the families."

"What do you mean?" Gene asked.

"That's the bad part. They separate all the men from the women, husbands and wives, fathers and daughters, they don't care. It gives you a bad feeling."

It did not sound good to Gene, and his unease grew after he was taken to another classroom later that day and questioned.

"Are you a soldier?" the officer in charge asked through an interpreter.

"No."

"What is your profession?"

"Student."

"Why did you come here?"

"I'm going to Lwów to join my brother."

"Don't you know it's illegal to cross the border?"

"I didn't know it was illegal to go from one part of Poland to another."

"That was your mistake," the officer said coldly. "There is no Poland any more."

And that was all. No more questions, no more answers.

It was a noisy group of refugees in the school, and each had his own theory about what was in store. There were many rumors but no hard facts. Every day names were called. Their owners were taken outside, formed into rows of four, and marched away. Every night brought a new catch of miserable people hauled in from the river. On Sunday morning, Gene's name was called. Holding his bicycle, he stood outside the gate with about 50 other men.

"Where are we going?" everyone kept asking.

"Calm down, calm down!" shouted a Russian officer, an interpreter by his side. "We're just going to the station. When we get there, everybody will be able to buy a ticket to wherever they want to go."

"He's lying through his teeth," Gene thought to himself. "Why have they split up families like this? Why are they taking so much trouble if all they're going to do is let us go?" He knew he must not board that train.

Gene found himself toward the back of the group marching down the middle of the road. There were only a few guards, he noticed; they were stationed at the front and rear of the column. He started edging forward, changing places with men in the ranks ahead of him, and distancing himself from the guards at the back of the company. As the prisoners marched, they passed groups of Polish peasants walking in the other direction, all dressed in their Sunday best. Gene observed one particularly large group of 10 or 12 people approaching the prisoners, obviously on their way to church. He glanced back to see what the nearest guard was doing. He was on the other side of the column by the edge of the road.

"It's now or never," Gene thought. His palms were sweaty but he did not hesitate. As the peasants came alongside, he swung smartly around with the bike and wedged himself in the middle of them. He had been wearing a cap, which he snatched off to change his appearance. He looked the other way as they passed the guard and prattled furiously to one of the peasants. He had the horrible feeling that he might get a bullet in the back at any moment, but he kept up a one-sided conversation with the bewildered farmer as if he had known him for years.

"Wonderful weather we're having. A warm October always bodes well for the winter, so they say," Gene babbled.

"What did you say?" the peasant asked. They had passed the Russian guard at the end of the column. Gene glanced back. Just a few more steps and he would be safe. He breathed deeply, good country air. The prisoners receded into the distance.

"What did you say?" the peasant asked again. Gene looked at him. It really was a wonderful morning, an uncommonly beautiful morning.

"I said, God bless you, and could you please point me in the direction of Lwów."

CHAPTER 5

Hewers of Wood

Lwów, with its hodgepodge of Gothic spires, cobbled lanes, medieval alleys and baroque churches was a central European outpost perched on the borderland between the former Austrian and Russian empires. Over the centuries it had been ruled by Poland and Austria. Now, in the fall of 1939, it was held by the Soviet Union. In August 1939, before the outbreak of war, its population stood at 350,000. By mid-October, when Gene arrived, refugees fleeing the Nazis had swelled that number to about 1.5 million. Beggars haunted the town squares like flocks of pigeons, looking for scraps of food, while the town center was a Mecca for black-marketeers, wheeler-dealers, informers, and spies.

Gene located Henek's uncle, who gave him the boys' address. They were living in a cubbyhole scarcely bigger than a coat closet. When Henek and Mark saw Gene at the door, they threw themselves at him with relief. "It's Gene, it's Gene," Mark cried. "He's come to take us home."

"Hey, it's good to see you," said Gene, returning the embrace. "Well, you two kids don't look so bad," he said, giving them a quick inspection. Actually, he was appalled. The boys appeared scruffy and undernourished. Mark's skin had acquired a sallow, almost green tint, while Henek's round face was gray with worry.

"You both could do with a haircut, though," Gene said, tugging affectionately on Mark's thick black mop, which stood up in front like a cockscomb.

"Never mind about that. When can we start for home?" asked Mark eagerly.

"We're not going home. I've come to stay with you here," said Gene.

"Not go home? Why not? Is anything wrong?"

"No, everything's fine. I've brought some letters for you and some other stuff."

"You don't know what it's been like for us here," Henek interjected. "It's not easy."

"How have you been managing?" Gene wanted to know.

"I got hold of a violin and tried playing in the town square for money," said Mark. "But it was a miserable instrument and nobody gave us much."

"Right, it was all the instrument's fault," said Henek. "Maybe if you'd tried playing some popular tunes instead of Bach..."

"Never mind that," Gene interrupted. "Tell me what happened to you in the past month and how you got here."

They filled him in about their experiences in the weeks since their evacuation from Nowy Sącz. With about 50 other teenagers, members of a high school military training squad, they had been taken by train to a town called Brzeżany, 50 miles southeast of Lwów. There, they were marched to a local school, where they spent the next ten days waiting for orders. They had an ancient radio and could hear how badly the war was going. They knew Poland was being crushed, and they had to sit there, idle and useless.

Finally, on September 13, 1939, the sergeant in charge received an order to march them south into neutral Romania. The Polish government, realizing that defeat was inevitable, had ordered as many of its men as possible and anyone able to bear arms to escape abroad so they could live to fight another day. But it was too dangerous to travel by day. German aircraft strafed anything that moved on the roads. Poland was littered with burnt-out trucks and dead horses. So they marched by night.

"That sergeant major, he set quite a pace," Mark recalled.

"How long did it take?" Gene asked.

"Three nights. We spent the days in schools resting," said Henek.

"And then what?"

"On the third night, we reached the border. There was a small village called Gorodenka. They took us to a school to wait until dawn, when we were supposed to cross into Romania," said Mark. "But of course, we never made it." .

"What happened?" Gene asked.

"At around midnight, we heard gunfire. I was never so scared in my life. Then, a bunch of soldiers rushed into the school pointing machine guns at us and yelling in a foreign language," said Henek.

"It may have been foreign to you, but I recognized it right away," Mark said. "It was Mother's language—Russian!"

That happened on September 17, the day the Soviet Union hammered the final nail into Poland's coffin. Hitler and Stalin had cynically agreed to carve up Poland between them. Germany seized the western half, and the Soviets swallowed the east. Already facing defeat by the Germans, the Poles were in no position to resist. Thousands of Polish soldiers were captured by the Soviets, who moved quickly to seal the borders.

The next day, Mark's group was ordered to line up in the schoolyard, where an officer took their names and dates of birth. They stayed in the school for the next two days, growing steadily hungrier. The Soviets gave them no food, but some villagers took pity on them and brought them apples. Finally, they were hustled outside and marched to the train station, where captured Polish soldiers were being loaded into cattle wagons. "More, more," the Soviet soldiers kept shouting, shoving in the prisoners until they were squashed tight against each other. Then the doors clanged shut.

"That was the worst moment," Mark recalled. "It was like being entombed. I never want to experience that feeling again." He shuddered, remembering how the occupants of the train car had shifted against one another like parcels in a mail van. Four small slits at the top of the wagon provided the only light and air; no one could see where they were going. After several hours, the train pulled up at a small station and the boys spilled out, massaging their cramped muscles, shielding their eyes against the sunlight.

"Where were you?" Gene asked.

"It was a place called Volocyska, just across the old border, in the Soviet Union," said Mark.

"I'll never forget that place. What a shit hole it was," Henek added.

"So how did you get free?" Gene asked.

"Wait, we'll tell you," said Mark.

The boys were marched to an open field strewn with piles of beets. A few sheds belonging to a collective farm stood in one corner. On the other side, the field stretched far into the cold wastes of Ukraine. The field was blanketed with thousands of bedraggled Polish prisoners sitting on the ground between the piles of beets. Each group was guarded by Soviet soldiers, who circled them like vultures, rifles at the ready. They need not have worried about resistance or escape. There could not have been a more graphic portrait of defeat.

The boys found a space on the ground and sat down. Darkness fell; the temperature plummeted. Most of the boys wore only their thin summer uniforms. Mark had a light blanket from home. He and Henek threw it over themselves, hugging one another for warmth. "Still, it was the coldest night of my life," said Mark. "Until the next night," Henek put in.

Each of the eight days they were there, Soviet troops brought more prisoners into the field. Some were led away for questioning; still others were marched back to the station, presumably to be sent to prison camps deeper in Soviet territory. The authorities were particularly interested in identifying Polish officers, whom they separated from the rest of the prisoners. Later, the Soviets executed many of these officers.

On the third day, Mark's group received its first hot meal, thin stew with a few carrots and cabbage leaves. On the fourth day, they found space in one of the barns by the side of the field, their first piece of good fortune. It arrived just in time. The days were getting shorter; each night seemed colder than the last.

After the eighth day, they were brought for interrogation. The officer in charge questioned them individually through an interpreter. "But when he found out that we were just a bunch of school kids below military age, he seemed to lose interest," said Mark.

"And then?" asked Gene.

"Two days later, they let us go. They just marched us out of the field, past the station, and down the road a couple of miles to the old border, where they told us we were free. So then we came here to Lwów," Henek concluded. "And the rest you know."

Gene quickly took command of the situation. For Mark and Henek, his arrival was a godsend. He made them feel as if nothing bad could happen to them. They decided their quarters were too small and started looking for a new room the next day. The city had been badly damaged by German air raids. They soon found a bombed-out building with some empty rooms that were relatively unscathed. They moved into one, even though the building was scheduled to be demolished. "That's fine, too. It means we might be able to get jobs on the demolition team," said Gene. "This place will be okay until then. It's got everything we need—ceiling, floor, front door. What more do you want?"

"How about four walls?" said Henek.

When the building was torn down, the local authorities gave them a new room in another partially damaged apartment house. They bought two beds. One was only long enough for a child, but it was all that they could afford. Later, they acquired a chair and table. They took turns sleeping in the beds. Mark was appointed chief housekeeper, in charge of cooking and cleaning. The room had one drawback; there was no privacy. Two young couples each occupied a room in the same apartment and had to walk across the boys' quarters to reach their own. The boys got along well enough with one couple and the husband of the second, Max Novak. But his wife Zofia seemed to take an instant dislike to them. She was a sharp-faced woman with small gray eyes and narrow, almost bloodless, lips. Angry with life, she was best left to herself.

It was now November, and they needed jobs. Winter arrived one morning with a drum roll of rain, drops as hard as pellets beating out a tattoo on their only window. Soon, snow would come. The boys noticed trucks dumping piles of firewood outside buildings. This gave Gene an idea. The beech logs were delivered in four-foot lengths, which had to be sawn into smaller pieces, chopped up, and stored in cellars. "We could do that," he said.

"But we don't have tools," Henek protested.

"We'll buy some. I still have a little money from home, and we've earned a bit on the demolition job."

"Isn't it a bit risky spending all our money like that?"

"We must take a chance. There are so many refugees here it's frightening, and there's hardly any work. A lot of people are already begging in the streets or thieving. We must find work if we're going to survive," Gene said.

So they bought axes and saws and started knocking on doors of houses and restaurants, hiring out their services as woodcutters. They had no trouble finding work. Restaurants were best, because there was the chance of a free meal in addition to the money. Mark was particularly good at finding jobs. Housewives found his baby face difficult to resist. It was hard work. Their arms and bodies ached with the effort, and their hands were covered with blisters. They started to toughen up.

One day, they were cutting wood outside an apartment when Gene heard someone calling him from a balcony. He looked up and saw Nusia. It turned out that she and her family had fled Sanok a month before and were staying with a cousin in Lwów. After half an hour, when the boys got up to finish cutting the wood, Nusia edged Gene into a corner. "How is it with us, Gene?" she whispered.

"It's just as I said it would be. We're friends, best friends, and will always remain so," he said.

That winter was one of the harshest in memory. Cold wrapped itself around the city, squeezing the vitality from many of the miserable refugees shivering within its tenements. The boys did not always have firewood, feeling obliged to share some with their freezing co-tenants, and their spirits, too, began to drop in the dark days of December and January. Occasional letters from home brought little cheer. Their parents and Nunek missed them deeply; they reported that life under the Nazis was a constant round of hardship and humiliation. Jews were forced to wear armbands with Jewish Stars. Jewish shops were marked with the Star of David, targeting them for frequent attacks and robberies. Some businesses had been expropriated and handed over to ethnic Germans. Jews were forbidden to buy food from the market. Mark and Henek were very homesick. The idea of going home became an obsession. They talked about it all the time. On January 20, 1940, the three celebrated Mark's 17th birthday. "Make a wish," Henek urged him.

"That's easy. I want my next birthday to be at home," Mark said wistfully.

Many of the Jews who had fled to Lwów the previous September were talking about going home. At least they would be in familiar surroundings. Conditions could not be much worse than under the Russians. Life in Lwów was increasingly tenuous. Food was short and there were long lines for bread and other staples. Mass arrests were taking place, and entire families disappeared. The boys became familiar with the dread initials NKVD, which stood for a shadowy, all-powerful organization, the People's Commissariat of Internal Affairs. Its officers, with their royal blue and scarlet hats, had taken over a prison near the city center. They worked under cover of darkness. One sometimes heard their trucks bumping through the streets in the frigid, predawn hours. Their initial targets were members of the intelligentsia—property owners, businessmen, lawyers, priests, policemen, clerks, and students. As time passed, the net widened. Gradually the NKVD emptied Lwów of Poles, making sure it would never again be a Polish city.

In April 1940, a German delegation arrived. A few days later, it was announced that a limited number of Poles would be allowed to return to their homes in the German zone.

"What are we waiting for? Let's pack," cried Mark, when he heard the news.

"We're not going," Gene said.

"Why not?" asked Henek.

"Like Mother said, I don't trust the Germans. It's safer waiting here."

"What makes you such an authority?" Mark snapped, uncharacteristically heated and belligerent.

"I was sent here to look after you and that's what I'm doing."

"I'm not a baby. I'm 17 and I'm capable of making my own decisions."

Mark was shouting now.

"You are not behaving like an adult and your behavior just proves it," Gene answered frostily.

"What about you, Henek?" Mark asked, facing his cousin. "Don't you think we should go home?"

Henek fidgeted, his eyes refusing to meet Gene's.

"I'm for going home," he said finally. "I miss everyone too much. I keep asking myself, what are we doing here?"

"What we need to do is wait patiently until they tell us to come back home. You've read their letters and there is nothing in them about our return," Gene said.

"I still think we should be at home supporting them," said Mark.

"Don't you understand? We're not going," Gene declared, banging his fist on the table.

"Who the hell do you think you are, ordering us about like this? I can't stand it when you lay down the law like that. I'll do what I want. You just try to stop me," yelled Mark, jumping to his feet and aiming a punch at his brother.

"I will stop you, you silly ass," shouted Gene, trying to catch hold of Mark's flailing fists. One rapped him sharply on the cheek and he made as if to hit back. Henek stepped between them, grabbing Mark and pinning his arms to his sides.

"That's enough, that's enough fighting," he bellowed. "Sit down, both of you." Neither Gene nor Mark had ever seen Henek like this, his face red, his usually gentle eyes blazing. They backed away from each other and sat down. "Now listen to me, Gene," Henek said. "We know you're the oldest and all that, but we're not babies and we can think for ourselves. We are not likely to help our families chopping wood here in Lwów, are we? Let's go home."

Gene looked at them both shaking his head. "It's a mistake to go back. It's a terrible mistake. But you two blockheads think you know best. I can't stop you from going, and unfortunately I can't leave you either."

They took the train to the town of Przemyśl, where the border crossings were taking place, and found it inundated with refugees trying to return to the German zone. Most were Jews. They joined a line of thousands of people snaking down to the San River Bridge, where the refugees were being processed. Gene was dejected. Having risked his life to cross this same river only a few months before, it was humiliating to now beg the Germans to cross back again. German officers sauntered by jeering at them as the boys waited in the spring sunshine, barely talking. Night came; they lay down to sleep where they were. As the line inched slowly forward, they took turns leaving it to buy food and drink. Another night fell, and nearly 1,000 people were still ahead of them. Mark and Henek spoke excitedly of going home the following day. Gene kept his gloomy thoughts to himself.

The next day the line continued to creep forward. There were only about 400 people ahead of them. Suddenly, there was movement ahead. The Germans closed the barrier. Soon, officers started walking down the line shouting, "That's it. That's it. We're not taking any more. The border is closed." There was a rumble of dismay from those still waiting.

"What's that? What does he mean?" cried Henek.

"They must have filled the quota," said Gene. Mark was almost in tears. Gene felt a huge wave of relief. "Thank God," he thought. He had not wanted to face his mother with the boys. He hugged Mark gently. "It's for the best. I promise you. We'll all be together again when this stinking war is over," he said. There was nothing to do but take the train back to Lwów. That night, they were back in their bare room. They did not know it, but they had just escaped almost certain death. Virtually all those who crossed the bridge that day were later murdered by the Nazis.

Back in Lwów, they resumed their previous routine. In spring 1940 there was still hope that the war might not drag on for too long. After all, the British and French had yet to seriously engage the German forces. But that hope died in May and June when the Germans overran Belgium and Holland and crushed the French. On June 14, the Germans marched through Paris in triumph. That same week, the Soviet Union swallowed the Baltic republics of Estonia, Latvia, and Lithuania. The Soviets were busy in Lwów as well. In late June, they launched a massive wave of arrests and deportations. They picked up refugees as well as the city's original Polish residents. Among those rounded up were Nusia and her family. They were loaded into wagons bound for Siberia.

To escape arrest, the boys left their room and spent three nights sleeping in parks. On the fourth night, they figured the arrests were most likely over and it was safe to go back. Relieved to have a roof over their heads, they went to sleep early. As dawn broke on June 29, 1940, there was a sharp rap on the door. Gene heard it as if in a dream.

"They've come for some poor buggers in the building," he thought groggily and turned over. There was a second knock, and he realized that they were the poor buggers. There was no question of escape. Shivering, he shook Mark and Henek awake and opened the door. Four uniformed NKVD men marched into the room. Now that the worst had happened, the boys were calm. How long could they have gone on hiding? Eventually they were bound to be picked up.

"Documents," said one of the officers in a flat voice. Gene handed over their Polish identity papers. The officer examined them in silence.

"You are all stateless aliens illegally in the territory of the Soviet Union. You will come with us. You have ten minutes to prepare," he said in broken Polish. The boys did not need ten minutes. They did not have much to bring, and their rucksacks were already packed.

"Can I take my bicycle?" Gene asked.

"Bring it," said the officer.

They were driven to an army barracks in town. Dawn was coming. Gene kept asking about the charges against them. The NKVD men ignored him. The barracks were crowded with hundreds of others who had been arrested that night.

"At least we're together. Most of these others are on their own," said Henek.

"That's right," said Gene. "And whatever happens, we must stay together. We must always stay together. That way we'll get through this."

Eventually they came to a desk where an officer recorded their names and personal details. Another NKVD man grabbed Gene's bike.

"Where are you taking that?" he shouted.

"You won't be needing it where you're going," said the officer.

"But you can't just take it like that. It's mine," Gene protested.

"I'll write you a receipt," the officer said. "Don't worry. The Soviet people are not thieves. You'll get it back after your release."

But Gene was upset. "I promised to return it," he kept muttering.

CHAPTER 6

Stalin's Meat Grinder

The boys were held in Lwów's Peter and Paul army barracks for two weeks. They filled out endless forms, answering the same questions again and again: Where were they from? Where were their parents born? What were their occupations? They could hear the distant hum of the city going about its business, but they understood that their lives in Lwów were over. They expected to be interrogated and accused of some crime, but the days passed, and they were neither formally charged nor sentenced. Gene took this as a good sign. "Maybe we'll be resettled somewhere not too far away and earn some money to send home," he said, trying to raise the boys' morale.

"Yeah, yeah," said Mark, who had become used to his brother's unrelenting cheerfulness.

Gene need not have worried. Mark and Henek were handling the situation well. They had the resilience of youth and a fighting spirit, which was more than could be said for many of the other prisoners crowded into the compound. Some members of the local elite—lawyers, journalists, bookkeepers, civil servants—already seemed to have lost hope. Some sank deep into private lethargy; others pestered indifferent guards with grievances. They had not yet grasped the fact that they no longer had any rights. Officially, the prisoners were classified by the NKVD as "anti-Soviet fascists." More accurately, they were nonpersons, carcasses about to be fed into Stalin's meat grinder.

More than a million Poles were deported by Stalin from eastern Poland to the Soviet Union between October 1939 and June 1941. Only a fraction would ever return. Many, dumped on distant steppes and left to fend for themselves, died during their first winter in exile. Others disappeared into the vast labor camp system known as the gulag, never to be seen again. Yet for the boys, their arrest paradoxically offered a slim chance of survival. If they had stayed in Lwów, they probably would have died. A year later, Germany attacked the Soviet Union and quickly overran Lwów. The invaders were greeted by cheering Ukrainians, who had already decked the streets with swastikas. Within a week, the Nazis had rounded up and shot 3,000 Jews, while an additional 3,000-4,000 were killed in pogroms. The rest were later sent to extermination camps. By the time the Red Army recaptured Lwów in July 1944, virtually all its Jews were dead.

Water was strictly rationed in the barracks, but Gene insisted that the boys reserve a small amount for washing. It did not help much. At the end of a week, their hair was stiff with dirt and their scalps and bodies itched furiously. Mark trawled through Henek's hair and came up with a tiny wingless creature, gray and flat. "What is it?" asked Henek.

"It must be a nit or a louse or something. Do you know, Gene?" Mark asked, clasping it between thumb and forefinger and thrusting it under his brother's nose.

"It's a louse," said Henek, looking at the six-legged creature.

Two days later, everyone had their hair shaved almost down to their scalps. It was a purely hygienic measure, the authorities said. It did not mean that they were criminals. But it was unsettling. Everyone suddenly looked alike, stripped of individuality. Shaving made little difference to the lice, which continued to torment them.

After two weeks in the barracks, their names were called as part of a transport of more than 1,000 prisoners. At night they were brought under heavy guard to the Lwów freight yard. Scores of boxcars stretched into the night. Half dazed by the unnatural glare of floodlights, Gene saw the endless line of rust-colored wagons and knew they were not going to be free laborers. The prisoners were divided into groups of 60. They waited patiently in front of the quietly hissing train until it was their turn to be loaded. The air rang with the sharp commands of guards hustling the prisoners along. "Davai, davai (c'mon, c'mon)" the guards shouted. They counted the men as they loaded each wagon, mashing them in layer by layer until there was no more room.

They found themselves lying on wooden shelves, jammed in on all sides by the rancid bodies of fellow prisoners lying in two tiers. When the boxcar was full, metal doors slammed and heavy iron bars clanged into place. They could hear the curses of the guards outside and the doors of other wagons sliding shut, but the sounds came to them smothered and indistinct. Inside, all 60 men seemed to breathe as one. As his eyes adjusted, Gene saw there was a thin trickle of light seeping through two closely barred windows just beneath the ceiling. "Mark, Henek, where are you?" he called out.

"Here," Mark answered from the board above him.

"I'm here," came Henek's voice from the right.

"Are you two all right?" Gene asked.

"Wonderful," said Mark. "Don't forget, I've already had one of these train rides. I already know how a sardine feels."

"It's more like a coffin than a sardine can," said Henek grimly.

"Sour grapes, grumble, grumble," someone interjected. "Think instead of the joy that awaits you in the worker's paradise they're taking us to."

The train lurched into motion, ending the conversation. Gene shoved his rucksack under his head to serve as a pillow and fell asleep as the train swayed and rumbled through the night.

He woke up with a raging thirst. He was aching to relieve himself. He seemed to have slept in one position all night, literally like a log. Now, he was stiff all over. The train was no longer moving and jagged splinters of light thrust through the two small windows. "Mark," he croaked, through dry lips. "Are you awake?"

"Yes, what is it?" came a faint reply.

"Can you see anything out the window?" Mark stretched his head to peer out.

"They've got to open the door soon or my bladder will blow up," Gene said.

"Do what we do," someone suggested. From the smell of urine it was easy to know what that was.

Eventually they heard the doors of an adjoining car sliding open. The men in Gene's car began to yell "open up, open up!" Guards approached, banging on the metal sides with rifle butts. "Shut your mouths, we'll open when we're ready," they snarled. Finally, the bolts were lifted, and the doors opened. Men were so stiff they needed help to climb out. The guards threw a cordon around the train. Gene hurriedly unbuttoned himself, screwing up his eyes against the brilliant morning sky, and surveyed the scene. The sun was as white as a vision. His brother and cousin were stretching their limbs. "How are you doing?" he asked.

"Not too bad," Henek replied. He managed a faint grin, his eyes puffy and bloodshot. "Don't worry about us," he said.

The guards brought a bucket of water. It tasted of train oil, but they all drank thirstily. After that, they each received a lump of black bread and thin soup with fish entrails floating in it. Gene examined the Russian writing on the outside of the boxcar, wondering what it meant. "It says perishable cargo," volunteered a prisoner, who could read it. "Russian joke I suppose."

"I guess we'll have to learn some Russian to appreciate their brand of humor," remarked Henek.

"Don't worry, you'll learn," said the man. "They'll shoot you if you don't." He pointed to the guards stationed on the flat roof of the railcars, watching their every move. All too soon, the prisoners were loaded back into their stinking metal box and the doors sealed.

They spent three weeks in the train. After a few nights, they passed the lights of Kiev. They traveled mostly at night, past sleeping towns and villages. Daylight would find them halted on branch lines, where they were fed and watered and made to wait until dark. Occasionally the prisoners were allowed to gather branches to sweep out their cars. Most days they were issued dry rations, mainly black bread. Fish soup was a special treat. The boys began to get to know some of the other prisoners. They included German Jews who had been expelled before the war. Mark got talking to some of them who said they had been in a German concentration camp.

"What was it called?" Mark asked.

"Buchenwald," one of them replied. "And I tell you, anything the Russians have in store for us will be like a rest cure compared to that place."

"Don't be so sure," called out another man. He was in his mid-forties, overweight, with an unhealthy complexion and a persistent wheeze. "I fought for the Germans in the last war, and I was held prisoner by the Russians."

"So was my father," cried Mark.

"Well, they brought me to this place up north, nearly in the Arctic Circle, the land of white nights," the man said. "It was 1916. What a place. In summer, it never got dark, and in winter, it never got light. The snow lasted eight months of the year; the cold never ended. It was a cold like none of you have ever felt, like whips and scorpions, as it says in the Bible. And the darkness, months of darkness, never seeing the sun."

"Where was this place?"

"In the province of Karelia, a little town called Medvezh'yegorsk. It means 'bear city' because of all the bears that live in the forests around there. The people even keep them as pets."

"That sounds exciting," said Mark.

"Exciting? It was hell. It damn near killed me. Pray God none of us ever sees it," said the man.

They could tell by the sound of the tracks when they were passing major junctions, but they had no idea where they were. How long had they been shut up in this nightmare? They no longer knew. Mark tried to keep count, but even he was confused. Was it 14 or 15 days?

Their thirst was unending. Each day they waited for the doors to slide open so that they could pour some of that blessed oily water down their throats. Illness began to spread among the prisoners—diarrhea, dysentery, and fevers. Some were too sick to eat. The weakest slipped away quietly at night, their final breaths merging with the rattle of the train. They were buried in shallow graves dug by the prisoners by the side of the tracks and promptly forgotten. Each death created a little more space for the living in the wagon. The prisoners were in their own universe. There was no telling if the rest of the world still existed. Once some ragged children begging for food approached them. The guards quickly chased them off. Then one night, the trains passed the lights of a big city. The men were excited. It was Leningrad, St. Petersburg of old. How romantic! "No better place to visit," they were saying, as if they would soon disembark to stroll down its avenues admiring its sights.

But the train rumbled on; the lights died. "We're going north; it won't be much longer now," prisoners told each other. The lookouts peering out the windows described a new landscape, flat and forested, covered with silver birch and pine. Still the train clattered forward. They passed another town by the side of a great lake. A day later, the train halted and the doors opened. "Take your belongings and get off," the guards shouted. They had arrived.

First the recent dead were dumped on the platform. Then the men were formed into columns. Finally they began to march. They were in a small town of crude wooden shacks on the shores of a wide lake. Its blue was so solid it looked as if it would still be blue if you scooped up a few drops in your hand. It was Lake Onega, one of the largest bodies of water in Europe. Peasant women, their hair wrapped in brightly colored scarves, came out to the dusty street and gazed sympathetically as the prisoners went by. One of them grabbed Gene's sleeve. "Poor boys," she cried, "where have you come from? You'll all perish here." A guard pushed her aside.

Mark, marching alongside his brother, was transfixed by something he saw standing in the yard outside one of the houses. It was dog sized, with a metal chain around its neck, but it was no dog. "Look at that," he exclaimed, pulling at Gene.

"What are you talking about?" Gene said. Then they both saw another one, a little bear sitting in a chair outside a house. "This must be the place he told me about. He said it was called bear city," Mark cried excitedly.

"Who said?" asked Gene, catching sight of some more pet bears.

"You know, the German guy in our carriage. What's his name? Herman. They keep bears as pets; it's just as he said." Mark was entranced by the bears and hardly noticed when the line of prisoners eventually reached a wooden stockade. There were machine-gun towers at all four corners. They marched through the metal gates and were told to sit in the middle of the compound and wait.

Instantly, swarms of mosquitoes were buzzing around them. Gene swatted one, and his hand came away smeared with blood. The men started jumping about like demented clockwork dolls, yelling and slapping at their tormenters. These were not like the mosquitoes they had known at home, which were small and agile and attacked in ones and twos. These were large, lumbering, and relentless. Singly they were easy to kill, but they came in huge kamikaze waves. The men were overwhelmed by numbers. The sound of slapping gradually died away like applause at the end of a concert; they were helpless and they knew it. "We'll be eaten alive," moaned Henek.

"They probably won't last long. Summer must be very short here," said Gene.

"It can't be too short for me if this is what it's like," said Henek.

"Don't speak too soon. I remember what that German fellow said about the winter up here," Mark chimed in gloomily. "Like whips and scorpions, he said it was."

Eventually, the men were taken into barracks. After they settled down, Mark went off to ask the German if it was the same place where he had been imprisoned more than 20 years before. "What a chance in a million if it is," he thought. "He was here in 1916 and now he's back again." Mark found the man lying on his back like a beached whale, his eyes closed, his breath coming in thick bubbly gasps. "Hey there, Herman, is this the place you were telling us about?" But Herman would not answer.

"Leave him alone, he's not feeling well," said another prisoner. "He hasn't said a word to anyone since we got here."

"I'll talk to him tomorrow," Mark thought.

He rejoined Gene and Henek. They waited for darkness so they could go to sleep. But darkness never came. Around eleven at night the light faded a little. The twilight did not last for more than an hour or so. Soon the sun was out again with a pale, shimmering light that softened the lines of fatigue on the prisoners' faces.

"We're in the land of white nights," Mark said. "The German guy talked about that too. I'll ask him more about it in the morning."

But next morning Herman was gone. "Dead," said his bunkmate laconically. "One minute he's up there wheezing like an express train, keeping the whole room awake; the next, he's clutching his chest and turning blue. By the time the guards came, he was gone. I guess the shock of coming back here again was too much for the poor sucker."

Next day, the prisoners were split into smaller groups. Gene, Mark, and Henek stayed close together as their band of about 200 left the compound. They traveled for several hours on a narrow-gauge railroad through dense pine forests. Eventually they reached a canal, where they were loaded on boats. They did not know it at the time, but they were traveling on one of the proudest engineering achievements of the Soviet Union, the White Sea-Baltic canal. Many thousands of slave laborers died building it in the early 1930s.

That afternoon, the prisoners finally arrived at their destination on the shores of a small lake. They were now in the hands of a shadowy organization called the Main Administration of Corrective Labor Camps, better known by its acronym—the gulag.

CHAPTER 7

The Gulag

The confines of the planet on which they were now marooned were narrow, consisting of the camp, the lake, and the forest. The camp compound was small and square, bounded on three sides by several lines of wooden and barbed-wire fences. There were watchtowers in each corner. Inside the perimeter were wooden buildings that included a row of barracks, each housing about 80 prisoners; a kitchen and mess hall; guard quarters; a small administrative building and a four-bed clinic; a solitary confinement hut, a bathhouse, and latrines. The camp's fourth side abutted a small lake that gave the place its name— Vanczozero, or Lake Vancz. Wooden rails stretched from deep in the forest down to a landing point on the shore, where timber was loaded on barges bound for the long trip to the Baltic Sea. The forest was impenetrable; the lake was the camp's only lifeline to civilization. Occasional boats would bring eagerly awaited letters and parcels, reminding the prisoners that there was still a world somewhere beyond the forest where people smiled at one another and ate regular meals.

In the camp, they were soon to learn, only a privileged few and the rats ate regular meals, and sometimes only the rats. The camp had been hacked out of the forest, and tree stumps protruded from the ground like tumors. Rats congregated around the stumps, scores of them. When disturbed they charged into the water, which writhed with their glistening bodies. Still, the boys liked the lake. It provided their only view of the world unimpeded by barbed wire. Reflected images of clouds, white and puffy, floated in its placid waters. But soon enough, summer would fade and the lake would turn dark and taciturn and begin to acquire the mysterious velvet stillness of water about to freeze. It would cease its gentle lapping against its rocky shore and hold its breath. Then winter would slip a straitjacket over its surface, snow would fall on top of the ice, and the lake would turn white. No more boats would reach the camp for seven months. The camp would be an island, cut off from the world except for the occasional caravan of horse-drawn sleighs, slithering across the frozen lake with supplies and outdated news.

Beyond the fences and the lake was the forest. It was no friend to the convict. From afar, it appeared as smooth and inviting as a tightly woven green carpet. Close, it presented a different aspect, tangled and spiky. It was mostly spruce and pine; great, straight trees huddled together. On mild summer days, the trees touched gently in the soft breeze. But when the wind was up, their upper branches clutched each other and moaned. Occasional clumps of silver birch were visible, tightly encircled by the firs. Undergrowth sprouted in matted strands near the ground, which was uneven and treacherous, concealing little mounds and hollows, huge slate boulders stained with lichens, and moss, and bogs and puddles where mosquitoes bred. In winter deep snow hid these pitfalls. Just walking through the forest became hazardous.

Prisoners soon found themselves waging a grim battle for survival. Cutting down trees would have been a tough job under any circumstances. When it had to be done in the dead of winter by starving, worn-out convicts standing up to their waists in freezing puddles and snowdrifts, wielding half-blunt tools, it became an impossible task. Gustav Herling, a Polish writer who was imprisoned in a camp in the same region at around the same time, later wrote that he never came across a fellow prisoner who survived for more than two years working in the forest. The work wore down even the strongest. The fewer trees they cut down, the less food they received. Finally, they lost all their strength and were "retired" to the mortuary. Of course, not everybody starved in the camps. There was one group who usually ate well. Known as *urki* they were the hardened criminals, murderers and gangsters, who ruled the camp at night when the guards disappeared. Everybody, including the guards, was afraid of them.

The Polish arrivals, exhausted by the long journey, spent the first night sitting in the open devoured by insects, waiting for darkness to fall. It was late and still the night would not come. They were slowly surrounded by other convicts. A few with swollen legs and toothless mouths looked so emaciated it was a wonder they could stay upright. They stood swaying from side to side, staring out of hollow eyes. The boys were soon to learn that these were the symptoms of scurvy and pellagra—diseases caused by vitamin deficiencies. But others, some adorned with weird tattoos, seemed strong and healthy. They stood there, leering at the Poles, snickering and cackling at private jokes.

"I don't like the look of this lot," whispered Mark.

"They look as if they're sizing us up for dinner," Henek said. He was not far wrong. The *urki* were assessing the newcomers' clothes and possessions for what might be worth stealing.

Gene's eye was drawn to a swarthy man with a scarred face. He was standing next to a young boy of 17 or 18, eyeing the newcomers with a predatory gaze. When he noticed Gene looking at him, he bared his teeth in a grotesque grimace, wrapped his arm possessively around the boy and squeezed hard. Gene looked away.

"They don't seem too friendly. We have to watch ourselves in this snake pit," he hissed to Mark and Henek.

The *urki* were tightly organized into fraternities with their own codes of criminal "honor." Many were convicted murders, psychopaths who thought nothing of killing again, who actually took pride in each new murder. They played cards with one another for the right to steal newcomers' possessions, including their shoes and the clothes on their backs. It was not unusual to see newly arrived prisoners stripped to their underwear and shivering in the cold after the *urki* had finished with them.

Most prisoners were helpless against the criminals. Anyone who received a parcel had to pay them off by giving them a share of its contents. No one wanted to antagonize them. Those who did usually ended up with a slit throat. The *urki* received the sharpest tools and the best rations; even so, they only worked when they felt like it. Other prisoners would see them in the forest lounging about and smoking. The supervisors were too intimidated to do anything about it. Once, a foreman ordered a gangster to work harder. The man picked up an ax and hacked the foreman to death while the guards quietly made themselves scarce.

In Vanczozero, the dominant criminal gang came from Georgia. Its leader,

Glusha, was the man Gene had seen that first evening. Gene, Mark, and Henek were careful to avoid him and his friends. The boys were largely left alone. There were easier pickings for the criminals among the other prisoners. The boys were young and strong, and there were three of them, which afforded some protection.

Several hours after their arrival, the Polish prisoners were given camp clothing and allocated barracks. The boys found themselves in a long building with four rows of double-tiered boards. Some twenty prisoners slept on each board, side by side in a row. At one end of the room, there was a single window and a small stove to heat the whole barracks in winter. In the space separating the lines of sleeping boards were six primitive washstands and two buckets of water. Another pail served as a latrine bucket. It was a profoundly depressing sight. The boys had at least expected their own beds. Even Gene was momentarily lost for words.

One German who had survived Buchenwald was nodding in approval as if the scene was what he had expected. A few of the younger Poles appeared defiant. The professional men were abject. Some were still wearing the smart clothes in which they had been arrested, now filthy and threadbare from the train journey. Their troubles had not even begun, and already they were shadows. Soon, unable to even approach their assigned work norms, their rations would be reduced to virtually nothing. They would grow crazy with hunger, begging other prisoners for scraps of food, but nobody could afford to share their meager rations. They would be seen rummaging through the garbage for rotten cabbage leaves or potato peelings, their eyes encrusted with filth and mucus. One by one they would disappear. That is how the dead died in Vanczozero. First they died inside from despair. Then they became human skeletons. Finally they vanished. Nobody knew or cared what happened to them; nobody mourned them; few even noticed that they were gone.

At 5 a.m. the day after their arrival, the Poles were lined up with the other prisoners for their first trek to the forest. They were surrounded by armed guards and camp administrators and divided into work brigades of about 40 men. The prisoners were counted before leaving the compound. They stood in rows of five to make the counting easier for the guards. Even so, it took a long time to check the numbers against the list. The gates were eventually opened and the prisoners allowed to move through, still in groups of five. The guard in charge of the gate counted them as they went through; then an officer in charge of assigning work counted them again. Finally, when they were lined up outside, the officer in charge of the escort counted them one last time. If all the numbers tallied, they began the long march to the forest. If not, they were recounted until the figures matched.

While these activities proceeded, guards with dogs positioned themselves along the column. "Attention prisoners!" the chief escort yelled. "While we march, there is to be no straggling, no talking, no picking up anything off the ground. A step to the left or right is considered an escape attempt. The escort will fire without warning. Understood?" The prisoners responded in a monotone. They had heard the warning thousands of times before and would hear it thousands of times more. Sometimes if a prisoner deviated from his course along the route, a guard would growl "a step to the left, a step to the right." That was usually enough to get the prisoner back in line.

The prisoners moved like phantoms through the early morning mist, marching along the railroad tracks into the heart of the forest. It took over an hour, longer in winter, to reach the work site. There the men divided into teams of four. The fourth member of the boys' team was a Pole named Jan Tomczuk, a stocky, fair-haired man in his thirties with a vivid purple scar down one cheek and an enormous grudge in his heart. Tomczuk had been a communist in Poland and had served six years in prison for his convictions. He was set free at the beginning of the war and headed straight for the Soviet zone, where he was promptly arrested for illegal border crossing and shipped to the gulag. Now he could hardly contain his rage against the Soviet gods he had once worshipped.

Each group was issued two thin, curved saws, one wide two-man saw, and two axes. They were assigned work quotas that they were required to meet to obtain full rations each evening in camp. "If you don't work, you don't eat," the norm-setter said brusquely. Their assignment was to fell 30 trees a day, each one at least a foot wide. They had to clear each tree of all its branches, cut it into specified lengths, roll it down to the railroad tracks, and stack it. Later, the trees were loaded on horse carts and dragged back along the rails for shipment. The prisoners were also required to collect and burn all the branches. At the end of the day, the foreman stamped the timber with the camp seal and recorded the amount of cut wood. He determined how much of the norm each group had filled.

Gene gathered his group that first morning. "Let's see what we can do," he said. "We've had almost a whole year sawing wood in Lwów. This shouldn't be too difficult."

"Not too difficult?" said Tomczuk morosely. "You are naive innocents. You don't know the goddamned Russian bastards like I do. We are here to get punished, don't forget."

"Shut up," said Henek. "This place is crawling with guards. All we need is for them to hear you talking like that." The boys had been told there was a particular way to address a guard. "Citizen supervisor" or "citizen guard," they were supposed to say, "permit me to ask a question."

They flung themselves into their work. No one showed them how to do it. Over time, they learned that there was a technique. One of the team made an ax incision on one side of the trunk while another used the saw on the other side, slightly higher. That enabled them to direct the tree to fall in the desired position. But it took a while to figure out the process. The first tree they felled almost hit another group of prisoners.

At first, they almost felt sorry for each graceful tree as it toppled, but that feeling soon gave way to the need to hurry. They took turns at the various jobs. Two of them cut down trees while a third lopped off branches and the fourth cut the logs to the required lengths. Soon they discovered a major problem. "These tools aren't even sharp," moaned Henek. "We'll never do 30 trees with these bloody useless things."

"Those Russian bastards, I told you so," growled Tomczuk.

"But the norm must be reachable, why else would they set it?" asked Mark.

"Because the Russians are shits. They like to see us suffer," said Tomczuk.

"No, it must be because we're new here. We're just not used to it. It can't be totally impossible to reach the norm," said Gene.

But it was. After a few hours, the four were exhausted. There was a brief midday break, when those with tobacco smoked and the few who had saved part of the previous evening's bread ration ate. Then work resumed. It was nothing like chopping wood in Lwów. Often the trees were wedged between boulders or in boggy ground so that it was difficult to even get close to them. They spent hours up to their knees in brackish water, which did not make matters easier. At the end of the ten-hour workday, the results were disappointing. They had only fulfilled 40 percent of the norm. That meant that their rations would be reduced accordingly. The boys had a lot to learn about the gulag, where there was no reward for honest labor. The harder you worked, the quicker your health collapsed. Hard work was the shortest route to the morgue.

The eighth day in the forest was their worst yet. They worked a narrow strip on a steep hill, the norm a distant mirage. That night they were very low. Their muscles ached and their hands were covered with blisters. They flopped down on the bare boards exhausted and dejected. But most of all they were hungry. How were they to carry on, they each wondered.

"It's just beyond understanding," Mark said in desperation. "What are we being punished for? We never did them any harm."

"We don't even know how long we'll be here. It's not like we're serving a sentence. We could be here for ever, until we die." Henek added.

"That won't be long if they don't feed us," Mark agreed.

"God I'm hungry. Is that all we can expect to get from now on?" Henek muttered. There was a long silence.

"Gene," Mark whispered later so that not even Henek could hear. "Gene, do you think we'll get out of this place?" Gene sighed. He too felt depressed. He tried to imagine what they might look like after a few more weeks on this punishment diet. Would they too turn into disease-ridden wrecks? He shuddered. No! There had to be a way to survive. He turned to his brother and reached out to touch him. "Sure we will," he said.

Hunger was the prisoner's chief enemy and constant companion. It was a persistent dull ache in the stomach, a weakness that spread from the body to the brain and back again. Hunger meant working like slaves all morning for no lunch, unless one had the willpower to save a pathetic crust of bread from the previous night. Malnutrition turned proud men into scavengers, reduced muscle to blubber, caused teeth to rattle in their sockets, swelled legs with pus, turned bowel movements into blood and water. Men who had once pondered profound theories, acted on tender impulses, or savored erotic fantasies thought only of food. Food haunted their dreams at night and was the object of their desires by day. After work, they lay in their barracks talking about food. Their imaginations nearly drove them crazy. One young Pole in the boys' barracks did go crazy and threw himself into the sewage pit. They never saw him again.

As they lined up for their one meal each evening, the prisoners watched anxiously as the server ladled out the fish soup or porridge. It was the most important moment of the day. Would he skim from the top, giving them nothing but barely flavored water? Or might he stir the bowl first and dip the ladle to the bottom, where the soup was thicker. Soup and porridge, porridge and soup— their lives revolved around them. The other main component of their ration was a hunk of bread known as *paika*, which was soaked in water to increase its weight and to profit some of the camp's crooked administrators. It accounted for more than half the calories the prisoners received. Gene insisted that the boys save at least half their *paika* every night for lunch the next day. Sometimes they succeeded. Other nights, hunger overcame them, and they wolfed down the entire portion in a few bites, regretting that they had done so as soon as the bread was gone.

Camp rations were distributed according to the cauldron system, a concept used all over the gulag. Those who surpassed their norms were known as "Stakhanovites" after a famous Soviet coal miner and hero of communism, Aleksei Stakhanov, who was credited with having produced 14 times his quota in the Donetsk mines in 1935. Stakhanovites lined up for their soup or porridge at one cauldron where the brew was thicker and even contained some fish and vegetables. Those who achieved most but not all of their quotas had their cans filled with a somewhat thinner soup at a second cauldron. The rest were served from a third pot where the soup was mostly water. Those in the third line were not long for this world.

The boys struggled to achieve their norm, but it was beyond their reach. With good tools and a flat area in which to work, they might have been able to achieve 80 percent of the target. Yet night after night, they saw a line waiting for rations at the cauldron reserved for Stakhanovites. Many were *urki*. Some gangsters did not deign to collect their own food, but sent their young male lovers or junior gang members to fetch it. As soon as he saw one of them, the server made sure to stir the soup vigorously and dip the ladle as far down as it would go. But the *urki* were not the only ones eating from the first caldron. Other prisoners also enjoyed the honor. Gene wondered how they did it. He knew it was not by honest work. What was their secret?

He discovered it a few days later when the norm-setter took him aside. "I've been watching you for a good while," he said spitting some chewing tobacco on the ground. "You boys fancy yourselves good workers, eh?"

"We're trying the best we know how," said Gene.

"If you carry on working like that, you'll kill yourself and those young lads along with you by the end of the winter," the man said sourly.

"What do you mean?" Gene asked.

"I mean, young fellow, that the harder you work, the quicker you'll die. Isn't it obvious? Haven't you heard the saying that work loves a fool?"

"No, I never heard it before."

"There are some very wise sayings in Russian that you ought to learn, especially that one. Work loves a fool." The man spat again.

"You're telling me that we're fools for working too hard," Gene said, beginning to catch on. "But if we don't work harder, we'll never reach the norm. And if we don't reach the norm, we'll stay hungry. Unless there's something I don't understand?"

"Ah, now we're getting somewhere," said the norm-setter.

"What do you mean?"

"Let's take it one step at a time. You all want to be Stakhanovites, don't you?"

"Sure we do."

"Well, I want you to be Stakhanovites too. I have norms too, you know. If you fulfill your norms, I fulfill mine, and everybody's happy. That's what we're aiming for here—happiness all around. That's socialism."

"Absolutely," Gene agreed.

"Teamwork. That's the secret. We have to work together. Like partners, like a soccer team. You pass the ball to me, and I score a goal. I pass it to you, and you score a goal. Ask me, how do you achieve norms, and I'll tell you, through teamwork—that and good comradeship."

Gene nodded, waiting for more to come.

"For instance," the man said, lowering his voice. "For instance, say you had some tobacco you don't need, 'cause you don't smoke, or a spare bit of your clothing. What would you do, a sensible lad like you? You'd share your good fortune, give a little something to your friends. That's what you would do, right?"

"I'm sure I would," said Gene.

"Of course you would. And that would be the right thing to do. It would be solidarity, it would be socialism. Now you, coming from a sick bourgeois society, may not understand it. That's why I'm explaining it to you. You see, if you remember your friends, they'll remember you. It's a lesson for life. So my question to you is this—are we going to be friends, you and me?"

"I would be honored, comrade norm-setter," said Gene piously. "Would you like a cigarette?"

That's how Gene was introduced to the important Soviet concept of *tufta*. *Tufta* meant cheating; it meant cooking the books so that it appeared more had been accomplished than was actually the case. *Tufta* was the grease that made the Soviet Union's wheels turn. Everyone did it. One saying had it that the Soviet Union was based on "padding, cussing, and *tufta*." In the forest, there were various ways of applying *tufta*. The most common one was to stack the logs with a hollow middle, making the pile appear larger than it was. Sometimes, "mistakes" could occur when the foreman counted the logs and he counted the same one two or three times. *Tufta* was Gene, Mark, and Henek's passport to life. The day after Gene's conversation with the norm-setter, they suddenly achieved 102 percent of their norm. That evening they received a slightly more satisfying meal than usual.

"Mark, I anoint you a true Stakhanovite," Henek announced as they ate their bread and soup.

"And I anoint you a true hero of socialism," said Mark.

"And Tomczuk too, don't forget Tomczuk," said Henek.

"Tomczuk, I award you the medal of a hero of the Soviet Union," said Mark.

"Screw the Soviet Union," said Tomczuk.

In the days and weeks ahead, Gene and the norm-setter became true socialist friends. In exchange for most of their tobacco rations, or other suitable bribes, the norm-setter saw to it that they remained Stakhanovites. Suddenly they started achieving 110 percent of the norm, even 120 percent if the gift was really good. They got used to lining up at the first cauldron and receiving the full bread ration and extra tobacco, some of which they exchanged for more food. But they still remained very hungry.

Tobacco was a key component of gulag life. All the prisoners smoked; so did the guards. Stakhanovites were issued a weekly tobacco ration, and tobacco was the most stable form of camp currency. Many kinds of items were good for bartering: sugar, food, clothing. But tobacco was best. It was not like the kind of tobacco known in the West; there was little leaf in it. It mostly consisted of coarse tobacco stems chopped into small pieces that were then wrapped in newspaper or whatever else was available. The clinging, noxious reek of those homemade cigarettes was one of the characteristic smells of the Soviet Union.

In the camps, men would kill for tobacco. Many prisoners were so addicted that they would exchange their precious bread ration for two matchboxes. Tobacco was their only pleasure. It stunted their appetites; it helped them stay alive. If a prisoner slacked on the job, guards would shout or set dogs on him. But if he asked permission for a smoke and was willing to share his tobacco with the guard, he might gain a few minutes of rest. When they ran out, some prisoners smoked bits of straw from their mattresses or cotton wool from their coat linings. Or, they mixed breadcrumbs with their tobacco to make it last longer.

Summer fades quickly in the northern forests and fall does not linger long in its wake. The first winds of October made the trees shiver in fearful anticipation. Soon the prisoners were trudging to and from work in the cold and dark. Breaths came quick and shallow. The air was as sharp as pine needles, pricking them in every exposed spot. The inmates were issued winter clothing—felt boots and *kufaikas*—thigh-length padded coats stuffed with cotton wool. Even so it was achingly cold, especially during the endless counts each morning and night.

That was the worst part of the day, the evening roll call when the prisoners were counted by different officials again and again on their return to the camp after a long day in the forest. By that time they were almost nauseous with hunger. Often they were individually searched. Sometimes it took more than an hour and a half to pass through the camp gates. The guards were paranoid about anything the prisoners might have picked up in the forest, especially sharp objects. The prisoners were equally determined to smuggle things inside. In their society of have-nothings, even insignificant items could have a high barter value. Gene managed to sneak in an old nail one day. After hours of work, he converted it into a makeshift razor. It was a point of honor for Gene, Mark, and Henek to be clean-shaven. It raised their morale and proclaimed to friend and foe alike that their spirit was not faltering.

Occasionally, guards would search the barracks for knives and other sharp objects. The prisoners were forced to wait outside while the search proceeded. Then they were individually searched as they returned to the building. The first time such a search occurred, Mark panicked. He was afraid the guards would find his precious collection of mementos, including letters and photographs of his family. So he took most of them outside and buried them. When he was allowed back into the hut, he found that the few things he had left inside were untouched. But when he tried to dig up the buried items, they were gone. For several days, Mark was inconsolable. It was as if another part of the happy child he had once been had died.

When all the counts were done, their rations collected and their bellies partially filled, the prisoners were free to loll in their barracks, talking or dreaming. That was the best part of the day. Sometimes when their hunger was not too acute, some German prisoners would sing mournful songs. Mark never forgot the tune and words of one: *"Oh Buchenwald, ich kann dich nicht vergessen, weil du mein Schiksal bist"* (Oh Buchenwald, I cannot forget you, for you are my fate).

The boys sometimes slipped into one of the barracks housing Russian political prisoners where they could satisfy their curiosity about the Soviet Union. Everything they encountered so far was new, strange, and often hard to fathom. They were becoming fairly fluent in Russian, and they learned about the Soviet justice system from these embittered men. One was serving a ten-year term after being sentenced for fighting against the Communists in the civil war some 20 years before. He was only three years old at the time.

While the criminals would readily boast of their real or imaginary exploits, the "politicals" were wary of informers and reluctant to talk to foreigners. One evening an opening presented itself. Fedor Kovalev, an elderly prisoner and no mean chess player, informed the Polish visitors that he himself had visited Poland. "It wasn't exactly a visit," he added. "It was in the year 1920 when the Red Army marched toward Warsaw."

"My father was one of those that stopped you," Mark blurted out. "He was there in the Polish army."

The room went silent. Much later Kovalev whispered to Gene, "You tell that young lad to keep his mouth shut, or he'll soon come to grief."

Once during a roll call, Gene found himself standing next to a tall, thin prisoner with fair hair and a bony, angular face. He seemed deep in thought, whispering to himself as if in prayer. When his name was called, the man muttered something, then corrected himself and answered in Russian. Gene was intrigued. The man's first answer had sounded like Latin. "*Adsum*," he had mumbled, if Gene were not mistaken. That was Latin for "I am present." Gene looked at the man with interest. He was peering around as if he were trying to read something. Gene later learned that he was nearsighted and had lost his glasses. A few days later, Gene found himself waiting in line next to the man again.

"You're a priest, aren't you?" Gene said. The man jerked upright, clearly alarmed.

"Who says I am?" he answered.

"Relax, I'm just curious. I'm not an informer," Gene said.

"Well mind your own business," the man said, turning away.

Gene left him alone then. But the two were thrown together during roll calls and counts, and Gene kept trying to engage him in conversation. For some reason, Gene felt drawn to him. He took to calling him Adsum. Gradually, Adsum opened up. He was a priest, not long graduated from the seminary, which explained his reflex response during roll call. "But I was anxious to keep the fact a secret. Now because of my carelessness the secret is out. However, *factum fieri infectum no potest...*"

"What's that?" asked Gene, whose Latin was sketchy, despite the hours he had spent studying it at high school.

"It means there's no going back. What's done is done. However I would appreciate it if my secret did not reach the ears of our masters. I fear that they have a special way dealing with Polish priests."

Adsum had a habit of peppering his conversation with Latin quotes. Gene enjoyed trying to work out what they meant, although Adsum had to translate some of them into Polish. One night in the barracks he told Gene his story. After graduating from the seminary, he had been sent to a village in eastern Poland to assist an elderly priest. Soon the war started, and the area was occupied by the Soviet Union. "The Russians came and arrested the old priest. I wasn't there that day. When I returned, the villagers warned me, so I ran away to Lwów," he said.

"You still feel guilty about it, don't you?" Gene asked.

"I should have stayed with my flock. That's what my conscience tells me."

"You did the right thing. If you had stayed you'd only have been arrested as a priest. Are you seeking additional suffering, martyrdom, perhaps?"

"No, it's not like that," Adsum responded after a long pause. "I was arrested anyway. I keep thinking perhaps I should have gone to the German zone. At least there I could have helped people in some fashion, however modest." Despite his height, he had a vulnerable quality. He was so thin that he almost seemed two-dimensional, a cardboard cutout of a man.

"Things are even worse under the Germans than they are under the Russians," said Gene.

"I have heard terrible stories about the Germans and their *furor Teutonicus* (Teutonic fury), but I must admit I take them *cum grano salis* (with a grain of salt)," said the priest.

"You're wrong," said Gene. "I was there only briefly, but I saw enough to convince me that the Nazis will stop at nothing to crush anyone who dares oppose them."

"Tell me what you saw," said Adsum. So Gene recounted his escape in Jasło when the Jews were rounded up and the synagogue set on fire. Adsum listened intently.

When the story was over, he looked at Gene asking, "Why are they doing this? Why?"

"I don't know. Some say they're possessed by the devil. But I think it's hatred and greed that drive them. They are human but they have become savages and they enjoy inflicting pain. I sometimes wonder if we're going to make it through all this," Gene said.

Adsum assured him, "I'm sure you will. It was a miracle you escaped in Jasło. There must have been an angel watching over you."

After that, Adsum sought out the boys as often as he could. Others also gravitated to their group. One was a man named Saltzman. He had served in the merchant navy before the war and took great pride in his physique. He was stocky, with bright rosy cheeks, muscular and aggressive. He had somehow gotten himself a job in the camp kitchen, so he was comparatively well fed. Saltzman wandered the barracks at night challenging other prisoners to bouts of arm-wrestling. Gene decided to take him on. Saltzman could hardly believe it when Gene won. The next contest was close, but Gene won again. But within days, Saltzman began defeating him, at first with difficulty and then with increasing ease. An exhausted forest worker was no match for a kitchen operative. But that made Saltzman a good friend to have. Working in the kitchen, he was able to pick up the latest gossip and even an occasional bag of sugar for his friends.

Some weeks after their arrival, Gene became a brigade leader in his barracks. Now he had to deal directly with the foreman and guards, get his men out in time to be counted, oversee a fair distribution of tools, and if possible negotiate an even allocation of working plots. His added responsibility entitled him to a slightly increased food ration. By this time, winter had arrived. Blinding snow swept the forest, stinging the prisoners' frost-encrusted eyes. Sometimes they had to walk two hours to get to and from the work site, roped to each other, staggering through snow so thick they could barely make out the shape of the person ahead. They wrapped rags or spare clothes around their heads and necks so that only their eyes were exposed. Despite this, men lost fingers or the tips of their noses to frostbite. Their feet were so heavy they seemed encased in concrete. Some suffered from snow blindness. They saw dazzling visions of big red rings gyrating before their eyes. They began falling behind on the march to and from the forest, calling pathetically to their workmates, "Where are you, where are you?" The onset of snow blindness was usually a sign that the victim's decline was irreversible. If you were snow blind, the guards would soon discover it and would no longer allow you to work in the forest. If you did not work, you did not eat. If you did not eat, you died. In that sense, life was simple in the camp, stripped down to bare essentials.

Felling trees became agony. The only way to stay warm was to work furiously and keep moving. It was hard enough chopping branches off a tree in sunshine, but virtually impossible when a felled trunk was half-buried in snow. The boys began falling so far below the norm that even *tufta* could not make up all the loss. Some of the kinder guards occasionally allowed the prisoners to warm themselves by the fire in exchange for a smoke. But that was also dangerous. As soon as they got warm, the prisoners would fall asleep. A spark from the fire could jump onto a *kufaika* and burn a hole in the lining. There was no cotton wool to replace the burnt material. From then on, a prisoner would really be exposed to the elements.

How to describe the anguish of those days? Gulag rules decreed that work was called off only if the temperature fell below minus 40 degrees Celsius. The prisoners prayed for the mercury to slide below the magic number, so that they could stay in the barracks wrapped in everything they possessed. But more often, the thermometer remained stuck in the minus 30s. Just getting up in the morning was hell. The three of them tried to urge each other out of bed. The punishment for malingering was a night in the punishment cell, which could be fatal. The cold there was infinitely worse than in the barracks or even the forest.

The sun occasionally made a brief and hazy appearance. A deep orange ball low over the horizon, it provided no warmth at all and less and less light. Outdoors it was the wind that stopped one's breath. And it was still only November. Gene hated to think what it would be like in January. But the three of them were holding up better than most. They were young and not yet ready to quit. They also had each other to keep, their spirits up, to share their thoughts, their food, and their body warmth on cold nights.

The boys only fully realized the effects of their meager diets when they had a bath every ten days. First they were sent to the delousing chamber, where they had to strip and surrender their clothes. Then they ran as fast as possible to the hot water. Only then did Gene realize how scrawny he was becoming after weeks on camp rations. Henek was getting very skinny, his ribs standing out like the wooden frame of a sailing ship. Mark still had some cover on his bones. Of the three, he seemed to be getting through the ordeal the best. When the bath was over, the prisoners ran back to recover their clothes from the heated delousing chamber. The heat killed the lice to bring temporary relief, but by the time of the next bath they would be lousy again. They shook the dead insects out of their clothes before dressing. The lice fell out like snowflakes.

Bad as camp conditions were, the authorities tried not to let them deteriorate completely. They did not want to exceed their mortality norm. Yes, there was even a norm for death in the Soviet Union, a centrally planned number of prisoners who were supposed to die each month and year. The prisoners' work was vital to the Soviet economy. If too may died, it would be jeopardized. One day a commission arrived to examine the high percentage of disabled prisoners at Vanczozero. On the day of arrival, each inmate received a bun for breakfast, an unbelievable treat. Then everyone lined up in the compound for inspection. The commissioners asked, "What did you get for breakfast today?" There were no further questions.

One day, Gene objected when his team was given an especially rough patch of land to work in the forest. Backed up by Tomczuk, he found himself in a furious shouting match with the norm-setter. "How do you expect us to cut trees in snowdrifts up to our bellies?" he yelled. The disturbance alerted the guard, who at once started to swear and bark menacingly, "Sabotage, mutiny, disperse or I'll shoot." At the end of the day Gene was taken away for a night in the dreaded punishment cell. He sat inside the crude log hut on the bare earth, regretting his outburst. It was deathly cold and black as a tomb inside the hut. A stove in the corner flickered ineffectually, providing only enough heat to melt the ice on the wall above. The water dripped down, forming a puddle that promptly began to freeze again.

For good reason, all the prisoners feared the punishment cell. A week inside could destroy a man's health forever. Two weeks and he was as good as dead. And there was also the risk of being raped by guards or *urki*. Gene thanked his lucky stars that he was in for only a night. For some reason, one of Adsum's favorite Latin sayings came to mind, *qui male agit odit lucem* (the evildoer hates the light). The thought made him laugh. It was a slightly insane kind of laugh, more like a whimper. Here he was in a Russian prison thousands of miles from home, in solitary confinement, and thinking of quotations in Latin. He lay down with a brick under his head for protection and waited.

Suddenly he heard screams coming from an adjoining room. It was all too easy to imagine what might be happening there. Would they be coming for him next? The cold was excruciating. It was the kind of cold that sits on your body and sucks the warmth out of you. Gene bent himself into a small ball, his knees up against his chin. The screams in the next room died away and were replaced by more cold. All his senses were frozen. Slowly, the night crept by. In the morning, still shaking, Gene was released back to the barracks. Mark ran up and hugged him.

"Are you all right?" he asked jerkily. "We were worried sick about you."

"I'll be all right. I never knew how warm and cozy our barrack is. Now I do," said Gene patting his brother.

"What was it like really?" asked Henek. "Come closer to the fire. You look done in."

"It was just very dark and cold," said Gene.

Later, he found Adsum. "I was thinking about you last night," Gene said.

"And I about you. I prayed for you."

"In Latin or Polish?"

"In Latin, of course."

"I appreciate that," said Gene, touched by the gesture.

"Oh no. It is I who should be grateful. Since we have been here together, I have realized that your God and mine really have the same address."

Toward the end of November, a rumor began circulating among the prisoners. A new word, *Etape*, was on everyone's lips. In camp language, *Etape* meant transfer; it meant some of the prisoners were about to be sent to another camp. Everyone was sick with excitement and dread. Perhaps the new camp would be better. They could scarcely imagine that anything could be worse, although old-timers would tell them there were many degrees of hell. One day, all the Poles were told to assemble outside the barracks with their belongings. An officer started reading out names. Gene was called, then Tomczuk, then Adsum and Saltzman, then Henek. They stood to one side as the officer went down his list. When he finished, Mark's name had not been called.

"Wait, there's been a mistake," Gene shouted.

"No mistake," said the officer firmly.

"But my brother…"

"No mistake," he said again.

"But we can't leave him. We won't go anywhere without him," yelled Henek frantically. The officer gestured to the men whose names had been called to march toward the camp gate. It was too much for Mark. "What about me?" he screamed, trying to run after them. Two soldiers blocked his way. He tried to shove them aside, shrieking in desperation. "My brother, my cousin," he howled.

Gene and Henek were yelling back, trying to reach out to him. The other prisoners were already marching off, but Gene and Henek refused to move.

"Gene, Henek, don't leave me," Mark cried. One of the guards grabbed him by the arms, the other by the waist. He tried to throw them off, bucking and kicking. But it was no good. One of them punched him in the face. "Take him to the punishment cell," the officer snapped as they slowly dragged him away.

The officer looked at Gene and Henek. "Either you join the transfer or you can have ten days in isolation. Which is it to be?" he asked coldly. They could still hear Mark screaming their names as he was marched toward solitary confinement. Gene looked at Henek, who had tears in his eyes. There was no real choice. Ten days in the punishment cell would destroy them both, and they would still not be together.

"Come on," he said. "We'll find a way to get him back."

CHAPTER 8

Transfer

Mark struggled as the guards dragged him to the cooler. They opened the door, gave him a few parting blows, and shoved him in. The lock clanked into place. He lay on the floor shaking and sobbing silently. He was in despair, completely alone for the first time. Gene and Henek were on their way, to where he knew not in this enormous country. To the Urals? To Siberia? Would he ever see them again? How would he survive in the camp alone? Gene and Henek had made all the difference. There had always been someone to share the hardship and fear, to ease the anguish. Now what would he do?

The cold began to ease its way under his skin. Trying to stay warm, he curled up into a tight ball next to the stove in the corner, which burned feebly. But it did not help. His extremities were turning numb. He forced himself to his feet and started pacing. "I must not quit, I must not freeze," he told himself. The chill was eating into him. He stamped his feet. Nothing seemed to help. To distract himself, he imagined that he was playing the violin. It was difficult when his teeth were chattering and his hands and feet were deadened. His imaginary audience clapped enthusiastically. In his mind, Mark tried to remember pieces he had played. Eventually it calmed him and he slipped into an uneasy sleep. Next morning, although he was stiff with cold, melodies lingered in his head as the guards released him. But he was still alone.

Because so many prisoners had been transferred, the works brigades were reorganized and Mark's luck changed for the better. The camp authorities seemed to realize for the first time that he was not yet 18 years old. Technically, as a minor, he should not have been felling trees, the toughest of all camp jobs, in the first place. He was released from the forest-working brigade and sent to do odd jobs for the foremen who lived in a large timber shack outside the camp perimeter. It was a big improvement. He left the camp each morning for the foreman's quarters and spent the day cleaning, emptying the grates, and chopping firewood. The work was easy, and some men showed their appreciation by rewarding him with a tomato or a carrot, the stuff of dreams. They even gave him a pear or an apple once in a while. But they could not help his intense loneliness, and his assignment would not last forever. What would happen to him next? For all he knew, Gene and Henek were in Siberia. How would he ever find them again in the vast Soviet Union?

In fact, Gene and Henek were only a short distance away in Volozero, a camp beside a largish lake of the same name. Volozero was the administrative center of all the area labor camps. It employed a large number of NKVD officials and other civilians who lived with their families just beyond the camp perimeter. Food and living conditions for the prisoners were better and the work slightly easier than at the previous camp. They slept in individual bunks instead of on long boards. There were issued new uniforms and rubber-soled shoes. The majority were political prisoners serving ten-year terms under the infamous Article 58 of the Soviet criminal code, which dealt with so-called counter-revolutionary activities. The prisoners included a large number of intellectuals, who spent their spare time passionately arguing the finer points of Russian literature or current trends in physics. They even had their own acting troupe and an orchestra conducted by a man named Grulov, a stubby fellow in his fifties who served as the camp pharmacist.

At first Gene and Henek were put to work in a sawmill, cutting logs into various lengths for railroad lines or telephone poles and chopping birch tree trunks into small pieces that would fuel the narrow-gauge locomotives that ran between the camps. It was hard work but nothing compared to felling timber in the forest. From the first, they tried to think of ways to have Mark transferred to their camp. They had become familiar enough with the ways of the gulag to realize that a little bribery, judiciously applied, could go a long way.

"We still have quite a lot of stuff left from home—sweaters, spare trousers, shoes, watches, lots of valuable stuff. It's just a question of finding people with the right kind of pull," said Gene.

"Do you really think we have a chance?" asked Henek.

"We have to try. We must."

"We should be careful not to throw our stuff away. Lots of people will swear they can help if we give them a watch. They would kill their own grandmothers for what a watch can buy. We've got to find officials who really can help," said Henek.

"We'll ask around among the prisoners. I was told many of them work in the offices outside. Some must have good contacts with the administration. Maybe some of them even work there," Gene said.

The political prisoners were very suspicious. They trusted no one, not even one another. They knew that the NKVD had planted informers in the barracks and no one wanted to risk having their sentence extended for careless talk. Gene was determined to gain their confidence. He started playing chess with a prisoner named Mikhail Kuznetzov, a handsome man in his fifties with steel-gray hair. Kuznetzov had been an engineer before his arrest. He was a man of few words and a fine chess player. He moved quickly and was at home with many openings and endgames unknown to Gene. His eyes behind steel rimmed glasses were probing, but his expression remained unaltered whether in victory or rare defeat. There was scant conversation during the contests, usually witnessed by one or two onlookers, but one evening when they sat alone, Kuznetzov pulled out a faded photograph of his wife and two grown-up sons and passed it to Gene across the table.

"Handsome boys," said Gene. "This one looks about my age."

"That's right. Sometimes I wonder how long they will remember me," Kuznetzov said.

"No, how can you think that?" Gene protested.

"It's the climate, the climate of the country," Kuznetzov said enigmatically. "Hang around the camps for a while and you'll know what I'm talking about."

"You'll get through this," Gene said.

"I'll be over 60 by the time I get out, if I live that long. Even then, I'll still be an enemy of the people. It might be better for my family if I go somewhere else. It won't be easy living with an outcast like me."

"Maybe they'll review cases like yours and you'll get a reprieve or an amnesty. The climate may change."

"I suppose miracles could happen. One can hope for such things, but one should not expect them," Kuznetzov said dryly. That was the closest he came to expressing a political opinion.

Through chess, Gene met other prisoners as well. One was a former university teacher named Mishkin, a tall, overbearing man with an enormous receding forehead and perpetual grimace. Mishkin lost no opportunity to correct Gene's rough-and-ready Russian. One day he lost patience.

"Yevgeny Adolfovich," he said, addressing Gene formally by his Russian name and patronym, "Something will have to be done. Your Russian is just too dreadful. Really, it's the Russian of the gutter."

"What do you expect? I learned it in the gutter."

"It just won't do. I'll have to teach you myself," Mishkin said irritably. "You have to know how to read and write. You just can't pick up the language from guards and hooligans. A language is a living organism with a soul. Only when you're ready to read the classics—Tolstoy, Lermontov, Pushkin—will you be able to say you know a little Russian."

They began nightly lessons. Mishkin was a good teacher despite his short temper, and Gene's Russian improved by leaps and bounds.

Mishkin seethed over his arrest and the inexplicable events that had plucked him from his post as a respected university professor and turned him into a traitor to his party and country. He idolized Stalin and the Communist party with the passion of a religious fanatic and could not imagine what sin he could have committed to have found himself excommunicated. "It's all a big mistake, a plot against Comrade Stalin," he would proclaim to the barracks. This was a sign for the other prisoners, who were tired of Mishkin's speeches, to turn their backs on him. But Mishkin would not relent. "It's nothing but a plot, do you all hear, a plot," he would shout, his voice trembling with emotion. "If our great leader really knew what was going on, we'd all be free tomorrow, I'm convinced of it. But there are evil men around him. One day, the truth will out, and Comrade Stalin will get rid of the traitors. Then we'll be released immediately and rehabilitated. It could happen at any time. We just have to keep the faith." Then he would subside into a long silence, while normal conversation resumed in the barracks.

Another inmate was Rykov, a tall, thin man with a scraggly beard who had been a geologist before his arrest. Some of the other prisoners poked fun at him. "Hey Professor, found any interesting rocks today?" they would shout. Rykov devoted his spare time to collecting rocks and minerals, which he kept in a canvas bag behind his bunk. He would trade his meager rations for rocks found by other prisoners. Often, he would rush back to the barracks brandishing his latest discovery. "Look at this rock, fellows. You see the minerals in there? It's extraordinary. It's so rare I don't even think it has a name," he would bleat. "They're going to be jealous of me at the Institute. They'll be quite amazed."

With these prisoners' help, Gene and Henek began to make contact with members of the camp administration. They completed forms requesting Mark's transfer. Clothing and other precious objects also quietly changed hands. Then they settled down to wait for the bribes to take effect. In the meantime, 1940 slipped away, and 1941 arrived.

Shortly after the New Year, one of the foremen offered Gene a job accompanying the convoys that regularly traveled across the ice to a distant camp to bring hay for the horses in Volozero. He accepted at once and a few nights after receiving a security clearance, found himself speeding across the frozen lake in a sleigh. The moon was nearly full, with a pale halo. It sailed high above them casting blue beams of light over the shimmering arctic landscape. The lake was as smooth and white as enamel. Gene was exultant. He was in the last of six sleighs, each pulled by two horses. Stars sparkled above like a distant fireworks display. Gene felt almost free. Although the convoy included four armed guards, nothing could dampen his spirits. Looking up, he suddenly saw incandescent purple flashes lighting up the sky; great swirls of red and mauve stardust shot across the heavens. "What's that?" Gene shouted at the sleigh driver. "Those are the northern lights," the man yelled back.

The trip lasted five days. At the end of the second, they reached a small settlement where they piled the sleigh with hay and other supplies. Next morning, as they prepared to leave, anticipation ran through the party. Everyone was in a good mood; guards and prisoners were suddenly sharing jokes and nudging one another in the ribs. One of them slapped Gene on the back. "Tonight's the night, Zjenya," he said, using the Russian diminutive of Gene's name.

"What do you mean?"

"Tonight, we all get laid. Hadn't you heard?"

"Heard what?"

"Tonight, we sleep in the women's camp. Not that any of us will get any sleep. They go crazy when men arrive. They'll eat a healthy young virgin like you alive. You're in for the night of your life. They'll screw your prick right off if you're not careful."

"Who are they? I didn't know there were camps for women."

"Who cares who the hell they are? They're just prisoners like us, only they're women, and they're dying for it. Just save your strength. Don't waste it all on the first one. Some of them get really wild if you can't get it up anymore. They can scratch your eyes out."

Women! Gene had hardly seen a woman for months. The only women who might occasionally cross a prisoner's path were the wives of camp administrators—they did not count. His sex drive had died months ago, killed off by hunger and cold. He remembered Nusia, soft and sweet-smelling. Did he really want to make love with these women, whoever they were? And what about diseases? He found he had little desire.

They arrived at the camp and were led to a large wooden shack. Gene, half hidden behind a *pechka*—a spacious Russian stove—observed the arrival of a large group of women, most of them much older then himself. They began picking men according to some kind of an accepted pecking order. The others were left to wait their turn. Gene stayed in his hideout. Nobody had noticed his absence. Soon the sounds of vigorous coupling spread through the house; shouts, cries, curses, giggles, moans, and grunts filled the night. The women swore and cursed along with the men. The door of the barrack kept opening and slamming shut all night. The orgy grew wilder and more violent. The men seemed almost glad when morning arrived and they could stagger into their sleighs. One of the other prisoners slapped Gene on the shoulder, saying, "Well youngster, how many did you screw last night?"

"I'm not quite sure," Gene stuttered. He did not want to confess that he had spent the night hiding. In the camps, sexual prowess was the ultimate proof of manhood.

"Lost count, did you? Good for you. Did you exceed the norm?"

"I don't know. What's the norm?"

"Five or six for a Stakhanovite like you. You look a bit pale. Prick a bit sore, is it? Mine feels as if it'll never get up again."

"Mine too."

"You're lucky they didn't tear you limb from limb." He sighed in satisfaction, "That's what I call a good night."

The miracle they had been praying for happened without any warning a few days after Gene's return to Volozero. The barracks door opened, and a familiar stocky figure entered. Henek saw him first. "Mark, Mark," he cried, jumping off his bunk and rushing to hug him. Gene was not far behind. The three clutched one another, jumping up and down with excitement.

"How the hell did you get here? When did you arrive?" Henek asked, his face alight with joy.

"Gene, Henek, I can't believe I've found you again. They just told me to get my stuff, and they brought me on the little train," cried Mark. "I arrived yesterday. I didn't even know that you were here. But I asked around and someone said you were." In his excitement and emotion, he grabbed the others again and kissed them. He was near tears. "I thought I wouldn't see you for years, if ever," he said, choking back a sob. "It's terrible being alone; you have no idea."

Gene stepped back and examined his brother with a critical eye. "You look better than when we left," he said, "Remember Henek, I told you he'd get through. How did they treat you?"

"I got a cushy job with lots of extra food."

"Thank God we're all together again. We're the three musketeers. All for one and one for all."

"What's it like here?" asked Mark.

"Wouldn't change it for a Swiss health spa," said Henek. "You'll love it. They even have an orchestra. You can play the violin to your heart's content."

That month, they received a letter from the outside world. The prisoners were allowed to write letters once a month. The three of them tried different routes to reach their families. They wrote directly to Nowy Sącz but also sent postcards to friends in Lwów, thinking that these might have a better chance of arriving. One day, a reply arrived. It was from Nusia. She wrote that her family had been deported to Siberia. A Lwów friend named Gina had forwarded one of Gene's letters to her and also sent the boys' address to their families in Nowy Sącz. Now the boys felt they had a thread linking them to their families and to Nusia. Slowly, a network was established with Lwów as the central post office. Most of their letters did not get through, but a few did and survived the war.

In mid-January 1941, Gene wrote Nusia a brief account of the months since they were arrested, although he had to be careful what he said:

> This is my second letter. I now have a lot of time since the temperature went a few degrees below minus 40, and we were left in the barracks. They assure us the temperature is likely to drop another ten or more degrees. They transported us with 1,500 others in sealed goods wagons to the north. From Medvezh'yegorsk we traveled many kilometers into the taiga. Then they took us along the White Sea canal and brought us to the camp. There we worked felling trees. When I think of those months I still feel shivers. If we fulfilled the norm, we received the prize—bread and water. Our team of Henek, Mark, and I were considered Stakhanovites and we more or less survived. We were separated and only after more than a month at the cost of most of our possessions we managed to get Mark here. We are sustained by hope. Read this literally! Write to our mother that we are in good health and we are all three together, nothing else!

Some letters from Nunek, Gene and Mark's younger brother, also survive. The first, written January 31, 1941, carries a return address in the America quarter of Nowy Sącz, where the authorities had established a Jewish ghetto. From this, the boys understood that their families had been evicted from their old home, although Nunek gave no details. "Dear brothers," he wrote.

> We are using every opportunity to let you have news about us. We got your address from Gina Spunier from Lwów. We have had no news from you for over seven months. You can imagine how worried we have been. We still haven't received an actual letter. We keep writing often. Be in touch with us via Lwów. We are all right. Your girlfriend Tonia has also written to you, Mark, and Henek's family has also written. Otherwise everything is all right. Please write a lot and often.

On March 4, Nunek wrote to Nusia: "Only six weeks ago, Gina Spunier gave us their address. I must emphasize that apart from their address we know nothing of their lives. I only know you from stories from Gene and from pictures. I am Gene's youngest brother. I will write to you every week. Please keep us posted."

There is one final letter from Nunek, dated April 29, 1941:

> My dearest ones, Gene's birthday is approaching, and we are using this opportunity to send you birthday greetings. I'm writing on behalf of Mama and Papa and all our friends. What a pity we can't celebrate Gene's birthday as we did in the old days. We received our last letter from you ten months ago and since then absolutely nothing. Otherwise everything is as usual. We are all right. We wish very much we could be together with you. I'm closing now and sending best regards from everyone. Mama, Papa, Tonia, and all your friends…

After this, there was no further word from home.

Soon after his arrival at Volozero, Mark sought out the pharmacist Grulov and volunteered to play in the camp orchestra. Grulov found an old violin and gave Mark an audition. The pharmacist was so happy to have another violinist that he also offered Mark a job in the pharmacy, which served all the regional camps. There were no pills, so Mark had to weigh various powders and wrap them in paper. The work was repetitive and rather boring but Mark wasn't complaining. Grulov was a Jew in his mid-fifties, originally from Leningrad. Like hundreds of thousands of others, he was arrested in the great purge of 1937 for no particular reason and shipped away to penal servitude. His face was long and melancholy; he looked a bit like a bloodhound, with hanging jowls and watery brown eyes. He treated Mark like a surrogate son and forbade him to work outside the pharmacy, loading and unloading supplies. "Your hands are too important to the orchestra. I'll get them to send another prisoner to do the outside jobs," he declared.

Grulov found escape and fulfillment in music. On the podium, an amazing transformation came over him. His eyes sparkled with fire as he threw his arms about like a man possessed and demanded more expression, more feeling, or implored his musicians, "Feel the passion, let it wash over you." He looked somewhat pathetic, this scarecrow of a man with his bald head and loose-hanging prison garb, waving his baton as if he were conducting a world-renowned ensemble. But nobody laughed at him, such was the force of his obsession. For months, Grulov labored over his masterwork, a Viennese-style operetta entitled *The Countess and the Cad*. He would sit behind his desk at the pharmacy mixing powders and humming arias from the ball scene, or the duel scene, or the wedding scene of his grand composition. "How does this sound Mark?" he would cry, singing what might have been a waltz in his tuneless falsetto voice.

"I don't know. I'd have to hear the orchestration," Mark would answer diplomatically.

The orchestra was actually quite good; it included a number of former professional musicians who had been cast into the gulag on the usual trumped-up charges. They practiced two or three times a week and sometimes were even excused from work to do so. During Mark's time at Volozero they performed two concerts for the entire camp that were rapturously received. They were a welcome break from the stresses of camp life. For two brief hours, everyone could escape reality.

Other prisoners also participated in these entertainments. Circassians and Georgians from the Caucasus performed folk dances to the balalaika. Mark became very friendly with some of them. One old Georgian who worked loading and unloading barges took a liking to Mark as well. Through his job, the Georgian had access to a great deal of food and sometimes brought the boys a can of sardines. "You ought to go to the Caucasus when you get out of here," he would tell them. "The food there is wonderful, out of this world. The white bread—I can smell it now, so soft and sweet and fresh." The boys would lick their lips. After months of soggy black break, just the thought of white bread made their mouths water. It became a symbol of freedom. When they were free, they would eat white bread again, they promised themselves.

One day in March, Gene set off on another of his sleigh trips. The months of total darkness were behind them, and there were now several hours of light each day. But the temperature stayed frigid, and the ice showed no sign of loosening its grip. The sun shone brightly as they set out, but as the afternoon lengthened, angry clouds covered the sky and the wind strengthened. Soon it began to snow. Night fell and they continued battling the blizzard in darkness. As usual, Gene was in the last sleigh with another prisoner who was driving and a guard. Their pace slowed, and they found themselves cut off from the rest of the convoy. They were cast adrift in an invisible ocean. The snow, as fine and gritty as sand, blew into their eyes and made breathing difficult. They could not see as far as the rumps of the horses pulling the sleigh. Gene could not judge how badly they were lost, or how far it was to the nearest human habitation, but the driver seemed confident as he kept the horses moving. Suddenly the guard clutched his eyes. "I can't see; I can't see," he yelled.

"What's the matter?" Gene asked.

"Maybe he's snow-blind," said the other prisoner. "It catches you sometimes if there's a sudden change from light to dark, like now. It will probably wear off in a bit."

But the guard was not listening. "I'm blind; I'm blind," he wailed in anguish. Then he bolted upright and clutched Gene by the sleeve. "Did you hear that?" he asked, his breath coming in short gasps of alarm.

"Hear what?"

"Wolves. There are wolves out there, I tell you. They're coming for us."

"I don't hear anything, do you?" Gene asked, turning to the other prisoner. There was only howling wind and horse bridles jingling.

"I don't hear anything either. It's just the wind, Citizen Guard," the other prisoner said soothingly.

"You see. There are no wolves," said Gene.

"They're getting closer. Oh God, what are we going to do?" the guard screamed hysterically. "They're coming closer, and I can't see anything. Here, you," he said, tugging at Gene's arm. "Take my gun and shoot them."

Gene turned to the other prisoner. The man shrugged at Gene as if to say, "Do it; humor him." But Gene hesitated. What if the guard later accused Gene of disarming him or of trying to escape and the other prisoner backed up the guard? He shivered with fear and cold, unable to decide.

"Take it, damn you, before it's too late. Can't you hear them howling?" the guard shrieked. Gene took the rifle but still hesitated.

"Fire, fire, what the hell are you waiting for?"

"I'm just trying to get one in my sights," said Gene. He fired some shots into the dark.

"Did you get them?" the guard asked.

"The shots frightened them off. There are no wolves now. You can stop worrying, Citizen Guard," Gene said in what he hoped was a calm voice.

"Are you sure the wolves are gone?"

"Yes, there are no wolves now."

"Let me listen … yes, I think they're gone."

The guard gradually relaxed as they blindly continued through the snowstorm. An hour later, to Gene's intense relief, they reached the shore and made their way to a settlement. By then, the guard had recovered. When they dismounted, he took Gene aside. "Listen here, lad, you know what happened out there tonight…" "Nothing happened," Gene responded quickly, "nothing at all."

"That's right," said the guard. "Good lad."

Meanwhile, at the camp excitement was rising thanks to the grand premiere of Grulov's operetta. Prisoners made costumes, set up a makeshift stage, and painstakingly copied the instrumental parts. Grulov himself was on the point of an artistic nervous breakdown. "Lighter, your singing must be lighter, like the bubbles in champagne," he begged the young man playing the part of the heroine, a prisoner who enjoyed the chance to dress in women's clothes and wear makeup. Mark found it all childish and ridiculous. Grulov's plot was an absurd variation of the Cinderella story, with many convoluted twists and turns. There were mistaken identities, star-crossed lovers, and an implausibly happy ending. The tunes were a banal parody of Johann Strauss. How could a bunch of malnourished convicts transform themselves into a Viennese orchestra?

But Grulov knew his audience better. The evening was a rousing success. Hardened criminals, convicted murderers, political prisoners, and intellectuals, as well as many self-invited NKVD men and administrators, all proved eager to suspend their disbelief and throw themselves into the story. The first appearance of the countess was greeted with a barrage of wolf whistles, but the audience soon seemed to forget that she was a man and settled down to watch his, or rather her, struggle for happiness. The final scene left many in tears. They greeted the end with thunderous applause. Grulov, mopping his brow with a tattered cloth, bowed again and again. He had finally achieved his ambition. He was a maestro.

As spring arrived, unsettling reports reached the camp. On June 11, 1941, Gene wrote Nusia:

> The ice cracked here at the beginning of June, but on the second day of the month there was a big snowstorm and an even bigger one on the ninth. There are persistent rumors we will soon be leaving the area of the White Sea canal. They are talking of releasing us or at least changing our status. That something is brewing is clear. Anything would be better than here. What terrifies us is the possibility that we will be parted from Mark again. The tension here is unbearable. Today or tomorrow it will be settled. Henek and I were taken to the railroad station today, but then they brought us back at the last minute. You can't imagine the tension. It's near panic....

It is impossible to know what the authorities had in mind for the boys. By now, the land was green and fragrant and they entered the period of white nights again. Gene realized that almost a year had passed since their arrest. It felt like a lifetime. They had survived while many had not. They had also gained in knowledge and self-assurance. If Gene had realized what lay ahead, he might not have been so complacent.

In the early hours of June 22, 1941, Nazi Germany launched Operation Barbarossa, a massive blitzkrieg against the Soviet Union. The German army rolled swiftly in the direction of Moscow and Leningrad. A week later Finland joined the attack, threatening to cut Soviet communications between the White Sea and the Baltic. Soviet authorities could not let the countless thousands of gulag laborers fall into enemy hands and ordered the evacuation of all camps in the region. For Gene, Mark, and Henek, a new chapter was about to open.

CHAPTER 9

Death by Inches

The boys learned about the German attack on the Soviet Union from prisoners working in the camp administration. At first, the news seemed hopeful. Because the Poles and the Soviets were now on the same side in the war against Germany, there was no longer any reason for the Soviets to hold Polish prisoners. But you never knew with the Soviets. They might choose to interpret the situation in their own convoluted way.

In fact, as the boys learned later, negotiations quickly began between Stalin and the Polish government-in-exile, resulting in an agreement to restore diplomatic relations. It was followed by publication on August 12, 1941, of a Soviet amnesty decree, stating that all Polish nationals held in Soviet prison camps were to be freed immediately and laying out procedures for their release. But those who had hoped for a speedy release of the captives did not take into account the slow-moving Soviet bureaucracy. It took months for the amnesty orders to seep through to camps in remote areas. Meanwhile, thousands of Polish prisoners who should have been freed continued to suffer and die.

None of this affected Gene, Mark, and Henek. A month before the amnesty was proclaimed, the authorities had already started evacuating prisoners from Volozero to camps deeper within the Soviet interior. The Soviet Union was also at war with Finland and the authorities decided the prison camps in this part of the country were too close to the Finnish border. The process began with marches to the shore of Lake Onega. There, thousands of prisoners were loaded into the cavernous barges usually used for transporting timber. They were packed like herrings, hundreds of men crammed into holds so tight they could not move. The heat was inhumane. The air smelled of filth and terror. Most of the prisoners stripped to their underwear. Even so, they were soaked in sweat. The only light and air came through a single open hatch. A ladder led to the deck and to a latrine. A long line of prisoners was always waiting to use it. When a prisoner finally emerged into the deck's fresh air, he was greeted by guards pointing machine guns. When he climbed back into the hold, he would have lost his place on the floor and would have to fight in the darkness to regain it.

The boys, as was their practice, kept close together. Few words were exchanged. From past experience they knew they could do little, but wait until the horror was over. Thank God they were not suffering from dysentery like some of the prisoners. Across from him, Gene saw Mishkin, his Russian teacher, muttering to himself. As Gene watched, he put his hands over his face in a gesture of despair. "Cheer up. This won't last long. We'll get through this all right," Gene called out. Mishkin looked up, his eyes gleaming weirdly through the gloom. "Don't you realize we're all dead men?" he declaimed, his voice trembling.

"Why do you say that? In another week or so, we will remember all this as yet another torment they put us through, that's all," Gene said.

"We haven't got another week. We'll be lucky to survive another day. Don't you realize how easily they could scuttle the barge in the middle of the lake? This is nothing but a floating coffin. They're just waiting until we get well away from shore, right in the middle of the lake where nobody can see. I tell you, we're dead men."

"They would never do that," Gene argued, trying to suppress his alarm. The tub did feel like a floating coffin.

"What do you know about it? Nothing! You are just a naive young Pole. They've done it before and they'll do it again. Start saying your prayers, young fellow. You won't have time once we start sinking. We're rats in a trap."

"You must be exaggerating, surely," Gene persisted. "Why would they do such a thing?"

"He's not joking," said another prisoner. "Haven't you heard the stories? They've done that and worse before now."

Other prisoners joined in, shouting over one another to make themselves heard. Several had heard accounts of barges full of prisoners being scuttled in Lake Onega or the White Sea. A heated debate broke out about whether they were likely to be drowned. Kuznetzov, Gene's chess partner, took a slightly hopeful line. "I don't think they'll sink us unless they have to," he said in his usual level voice. "After all, they could have just shot all of us back in Volozero. Our labor still has value, even more now that the war is going on." There was a rumble of agreement from some of the prisoners.

"But what if the Germans bomb us?" someone else shouted. "We're helpless, like babies in a cradle."

"Bombing isn't likely, it seems to me. But we'd better pray that no enemy planes come this way. If there's any chance of them sighting us, they'll scuttle us for sure," said Kuznetzov.

"Why?" asked Henek.

"The whole point of this evacuation is to keep us from falling into enemy hands. They want to keep the camps a secret. The NKVD never lets a prisoner go if it can help it. They won't let us fall into foreign hands at any price," Kuznetzov said. Gene had never heard a political prisoner talk like that aloud and certainly not a cautious man like Kuznetzov. By now he was thoroughly alarmed.

"I can't believe this," he said. "Why would the Germans come all the way up here? It's not very likely. Goddamn it, Mishkin. I thought you believed in the party and the system and everything. Surely you don't think they'd just drown us all?"

"Why not?" Mishkin replied in a low voice. "What's a few thousand lives more or less? You've been in the camps. You've seen how cheap life is to them. The individual counts for nothing in the greater scheme of things. We all accepted that when we joined the party."

Hours passed. Their muscles stiffened; they ached all over; the feeling of helplessness would not go away. But when the guard distributed food and water, their spirits rose. Why would the authorities waste it on them if they intended to drown them? The *urki*, who had congregated into one corner of the hold, had already gone into action, stealing bread from the other prisoners. They were the only ones who were comfortable, having shoved terrified prisoners aside to clear more space for themselves. The rest sat together, unable to move even a limb. The lucky ones dropped off to sleep. The throbbing engine and water gurgling under the deck gradually lulled the others into a kind of stupor.

For four days and three nights they were cooped up in that floating crate as it traversed the lake. Occasionally the boat tied up for a few hours, but the prisoners were not allowed ashore. Unwashed and unshaven, stinking and lice-ridden, the sense of degradation and impotence were almost worse than the pain, the fear, the hunger, and the thirst. "We're nothing but animals to them," Gene thought.

During his brief visits to the deck to use the latrine, Gene tried to stretch and smell the sweet breeze. They were chugging through an archipelago, some islands no more than outcrops of bare rocks, others covered with evergreens. They sailed so slowly that it seemed as if the islands were moving and the barge was still. He thought about diving into the water and leaping like a porpoise to freedom. But the guards became impatient, gesturing to him to climb the ladder back into the stinking bowels of the boat. He had no choice but to obey.

On the evening of the fourth day they disembarked somewhere on the lake's eastern shore. A line of snarling guards with machine guns was waiting. The prisoners were hungry and thirsty but there would be no delay. They were formed into columns and marched east on a track through the forest, goaded by the guards. Gene saw the geologist Rykov, struggling to lift a heavy pack onto his back. "What have you got there, professor?" Gene shouted.

"My rocks, my precious rocks," gasped the professor, "I'm not leaving them."

"Don't be foolish," said Gene. "How do you expect to carry them on a march? We could be walking for days. You'll never make it. Leave them behind."

"I'm a scientist. These are my life."

"They'll cost you your life if you try to bring them."

"But these are priceless. I can't leave them," wailed the professor. "Some of the minerals they contain aren't even named yet. If you carry some for me, I swear I'll name one of them after you. You would be serving the cause of science."

"Sorry, professor, my mind can't deal with the cause of science today," Gene said. For several hours afterwards, he occasionally heard Rykov's reedy voice imploring others to help carry his precious load in exchange for scientific fame.

There were no takers. Gene assumed the professor would eventually be forced to drop at least some of the rocks.

As the march proceeded, Gene, Mark, and Henek found themselves near the middle of the column. Guards strode on both sides, yelling at the prisoners to stay in line. "A step to the left or a step to the right and we'll shoot," they bellowed. As the prisoners tramped forward, they heard wild shouts and occasional shots coming from the rear.

"What the devil is going on back there?" someone called out.

"Maybe they're shooting the stragglers. I wouldn't put it past them. D'you think the bastards will ever give us any food or water? We haven't had a drop all day," panted Henek.

"It's a lot better than that hellhole of a barge. I'd rather march all day and night than go back there," said Gene.

"Me too, I'm just so thirsty," said Henek.

"You have to keep going. Eventually they're bound to feed us. I guess they want to get us as far away from the lake as they can," said Gene. He looked at Mark, who was marching along doggedly. "Are you all right?" Mark nodded without speaking.

Later their friend Saltzman, who had been a few rows behind, came up to them. "Do you hear the shouting back there?" he asked. "It's the goddamn *urki*. They're attacking people and stealing their things. We've got to organize against them. They may try to come at us at some point."

"What about the guards?" asked Henek.

"They never tangle with the *urki*. They probably work together. We'll get no help from them," Saltzman said.

"He's right," said Gene. "We need to get a group together."

After several hours they stopped to rest and were given bread and water. A small group of Poles, including Saltzman, Tomczuk, and the priest Adsum, organized around the three boys. They each took turns standing guard while the others slept. Tomczuk was on guard when a bunch of criminals approached. He quickly woke up the others. "Go to hell, you Russian bastards, you sons of whores, you scum," he yelled. Gene, Mark, and Henek were quickly on their feet rallying to his aid. Even Adsum levitated himself on unsteady legs and blinked shortsightedly at the attackers. There were four or five of them. One rushed at

Tomczuk flashing a wicked-looking blade. Saltman grabbed the man by the neck and wrestled him away while Gene tackled another one. Others joined in resisting the attackers, who left empty-handed after a short scuffle. "We'll be back," they promised.

After three days of marching, the scenery began to change. Between woodland clumps, they were crossing more open country. The soft, marshy ground slowed their progress. Mosquito swarms plagued them and the *urki* continued to attack. Twice, Gene's group briefly skirmished with the thieves, who backed off in the face of resistance.

Many prisoners had jettisoned all but their most precious possessions to lighten their loads. Gene, Mark, and Henek obstinately held onto their packs. Fair-skinned men like Adsum began to turn red and raw as the sun slowly fried them. Mark briefly glimpsed Rykov, still staggering under his load of rocks, his face a mask of pain and determination. An hour later, there was a commotion behind them. Mark turned to see Rykov clutching his chest and gasping. Then he keeled over. Guards ran toward him as other prisoners crowded around. The guards angrily ordered them to keep marching and dragged Rykov off to the side.

"Mark, keep up, why are you dropping back?" hissed Gene.

"It's Rykov. He just collapsed. I think he must have had a heart attack back there."

"Oh God! Poor old professor, I hope it's not the end for him," said Henek. They all turned back for a moment and saw Rykov's fallen figure surrounded by guards. But they could not stop. One of the guards angrily brandished his weapon at them and told them to keep moving. There was nothing they could do. They turned and began plodding forward. Saltzman eventually broke the silence. "Stupid bugger. I mean, bringing those rocks. What a fool," he said. It seemed like a harsh epitaph.

"He's a good man. Just a little crazy," Mark panted. He looked back one last time but could no longer see what was happening. They never saw Rykov again.

After several hours, they came upon a small lake. Like men possessed, the prisoners ripped off their shirts and plunged into the water, ignoring the cries of the guards. A black cloud of insects rose from the lake to greet them. By the time the men reached shore, many had blood streaming down their chests and backs. Afterward, their bodies were covered with huge, angry red blotches.

Now they spent the days mostly resting, hidden in the woods, and marched at night when the light was somewhat dimmer. There were no signs of human habitation—no roads, no houses, no domestic animals, no people. The guards stepped up the pace, as if they were in more of a hurry to reach their unknown destination. After months, and in some cases years, of starvation rations, many of the prisoners were weak and unfit and began to fall behind. The shots they occasionally heard from the rear were a grim reminder of what awaited those who dropped out. At least the thieves had stopped attacking the boys. Their small group began to spread out. Adsum was limping badly and falling behind. Gene tried to encourage him. "Come on, don't give up, you've come this far. You've got to keep going," he urged.

"You know, I never dreamed I might end my days in a wilderness like this," Adsum gasped, stumbling over a tree root.

"Nonsense. You can't give up now, Adsum. Another day or two and we'll be wherever it is that we're going."

"The spirit is willing, my friend, but the flesh is weak. You march with your brother and your cousin. They need you. I can take care of myself," Adsum panted.

They walked on in silence for a while. Then Adsum spoke again. "Isn't it funny that you and I should have found friendship and that you, a Jew, are the only person I can talk to at this of all times."

"What do you mean?" Gene asked.

"My whole life I was brought up to believe that Jews were evil. I never really knew any Jews before you; I only knew what I learned in church about how you Jews killed Christ and deserved to be punished. And now I see that millions of people in this world are being punished without deserving it at all."

"Adsum, dear friend, I think I know what you're trying to tell me, but this is no time to get morbid. We have to keep going and get through this," said Gene.

Adsum was still with them at the end of the next day's march. But some time the day after that, he disappeared. Gene looked for him in the evening but could not find him. He ran from one group of prisoners to another asking if anyone had seen Adsum. No one had. He had simply vanished. One moment he was spouting Latin; the next he had quietly slipped away. Gene never saw him again.

They marched on, always toward the east over an endless expanse of bog and forest. Finally they saw something shimmering like a mirage above the flat horizon. As they approached, it took on a definite form. They were advancing towards another outpost of the gulag—four watchtowers with machine-gun nests floating above the plain. The footsore prisoners began slapping one another on the back. They picked up their pace, eager to reach sanctuary, however grim. Seldom had a group of convicts been happier to see their prison gates open before them. Gene felt as if they had conquered another challenge. What could be worse than what they had already survived?

The boys learned that they were in a gulag region known as the Kargopol district, which consisted of half a dozen camps spread around a 35-mile radius. They spent the first night at Yartzevo, the administrative center. The next morning the prisoners were divided among other camps. Gene, Mark, and Henek were among 150 Poles who were sent to a place called the Second Aleksyevka Camp. As soon as they arrived, each was seized by unease. There was something about the place—the way prisoners lurched around the compound like scarecrows, the guards' expressions—that set their nerves on edge. When they entered their barracks they noticed that the names of hundreds of prisoners had been gouged into the plaster walls. Most had a small cross and a date scratched beside them.

Henek saw a prisoner dozing on one of the bunks. "What kind of place is this?" Henek asked. The man lifted up a filthy face and gazed at them through pus-filled eyes. His gums were an unearthly white, and half of his teeth were missing. "What's that? Who are you?" he asked.

"I said, what kind of place is this?" Henek repeated.

"New prisoners, eh? You'll find out soon enough, you poor fuckers. You'll find out," the man wheezed. He slumped back into his corner, ignoring all additional questions.

When rations were distributed that evening, the boys got a miserly portion of bread. The soup was a pale urine color with almost nothing in it. "Surely they can't expect us to live on this," Mark said.

"I'm sure we'll do better when we start working. We'll find a way to become Stakhanovites, and then we'll get better rations," said Gene. But when they went to work the next day they found there were no better rations. Everyone in the camp was on the same starvation diet. This was no usual camp, they were told. It was a special place for repeat offenders and troublemakers. The other inmates were hardened criminals or unfortunates who had fallen foul of someone in authority. In the confusion of war, the Poles had accidentally been handed what amounted to a death sentence. It was not a deliberate punishment. It was just bad luck.

They were put to work clearing weeds from a river, so that it would be ready the following spring when timber would be floated in it. There were no quotas to fill; the guards did not even bother to record how much work was completed. The work was secondary; the camp's main purpose plainly was to kill its inmates by starvation. Those crosses next to the names on the barrack walls were the pathetic attempts of prisoners to record their deaths. Convicts would scratch their names on the wall and ask their mates to add the date after they died. It was the nearest thing to a gravestone any of them would have.

July turned to August and August to September. They grew weaker and thinner by the day; each step seemed a step closer to the morgue. For a short time in the summer, they supplemented their diet by picking berries in the forest, but nothing assuaged their constant hunger. They received no fruit or vegetables in their camp rations—just watery broth and the occasional semolina cut into tiny portions. Mark once saw the cook carrying a jar of oil into the kitchen—one small container for 600 men.

There was never a moment when they were not hungry. They passed through distinct stages on the road to starvation. At first, the hunger was like being urged by a possessive lover for more and more attention. Then when the nagging pain could not be appeased, some prisoners were driven to eating grass, leaves, and twigs. At the Aleksyevka, that phase did not last long. As the prisoners grew weaker, they were overtaken by depression and lethargy. Their hands and feet felt cold even when it was warm. They could not get comfortable at night; every position bruised their abnormally sensitive skin. Their eyes turned dull, their necks seemed unnaturally long, their buttocks were thin and sagging. After work, they lay in the barracks, lacking the energy even to talk. Their hearts beat abnormally loudly. In the final stages, they would lose their appetites—then it was only a matter of days.

Even the criminals in the camp seemed different. Half men, half beasts, they seemed to communicate in some primordial language of snarls and grunts. One night Gene walked past their barracks and smelled meat cooking. His mouth watered as he made his way back to his own miserable bed.

"The *urki* have meat from somewhere," he announced.

"It's human meat," another prisoner said.

"What?"

"It's human meat. When they get really hungry they decide who they're going to eat. Then they play cards, and the loser has to kill whoever it is they've chosen. Normally they wait for the night to slit his throat. You can buy some of that meat from them if you've got anything to trade for it."

Gene felt nauseous. He felt as if he had entered a world he never imagined existed anywhere on earth. "What about the authorities? Surely they draw the line at cannibalism," he said.

"Why should they? We're all condemned to die here anyway, from natural causes or from work accidents. That was a work accident. The guards know what's going on. They don't care."

"I wonder who the poor bugger they killed was," Henek said. There was silence for a moment. Then the other prisoner gave a hollow laugh.

"One good thing is that we don't have to worry about going into their pot. We're all too skinny. They usually choose some new pigeon to slaughter, fresh from the outside world with a bit of meat on his bones."

The prisoners were isolated. There were no letters, no newspapers, no radio. They did not know that the Germans had captured Kiev and were at the gates of Leningrad. Nevertheless, in September a rumor seeped in from somewhere that Polish prisoners had been granted an amnesty and were about to be released. The rumor caused a brief upsurge of excitement. But nothing happened, and hope slowly drained away. The boys felt as if there was no outside world; it was just them and their hunger. The despair destroyed the prisoners morally as well as physically. Friends in the Polish group began quarreling with one another over minor items. There were fights over garbage scraps. Men died all around them.

Gene, Mark, and Henek tried to keep up their spirits. They knew that the more apathetic a prisoner became, the more quickly he died. They attempted to maintain a daily routine: washing the yellow crust out of their eyes every morning, shaving when they could muster the strength. But it was difficult. They began suffering from scurvy. Henek and Gene had swollen ankles and legs;

Mark's arms were covered with bleeding sores that did not heal. Their gums were swollen; their teeth were loose. Gene avoided looking at himself. October faded. The first snow arrived, and Gene faced the fact that they would not survive the coming winter. He wanted to live, that he knew. He could feel his will to survive still burning within him. But he had to face the facts. If the swelling in his legs reached his knees he would be immobile—a goner. The jailers would leave him to his fate.

Gene did not say anything to the others. He could tell that Henek saw the end coming, too, but Mark remained relatively cheerful and optimistic. Mark had shown an amazing ability to absorb punishment. Perhaps Mark would pull through, Gene thought.

November arrived with a foot of snow. Gene wondered if he would see the New Year.

CHAPTER 10

The Big Zone

D eliverance arrived on a cold November day. A camp official summoned the
Polish prisoners to hear an announcement. Most of the prisoners were too
weak to concentrate on the dry and legalistic language.

Circumstances had changed, the officer began. The Soviet Union was at war
with a cruel and powerful enemy. Poland, the first wartime victim of Nazism,
was now an ally. The Soviet and Polish peoples would fight together until the
German monster was vanquished. The officer droned on as the prisoners
coughed and shuffled their feet. He finished the first page of his statement and
went to the second. Accordingly, the government of the Union of Soviet
Socialist Republics had issued an amnesty, he stated. One of the effects would be
an immediate change in the status of Polish prisoners. Procedures were being
implemented. Over the next few days, groups of prisoners would take their
personal files and make their way to Yartzevo, where they would be issued new
papers. They would then receive further instructions and information about
their destinations.

As the officer left, the prisoners looked at one another through hollow eyes.
What did he say? What did he mean? Disjointed words drifted through Gene's
mind—"amnesty, changed status, allies, procedures, new circumstances…"
Slowly, it dawned on him. The officer had used the word amnesty. It had to
mean they were being released; whatever crimes they had been accused of were
being wiped out. Gene felt a hint of a sensation so foreign that he had to reach

back into his memory to identify it. It was hope. A path was opening before him. They were being released! They could leave the camp, walk out of the gates without being counted; they would no longer be surrounded by snarling guards and snarling dogs. If they took a step to the left or to the right, no one would shoot them. They might even get regular meals again.

Years later, none of them could remember how they managed to reach Yartzevo or how long it took them: they may have lurched down that road for four or five hours. They simply focused on the mechanical act of putting one foot in front of the other. Heavy snow clouds hovered above. They were in a slow-motion race to reach their goal before the storm engulfed them. Each step was a stab of ice. Every few minutes, they had to stop to rest. Yet the march was liberating. With each stride, they shook off the mental shackles of slavery and began to reclaim themselves.

In Yartzevo, women and children gave the released prisoners a wide berth on the sidewalks, unable to hide their disgust and fear of these human wrecks dressed in rags. But Gene held his head high. He looked at Mark, who was smiling like a kid on an outing despite the oozing sores on his hands, and Henek, his face set in a mask of determination. Gene thought about the way he had found them in Lwów—homesick schoolboys, with half the stuffing knocked out of them. Now, although their faces retained traces of boyish softness, their expressions were hard and wary. The three of them had survived as severe a test as Gene could imagine. They were battered but undefeated. And they were still together.

At Yartzevo they found a commission of three NKVD officers waiting. There were the usual questions: name, birthplace, father's name, profession. When they came to Gene, one of the officers raised an issue. "Born on Soviet territory in Odessa, eh? You'll have to stay. The amnesty only applies to citizens of Poland." Gene, rejuvenated by a few hours of freedom, was dumbstruck. He was not going back to the camps, not under any circumstances, not while everyone else went free. "I am a Polish citizen," he insisted.

"Not if you were born in Odessa you're not."

"My brother can vouch for me. How can he be Polish while I'm not?"

"Because he was born in Poland, and you were born in the Soviet Union."

"I was born in Odessa only because my father, who is a Polish citizen, was held there as a prisoner of war. He was never a Russian citizen and I was never registered as a Russian citizen." Gene raised his voice, his fury getting the better of him. "Why was I arrested in the first place?" he yelled. "Because I was a Polish citizen on what you called Soviet territory. Surely you have that written in your goddamned files. My father is a Polish citizen, my brother is a Polish citizen, my cousin here is a Polish citizen, and I am a Polish citizen."

The officers looked at each other. They had a long line of prisoners to process, and it was getting late. "Come back tomorrow, we'll review your case," one said.

"You'd better think about what you're doing," Gene shouted, trying to draw the crowd's attention. "I'm a citizen of a friendly state. Do you think you can keep me rotting here in secret? First you arrest me because I'm a Pole. Now you say you won't release me because I'm not a Pole. Everybody here knows I'm a Pole."

"Calm down, calm down," Henek hissed at Gene, who was now beside himself in fury. "They said they would reconsider. That's a good sign. Let's see what happens tomorrow. Come away now before they arrest you on the spot." Henek and Mark grabbed Gene's arms and dragged him off.

The three spent a restless night, worrying about what the next day would bring. But in the morning, the officers said that Gene could leave with the others. They gave no explanation for their change of mind. Each prisoner was given two loaves of bread and 30 rubles—a week's wages in peacetime, now enough to buy 8 or 9 loaves of bread on the local black market—and an identity document stating that the holder was a Polish citizen directed to travel to a stated destination only. On the boys' papers it said the destination was Arkalyk, a place in northern Kazakhstan. When they asked around, nobody knew anything about the place; few had ever heard the name before.

Although the Soviet government was releasing tens of thousands of Poles from the camps, the government's attitude toward them remained hostile. Almost all of those released were in poor shape—sick, malnourished, and exhausted. No doubt the authorities hoped that by sprinkling the prisoners around remote and inhospitable areas of the Soviet Union, most would quietly die. Thousands did.

Before they left, Gene had a parting shot for the NKVD. Extracting a tattered piece of paper from his bag, he brandished it under the nose of the astonished officers. "What's this?" they wanted to know.

"My bicycle. I want my bicycle back," Gene insisted.

"What bicycle? What nonsense is this?"

"When I was arrested in Lwów, the NKVD took away my bicycle. They told me that I would get it back after my release. Well now it's after my release, and I want it back or another one like it."

"Don't be ridiculous. Don't you know there's a war going on?" snorted one of the officers. "What do you think you're going to do with a bicycle? Go for a ride?"

"I'll do what I like with it. It's my bicycle. This is an official NKVD receipt. I expect you to honor it."

"You'll get everything back after the war. Now get the hell out of here before we change our minds. We're in no mood for more jokes," shouted the officer.

Once again, Mark and Henek had to pull Gene away.

In the Soviet Union, the "freedom" the boys had been granted was not exactly real freedom. They were leaving what prisoners called the "Little Zone" of the gulag camps but they were entering the "Big Zone"—the prison-like world of the Soviet Union at large, where people lived in perpetual fear, where a wrong word could be deadly, where lies masqueraded as truth, and where truth was treason. As foreigners, their position was especially tenuous. The NKVD was everywhere; the road back to the camps was short.

Saltzman and Tomczuk were released at the same time as Gene, Mark, and Henek. The five walked to the small railroad station at Yartzevo and caught the first train. It took them to Vologda, an important junction. Chaos greeted them at the huge station. Thousands of refugees were on the platforms, desperately rushing toward each approaching train. Some had waited for days, or weeks, sleeping in the station or nearby railway yards. Whenever a train arrived, hundreds of desperate people hurled themselves at it even before it stopped, waving tickets and documents in the air. Conductors used their fists to keep the mob at bay. The human tide surged forward, flinging women and children against the carriages like driftwood. A few determined individuals sometimes managed to fight their way aboard before the doors slammed shut. The rest were cast back on to the platform until the next train arrived.

The Soviet Union, reeling under the weight of the Nazi advance, had embarked on the most massive evacuation in history in a desperate effort to preserve its essential industries. Between July and November 1941, the Soviets dismantled and transported east of the Urals more than 1,500 complete industrial installations. Most were directly involved in armament production. Some ten million people were also shifted away from the war zone. The operation used 1.5 million freight cars. Locomotives dragging scores of trucks and carriages snaked across Russia's great plains toward the safety of Asia. Most government departments also relocated beyond the Urals. Meanwhile, entire ethnic groups considered suspect, such as the Volga Germans, were ruthlessly uprooted and sent into exile. No wonder bottlenecks developed at major railroad junctions.

Along with hundreds of other released prisoners and refugees, the boys spent four nights on the bare floor of a vast waiting room in Vologda. At night, thieves pilfered people's bread and belongings. By day, the authorities drove most of the refugees out of the station and into the town. Those who died the previous night were dumped outside the station each morning for removal.

The only food for sale in Vologda was soup and, for some reason, ice cream. The boys ate as much as their cash reserves permitted. It was obvious that they had to find a way out. With the papers that they had been issued, there seemed little chance of boarding a train soon. And they were in no rush to reach Kazakhstan, a place they knew nothing about. They thought there had to be another alternative.

Wandering around town, they met other Poles who told them that a new Polish army was being formed in southern Russia. It had been established in August as part of the Soviet-Polish agreement. Its commander, they learned later, was General Władysław Anders. Gene was eager to enlist. "What have we got to lose?" he said. "This might be our chance to get out of here. We could be stuck here for weeks and when we finally board a train, there is no telling what we might find in Kazakhstan. And won't it feel good to have a gun in our hands, for a change? What do you say?"

Henek concurred, they'd been downtrodden for too long. But Tomczuk and Saltzman were not enthusiastic. "I don't understand you fellows. No sooner do we get our freedom than you want to throw it away," Tomczuk said. "What makes you so keen to join up? We don't know anything about this army. If it's in Soviet territory, it's bound to be under Soviet control. I don't want to fight for those bastards after what they've put me through. I say screw them and their army."

"It's not a question of fighting for them. We'd be fighting for ourselves. It's a way out of this trap. Who knows, it might be a way out of this country," said Gene.

"It might be a way into a wooden box," said Tomczuk. "Maybe we should take a look at Kazakhstan first."

"I don't know anything about Kazakhstan, but it sounds awfully cold to me," said Henek.

"I think we should go to the army," said Mark. "The food might be better. After all, they have to keep their soldiers healthy."

"And there might even be meat on occasions. When was the last time you fellows tasted meat?" Henek asked.

"And white bread," Mark added.

"All right, all right, don't get carried away. How did we get started on food? Now we're going to be hungry all night thinking about it." Gene interrupted. "We need to decide, are we going or not?"

Tomczuk and Saltzman still had their doubts but said they wanted to stick with the others. Later that day, the five presented themselves to military headquarters to volunteer. Gene, as their leader, was issued a travel warrant that entitled all of them to travel to the Polish army and draw military rations along the way. The army was being formed near the small town of Buzuluk, about 1,600 miles away in the south of Russia.

"How long will it take us to get there?" Mark asked the issuing officer.

"In normal times, three days. In these times, better count on a couple of extra days."

Their military tickets enabled them to board a train, but they were not allowed to sit in a regular compartment with Soviet citizens. Instead, they were hustled into a car full of released prisoners like themselves. The train crept out of Vologda, heading toward the steppes. It rattled through the darkness for a few hours, then jolted to a stop.

"What's happening? Why have we stopped?" asked Mark.

"It looks like we're on a siding. There's a supply train going by," said Henek. They peered out as car after car thundered past. When the train was finally gone, another arrived. Then another. It was an endless procession, well into the next day. Entire dismantled factories lumbered by—contraptions as large as houses secured with ropes; twisted heaps of pipes and tubing piled like spaghetti; bulldozers, cranes, huge flywheels, massive metal girders laid carefully on their sides like sleeping giants. They loomed out of the fog, acquiring a fleeting form, then disappeared. Occasionally carriages full of people rumbled by as well, kaleidoscopes of ghostly faces, one or two pressed against grimy windows. If the train was moving slowly, one might capture a single cloudy image—the face of a young girl, a man asleep clutching a vodka bottle, a couple nestled in each other's arms—then it was gone. They watched until they were tired of watching and then, having nothing better to do, they watched some more. "I'm getting hungry," Mark said at last. "What's the good of food vouchers if you can't use them? What have we got left?"

"Nothing," said Gene, "we finished it all last night."

"Here comes another goddamn train. How long are they going to keep us stuck here?"

Eventually their train lurched forward. Several hours later it pulled into a small station, where they were able to get some food. They had not eaten for two days but were only issued a single day's ration. After wolfing down the food, they were still hungry.

"This is ridiculous," said Mark. "Listen, why don't I change the travel warrant to say there are 15 of us, instead of five? That way we would get more food."

"Good idea," said Gene.

"Cheating the Soviet state. It's against the law. I'm ashamed at you upright boys," said Saltzman sarcastically. They smiled, but Tomczuk was not amused. "Don't even mention law and this fucking country in the same breath," he snorted. Mark altered the number on the document, which helped the next time they passed a station and drew rations. Meanwhile, their progress remained painfully slow. Every few hours they would be shifted aside as a more important transport rolled forward. Sometimes, their carriage was decoupled from the locomotive, and they were told they would not move for at least another day.

They made their way east, past Kirov, past Perm, and into the Ural mountains, the dividing line between Europe and Asia. After two-and-a-half weeks they reached Sverdlovsk, a dreary industrial center. The train stopped there at an imposing station overflowing with refugees. The boys ventured into the city, to find muddy streets lined by shoddy wooden hovels. The town was filled with tired, miserable people standing in long breadlines. After two days, the boys were glad to board a train for Chelyabinsk. They were again segregated in a car with other released Polish prisoners. The wagon was unheated, the cold horrendous. One morning, they woke to find themselves parked on a side rail. It had snowed heavily, and the drifts rose halfway up the doors of the car. Gene tried to open the door. It would not budge; they were snowed in.

"Help me get this open, we've got to dig out," Gene called out to the others.

"What the hell for? To let the cold in?" growled Saltzman.

"We can scout around for food. We can't even see where we are like this. Maybe we're near a village or town," said Gene, his teeth chattering.

"Screw that," said Saltzman. "I'm not moving unless you can show me actual food." A few volunteers stepped forward and tried to push the door open. At last it released, and Gene immediately stepped out. Their car stood alone on the deserted siding; the rest of the train had disappeared. A cruel wind nearly bent him double. Gene beat a hasty retreat.

They sat for three days as trains rolled by on the main line. Once a train stopped in front of them. Men, women, and children poured out to relieve themselves. There were sides of frozen meat hanging from the train windows. "We could do with one of those," murmured Mark.

"Why don't we get one?" said Saltzman.

"But how?" asked Gene.

"Simple. I climb up on the roof of the car and cut the meat loose as the train starts moving. Then I jump down."

"It won't work, It's too cold out there. You'll get frozen rigid up on that roof," said Mark.

"It will work, and I want that meat," said Saltzman, licking his cracked lips. "If it gets too cold, I can always come back. But I don't think the train will be there much longer. If those people are fortunate enough to have all those sides of meat, they'll be too important to leave standing in the middle of nowhere. It's only trash like us that they leave hanging for days on end."

Saltzman was right. Less than half an hour after he swung himself onto the roof of the other train, it started moving. Saltzman began sawing at a rope holding the meat. As the train gathered speed, the rope broke. An entire quarter of sheep fell to the ground. Saltzman jumped off the train and landed in the snow, whooping in triumph. It seemed an eternity before the meat thawed enough for them to hack it into manageable portions. When they finally cooked it, it was the best meal they had eaten in their 18 months in the Soviet Union.

At Chelyabinsk, the boys lost Tomczuk and Saltzman. They took off one night without farewells. They had never been enthusiastic about the idea of joining the Polish army. Gene figured that they had decided to take their chances in Kazakhstan. After so many months of shared hardships, he was sorry to see them go. On the other hand, he was glad to be alone with Mark and Henek—three against the world—again.

They squeezed into a train for Orenburg, which put them within 100 miles of their destination. Orenburg was swamped with Polish refugees, most of them women and children attempting to join men with the army in Buzuluk. The refugees were a sad sight. Some had been living in the station for weeks as they laid siege to the ticket office, but station authorities refused to allow them to board trains without medical certificates declaring them free of infection. And the medical officer who issued the documents never bothered to show up. Leaving these desperate people behind, the boys boarded a train the next day. A few hours later, it rolled into Buzuluk. The date was December 11, 1941. What should have been, at the most, a five-day journey from Vologda had taken almost a month.

The Polish army was pitiable. The amnesty had unleashed an enormous human tide in the direction of Buzuluk, a poverty-stricken town ill-equipped to handle the onslaught. In his autobiography (*An Army in Exile*, London: Macmillan, 1949), General Anders wrote that his army spent the winter in thin tents pitched in temperatures that fell to minus 52 degrees Celsius. Most of the soldiers had neither boots nor shirts; many froze to death. The Soviets would not provide them with weapons, and recruits drilled with wooden rifles. By December 1941, 46,000 men had enrolled. Many brought their families, hoping they might be fed. But the authorities could provide rations for only 30,000 men and called for an end to enlistment.

Gene, Mark, and Henek reported immediately to the officer on duty and were sent for a medical examination. Their physical condition had improved since their release and they were pronounced fit to serve. They were sent to sleep in a tent full of other volunteers and told to report the next day for further instructions. It was a long and bitter night. There was a single stove in the tent, but it was too cold to sleep. They lay huddled together on the ground talking quietly. "What's going on here?" Gene asked one of the soldiers.

"It's a shambles. No food, no guns, no barracks. And wait until you see some of the other recruits. I thought we were joining a Polish army, but this lot here is a joke."

"What do you mean?"

"You'll soon see. It's overrun by fucking Yids."

"And that's not all," growled another man. "This army is under the control of the damn commies in Moscow. They've got us where they want us. Look at us, freezing to death here."

"What's that got to do with the Jews?" Henek asked.

"Everybody knows that the communists are Jews, at least most of them. The Jews can't fight, but everywhere you turn there's a Goldfarb or Silberstein, whining and chiseling, trying to sell you things. When they've taken all our money and our things, they'll leave us to starve. What kind of army is that?"

Mark and Gene looked at one another in the dim light, disturbed by what they were hearing. Gene put his finger to his lip. Everyone in the tent, it seemed, had a bad word for Jews—the cause of all their troubles. Their hatred seemed to be the only thing keeping them warm.

"Pity we don't have some Jews in this tent here with us. They wouldn't last long, I can tell you," another recruit said through chattering teeth. "If it wasn't for the Jews, none of us would be here. I mean, how did the fucking Russians come to invade Poland in the first place?"

"How?" asked Henek.

"The Jews invited them, that's how! We never had commies in Poland except the Jews. The Jews were waiting for them. I was in Lwów in '39...."

"So were we," said Henek.

"Well, you know what happened then. Who was waiting for the Russians with open arms? The Jews. Who took over all the best jobs and houses? The Jews. Who got sent to rot in Russian prisons? Not them!"

The tirade continued through the night. At one point, the boys heard screams from another tent. "What's that?" Gene asked.

"They probably found one. I wish I was there. I would teach them a lesson," said one of the soldiers. "Mary, mother of Christ, it's cold. I could do with a Jew to beat up; it would warm my blood." The screaming continued for a few minutes, then died. But the sound echoed in Gene's brain all night long.

"Let's get out of here right now," Mark said the next morning. "I don't want to fight alongside scum like them."

"I think we should wait," said Gene. "Maybe they aren't typical."

"How can you say that?" Henek exclaimed. "You heard the screams; you heard what they were saying. They'll kill us as soon as they find out that we're Jewish. How long do you think we can keep it secret? A week at most. I don't want to stay here another minute."

"I know, I know," said Gene. "But I don't think we should be in such a rush. You know as well as I do that there are all sorts of Poles. Not all of them are like this. Maybe we can find our place here, maybe not. Let's give it a chance before we decide."

The next day, Gene, Mark, and Henek struggled through the blizzard to the storehouse, where they exchanged their rags for decent clothes and proper shoes, even if Gene had to settle for a pair a couple of sizes too small. That night there was more screaming and yelling from neighboring tents. They did not sleep much.

The following day, the President of the Polish government-in-exile, General Sikorski himself, visited the camp. There was a Catholic Mass followed by a parade in his honor.

Later that day, Gene returned to the medical officials to complete more forms. As he walked back to his tent, he saw a group of soldiers viciously beating two men. One of the victims lay on the ground, unable to move. The second was on his knees, trying to protect his face. A corporal was leading the assault. "This will teach you, Jewboy," he shouted, aiming a blow at the helpless man's head. Other soldiers jeered, or walked past without stopping, some averting their heads. Nobody, it seemed, was about to intervene on behalf of a couple of Jews. Gene had seen enough.

"That's it, we're leaving," he told Mark and Henek when he returned to the tent.

They had not been sworn into the army and did not have uniforms, so it was easy to escape through the woods. Soon they were on the Buzuluk station platform, boarding the first train back to Orenburg. "Where are we going to head for now?" Henek asked.

"Somewhere warm, for a start," said Mark.

"We need to get away from all the refugees. We need to find someplace where we can find work, settle down for a bit," said Gene.

"How about Tashkent?" asked Mark.

"Why Tashkent?"

"I once read a book where it said that Tashkent was called 'the city of bread.' It's in Central Asia. It ought to be warm there."

"Do you know anything about Tashkent, Henek?" asked Gene.

"No, but I don't know anything about any other place either."

"I don't either. The main thing is to get well away from here," Gene said.

"Tashkent seems as good as anything else," said Henek.

"Right then, Tashkent it is," said Gene.

CHAPTER 11

The Steppes of Central Asia

The trains heading east from Orenburg were not as crowded, and there was no difficulty getting aboard. But they no longer had enough money left to buy tickets so they spent much of the next 48 hours dodging the conductors from carriage to carriage or riding on the steps outside. When the train was at full speed, that became a new ordeal, breathing the icy fumes from the locomotive and hanging on desperately with numbed fingers. Once, a conductor discovered them and kicked them off but they simply boarded another train a few hours later. As they moved east, the climate and the landscape changed. Snowy steppes gave way to scorched semi desert. Their wan bodies defrosted; color and circulation painfully returned to stiff limbs. They passed remote stations teeming with thousands of women and children with nothing to eat and no place to go. These were, they later learned, Volga Germans. Stalin suspected them as potential allies of Hitler so he ordered them expelled from their villages and deposited haphazardly in remote parts of the Soviet Union. Once, Gene saw camels outlined against the horizon. Thrilled, he nudged the others—they had never seen a camel outside a zoo before.

After two days they arrived in Tashkent, capital of Uzbekistan. They had hoped to find a place that was not teeming with refugees where they could perhaps find refuge and employment. But one look at the railway station crammed with people camping on platforms and in the waiting room told them that Tashkent was not that place. Just as many crowded the plaza outside the station. "So much for the city of bread," said Henek dejectedly, as they stood surveying the misery. "What do we do now?"

They needed money to buy food, so they headed for the market to sell something. They were immediately plunged into a world familiar only from *The Arabian Nights*. Mark kept stopping to smell the aromas: cumin, cinnamon, nutmeg, and animal dung. Old men sat smoking pipes or drinking green tea. Women with faces obscured behind black veils stepped aside to let animals pass. The boys followed the crowd and eventually found themselves in a large open-air market. After fierce bargaining, Henek sold a pair of trousers he had purloined from the Polish army in Buzuluk. They could eat.

Gene was reluctant to sleep in the station with the refugees, but there was nowhere else to go. They were used to battling the thieves who infested all Soviet stations, but in Tashkent the villains were in a league of their own. One tried to grab Henek's pack from under his head. He woke up just in time to save it, chasing the robber away with curses learned in the camps. Meanwhile, another thief managed to undo Gene's shoelaces while he was asleep. Luckily, the shoes were so tight that they could not be pried loose. Others in the station were less fortunate. Each morning the station echoed with the cries of those whose shoes had been stolen as they slept. Those with money bought replacements at the market. The rest had to hobble around barefoot.

No corner of Tashkent was safe from thieves. Someone stole Henek's backpack, which he had foolishly put down while sitting in a restaurant. As soon as they realized it was gone, the boys tallied the missing items. Mark was especially upset to discover that one of his original shoes from Poland had been in the pack.

"What am I supposed to do with one shoe," Mark wailed, holding up the other, which by chance had been in his own pack.

"We'll have to sell it," said Gene, grinning.

"Come on, don't be stupid. Who'd want a right shoe without the left shoe?"

"Lots of people. You can sell anything in this town. We could even sell you if we got really desperate. There must be lots of one-legged war veterans who would love a good Polish shoe. All we have to do is find one. It shouldn't be too difficult."

It was not. They soon found a man who had lost his left leg and sold him the remaining shoe for a decent price. But they were cheated later, when Mark tried to sell a sweater. Having first shown Mark a 100-ruble bill, the stall keeper managed to switch it with a 10-ruble note when he paid. It was a minor disaster in the greater scheme of things, but Mark was desolate for the remainder of the day.

In addition to regular thieves, Tashkent was overrun by street urchins. Ranging from eight to fifteen years old, they were organized in gangs and generally worked for one of the criminal clans that terrorized the town. Most were orphans whose parents had been swallowed up by the camps in Stalin's purges or by the war. Others had been separated from their families in the confusion of evacuation. They roamed the streets in packs as large as thirty, snatching refugees' belongings in broad daylight. At train times they haunted the station, waiting to plunder new arrivals.

One afternoon, an unusual group of travelers arrived. They looked like they belonged to a circus. A huge man, seven feet tall, stepped off the train with a suitcase in each hand. He was followed by several dwarfs. The giant led the way to the plaza outside. The street urchins did not hesitate. While the big man stood blinking in the bright sunshine, three or four small boys rushed up and kicked him in the shins. Taken aback, he dropped one of his bags to clutch his smarting leg. Instantly a youngster grabbed the suitcase and began dragging it away. The tyke could barely lift the heavy case, but his friends helped whisk it away. As the giant limped after them, one of the boys deliberately slowed down, allowing the man to collar him. The boy immediately started wriggling and kicking, forcing the giant to drop his second suitcase. Within an instant, that bag was gone as well, and the boy had slipped free. The giant had lost all of his possessions less than five minutes after arriving. He stood nearly in tears while a dozen young delinquents circled him, jeering.

"We can't sleep in the station any more," said Gene, as the urchins finally tired of their sport. "A few more days of this and we'll lose everything we have."

"If you ask me, we can't stay in this town at all. There's nothing for us here. There's surely no chance to find work, that's obvious," Henek said, voicing what they all thought.

"But where can we go? Everywhere we've been so far has been just as bad. This entire country stinks. If only we could find a way to escape," said Mark.

"Escape! Escape, yes, that's the answer," said Henek.

"Hold on, slow down, both of you. It's all very well to daydream if it makes you feel better, but this is the Soviet Union, don't forget. You can't just start walking in the direction of the nearest border and tell the sentries you've changed your mind about staying here. The whole country has always been guarded like a prison, probably even more so now that there's a war on," Gene said.

"You don't know that for a fact. You're the one who keeps saying that we can do anything we want as long as we stick together. I think Mark's right. This country is hell. We've been halfway across it by now, and all we've seen are starving people and NKVD wherever you look. God knows what might happen to us if we stay like this. If only we could get out," said Henek.

"Look, I don't disagree with you. But face facts. It's bound to be incredibly difficult to escape. Otherwise, lots of people would be doing it. Without a map, I don't even know how far it is to the nearest border and which country is on the other side," said Gene. "Do you know, Mark?"

"I'm not sure. Maybe China or Afghanistan. That's one thing it should be easy enough to find out."

"All right, let's ask. Maybe we can find some Poles who've been deported here and ask them. But just be very careful. The place is crawling with NKVD," said Gene.

"So what do we do in the meantime?" asked Henek.

"We stay here, but we try to find some other place to sleep. I've had it with the station," said Gene.

That night, they found an empty railroad car, but railway officials came by at midnight and rousted them out. The following night, the same thing happened. So the third night they tried sleeping in a car that stood on a siding farther away from the station, hoping the guards would not be eager to trek so far. No guards appeared that night. Instead, thieves came—two of them—wielding knives. Gene woke up when he heard them rummaging through his belongings. He half opened his eyes, then quickly closed them when one of the robbers turned his way. Gene could sense their unwashed bodies moving closer. From their regular breathing, it seemed that Mark and Henek were asleep. Gene prayed they would stay that way. If the thieves suspected that any of them were awake, there would be a fight and they might be badly hurt or killed. Gene tried to keep his own breathing even. After some tense minutes, the men took what they wanted and left. The next morning, Mark found two razor cuts on the back of his right hand.

The robbers apparently had been trying to pry something out of his pocket, but he had been so deeply asleep that he felt nothing. For weeks, the cuts oozed blood, Mark's vitamin-starved body incapable of healing them.

The boys stayed in Tashkent for several more days trying to get information about potential escape routes. They were still there as the terrible year of 1941 ended. The word among the Polish refugees was that it was impossible to reach the Chinese border. Some spoke of a possible escape pipeline further south, through Tajikistan, over the Pamir Mountains, and into Afghanistan. But the route was difficult, the mountains high and craggy, and all the passes were guarded. They would need a lot of money to tempt a guide and to bribe the guards. At present, they could barely scrape enough for the next meal. Another idea they talked about was to go southwest into the valley of the Amu Dar'ya River and try to cross the border there, though no one knew of anybody who had attempted it. The boys decided to head for the ancient Silk Road city of Samarkand and see if there was a better chance to find work or an escape route from there.

Samarkand! The name seemed to breathe romance; the reality of January 1942 was anything but romantic. They arrived on a miserable gray day, hungry after the overnight train journey, and virtually penniless. Splashing through streets lined with dilapidated mud-brick dwellings, they searched in vain for something to eat. Finally they found themselves in a magnificent central square, bordered by the deteriorating remains of a fallen empire. It was almost deserted. They were dwarfed by huge columns, minarets adorned with chipped mosaics and faded Islamic calligraphy, and a mosque, topped by a grimy turquoise dome. Indifferent to the grandeur, all they wanted was to eat.

"Gene," Mark eventually said, breaking the gloomy silence.

"Yes?"

"What's going to happen to us?"

"I don't know."

"I mean, how much longer can we go on like this, wandering from place to place?"

"I don't know, Mark," Gene sighed deeply, burying his head in his hands.

They eventually asked an elderly Uzbek where they might eat. All the shops were closed that day, he told them and suggested they try a sunflower oil factory on the outskirts of town, where he said there might be food for sale. At the factory, the only "food" available was compressed slabs of sunflower seeds usually used for animal fodder. They bought one. It was gray-green, cheap—and inedible. They had to use a rock to break it into pieces small enough to chew. One taste was enough—each of them quickly spat it out.

"This is too disgusting," said Henek. "I'd rather starve."

"You might have to. Maybe the first bite's the worst, and it grows on you," said Gene, taking another bite. It did not grow on him.

"I've got a better idea," said Mark. "We still have our travel warrant for the Polish army. Why don't we go to the station and try to draw military rations. They don't know we've already been to Buzuluk. For all they know, we could be on our way there from Tashkent or some other place in the east."

"It's dangerous," said Gene. "The last time we drew rations was in Sverdlovsk, which was in the opposite direction and closer to Buzuluk than we are now. And another thing, the document says there are 15 of us. How do we explain that?"

"You figure it out," said Mark, hungry beyond reasoning.

"We could tell them that there wasn't room on the train for everyone, so we agreed to meet up some place later," said Henek.

"It sounds awfully thin. If they decide there's anything suspicious about us, we could get into trouble," Gene worried.

"Do you have you a better idea? It's either that or starve. Do you want to eat this muck? How much lower can we fall?" asked Mark.

"No, I guess we don't have much choice," Gene conceded. "It's a crazy thing to do, but I'll do it if you promise to send me food parcels if I get sent back to the gulag," he added, only half joking.

Gene decided that he should go to the station commander's office on his own. If anyone were to be arrested, it should be him. There was no need to expose all three of them. He found a tired officer dozing behind a desk. The man eyed the document while Gene waited nervously. "You say there are 15 of you?" the officer asked apathetically. "No, there are only three of us here. The others got left in behind Tashkent. Some got ill and their friends wouldn't leave them." The man grunted noncommittally, scratched his head, and looked at Gene again. Gene held his breath, his heart pumping hard. Then, reaching into his desk, the officer wrote out a new warrant, which he stamped and handed to Gene.

"You can go and get your rations in the storeroom. The clerk in the office will give you some money for the next stage of your trip. I suggest you catch the first train out of here tomorrow morning." Like any good Soviet official, the man had not dared change the paper. It still said they should get enough food for 15.

They celebrated in the waiting room that night, stuffing wads of black bread into their empty bellies. There was also some dried powder, which, mixed with boiling water from a vat in the station, turned into an ersatz stew, a real feast. But it was a one-time treat. Having presented themselves as prospective Polish soldiers, it was too risky to remain in Samarkand.

They had just enough money to buy tickets to Kagan, the next big town to the west. They arrived the next afternoon and resumed the search for food or work. There was little of either. Their odyssey seemed increasingly pointless. They had traveled more than 2,000 miles since their release from the camp but were no nearer a destination than they had been at the start. They were dejectedly discussing their options when someone called out to them excitedly in Polish. "Gene, Mark, Henek, is it really you? It can't be!"

They looked up. For a moment they could not place the fur-hatted figure walking toward them. Then recognition dawned. It was Max Nowak, one of their neighbors in the derelict building where they had lived for six months in Lwów. The four of them met, yelling and whooping, hugging and slapping one another on the back.

"Let's have a look at you. You look thin. Where have you been?" Max bubbled. "You must come with me to my place."

"Where do you live?"

"Bukhara, it's just a few miles away on the train. But what an amazing coincidence. They say it's a small world, but I never believed it until now. Wait 'til Zofia sees you; she'll be so happy to see people from home."

Gene was not sure about that. He remembered Zofia as a sour-spirited woman who had never liked them in Lwów. But he was happy to visit. At least they might get a decent meal and a night in a proper bed. The train to Bukhara was not due for two or three hours, so Max suggested going to a bar. Mark was elected to stay behind to watch their belongings and buy tickets.

"Why me?" he yelled at their retreating figures.

"Because you're the youngest," came the usual answer.

The others were gone for what seemed like a very long time. Mark bought the tickets. Then he stood on the platform, growing more and more anxious. The train arrived, and passengers began to board. Still the others did not appear. Finally Mark caught sight of three figures weaving down the platform, tunelessly singing a lewd song in Polish. Mark's anger turned to fear when he saw what state they were in.

"Hurry up, the train's about to go," he shouted.

"Whassat, little brother?" came Gene's slurred voice.

"The train, the train. It's about to leave. And shut your mouths, for God's sake. You're all plastered."

"I will not shut my mouth. I'm sick of shutting my mouth. I'm sick of everything in this stinking, rotten country. Comrades, it's time to speak the truth," Gene proclaimed, throwing his arms wildly in the air. Mark had never seen him like this before. He could scarcely believe it.

"Let'sh drink to the truth," yelled Henek, who clutched a bottle. "Shcrew the Soviet Union and everyone in it."

"Scuse me, what did you say?" asked Max.

"I shaid, screw the Soviet Union and everyone in it," screamed Henek. Other passengers turned to look at the drunken trio.

"And d'you know what else I say? I say screw that motherfucker Stalin," shouted Gene. He began stumbling forward again, singing the words aloud to the tune of a Polish folk song. Mark was almost breathless with terror. He anxiously scanned the platform to see if anyone was paying attention. But drunks were a common sight in the Soviet Union and most of the other passengers ignored them. Luckily, there did not seem to be any NKVD men around.

"Shut up, for God's sake," Mark pleaded.

"Look, isn't it shweet? Mark's worried about us. He thinks we're drunk," Henek said.

"You are drunk," hissed Mark.

"We're not! We're just happy for a change. We're happy we found our friend Max, aren't we, Max old friend? When was the lasht time you were happy, little cousin?"

"I can't remember. And you won't remember either if you wake up back in the gulag. Come on, we've got to get on the train," Mark said, trying to manhandle them up the steps. He wrestled them into an empty compartment and slammed the door shut.

As the train moved off, Max threw up. Henek took one look at him and threw up too. The compartment seemed knee-deep in vomit. Mark was frantic, fearing the train conductor would report them for "hooliganism." He rushed out to the corridor, searching for something to clean up the mess with and finally used an old pair of trousers from his backpack. Gene and Henek fell asleep, snoring loudly. Mark stood guard outside the compartment until the conductor came to check their tickets. Fortunately the official did not insist on entering the berth.

They arrived in Bukhara with Gene and Henek still stone drunk. Max knew enough to hire a droshky. After Samarkand's mosaics, Bukhara was unrelentingly drab. Gene and Max kept up their singing all the way to Max's house, while Henek complained that his head was spinning. Finally they arrived.

Max staggered to the door and began thumping on it. "Zofia, Zofia, my bird, my sweetheart, look who I've brought you," he raved. The door opened to reveal Zofia, even more bony and disapproving than they had remembered. She did not seem happy to see them, especially in the state they were in. "Pigs, filthy drunken pigs," she spat, grabbing Max by the collar and pulling him inside. She told him in no uncertain terms to sober up. "As for the rest of you, I don't know what my drunken husband told you, but you can't stay here. We have no money and hardly any food."

"But beloved, that's no way to treat old friends from Poland. They gave us firewood that cold winter in Lwów, remember? You can't throw them out in the street," Max burbled.

"We are not running a guest house. I won't throw them out tonight but they'll have to leave tomorrow," Zofia hissed.

"Don't worry, we'll be on our way tomorrow," said Mark. "We just wanted to see how you and Max were managing and maybe have a wash."

"Well, you can stay tonight," Zofia said, her pinched face softening a little. "You could certainly use a wash."

By evening, Gene and Henek finally sobered up. Gene took Mark aside. "Look, I'm sorry about getting drunk like that," he said uncomfortably.

Mark waved him away. "No harm done. Just don't sing again. You have a terrible voice," he said with a grin.

That night, they quizzed Max about possible routes of escape from the Soviet Union, but he knew nothing. Other Polish exiles gathered; it seemed none of them had ever given a thought to trying to get out of the country. No one had a map; in the Soviet Union, possession of a map was not encouraged even in peacetime. The boys realized there would be no escape. They were trapped in the USSR and they had better make the best of a bad deal. But where in this vast country might they find work and a secure place to stay? Bukhara was even worse than Tashkent or Samarkand. The city was in the grip of a typhoid epidemic. Factories were closing and sending workers home until it abated.

"Maybe we should try the Caucasus," Gene suggested that night as they lay down to sleep. "We're already halfway there. It shouldn't be too difficult to get to from here."

"The only thing I've heard about the Caucasus is from that old Georgian in Volozero with his stories of white bread," Mark recalled.

"I remember him too. But what makes you think there won't be masses of refugees there as well?" asked Henek.

"Who knows, but it seems like most people are being evacuated to Central Asia," Gene reasoned. "Since we left Tashkent and started going west, the trains have been less crowded. Besides, the climate is bound to be better there. We might as well give it a try, unless someone has a better idea."

"What about documents? We need documents to travel," objected Henek.

"That's true. We would have to fix our papers somehow."

"Do you really think there's white bread there?" Henek asked.

"I don't know. It would be nice, but really it makes no difference. We can't stay here, we can't go back, and we can't get out of the country. So what's left? Take a look at the travel warrant, Mark. Do you think you can you do anything with it?"

"Maybe," said Mark. "I'd have to add a destination in the Caucasus if there's room on the form." He examined the document. The space set aside for their destination was quite small and mostly filled by the word *Buzuluk*. But there was just enough room to add another place name if it was short.

"What places do you know in Georgia?" Gene asked.

"I only know one that's short enough—Gori, Stalin's birthplace," said Mark. They laughed. It seemed an appropriate choice. So Mark carefully added the words "via Gori" on the paper. They decided that if challenged they would say they had been chosen for special technical training in Gori and were to join the rest of the Polish army in Buzuluk after the course.

The next morning, January 9, 1942, Gene wrote to Nusia before parting from Max and Zofia. It was the last letter she would receive from him during the war. "All these months we've spent on trains and in railway stations. But we cannot remain here either. We leave today, for where exactly we do not know," he wrote. "If, by chance any news reaches you from our families, I pray it won't all be bad."

Back at Kagan, they counted their money and discovered that there was only enough for two train tickets. So they wrapped Mark in a blanket, tied him up with string, and shoved him in the luggage rack, much to the amusement of the other passengers. Mark did not think it was funny.

"Why me?" he kept asking.

"Come on Mark, you're the smallest and the youngest," said Henek.

"I'm always the youngest."

"And you always will be. So shut up and stop moaning, at least until the conductor comes through."

The next major stop on the line was a town called Mary. All the way, Mark kept sticking his head out and complaining that he was hungry. Eventually he became too uncomfortable on the luggage rack so they shoved him under the seat. But the deception worked; the conductor never suspected a thing. They traveled for several hours, crossing the Amu Dar'ya River and heading into the Kara-Kum or "black sands" desert, which stretched to the shores of the Caspian Sea, the gateway to the Caucasus. They reached the Republic of Turkmenistan. When the train arrived at Mary, they got off. They needed food and money before they could push on, but that meant presenting their travel warrant to the local military, a new risk. Gene nervously took the document to the stationmaster's office and was directed to local army headquarters some distance away. The officer there was the opposite of the commander Gene had encountered in Samarkand, who had barely examined the paper. This one pored over it for a disturbingly long time, mumbling to himself.

"You say you are Poles?" he eventually asked.

"That's right," said Gene.

"And you're on your way to Buzuluk."

"That's right."

"But first you want to go to Gori in Georgia."

"That's right."

"What's in Gori?"

"It's a technical training course."

"For Poles?"

"Correct."

The officer stared at the paper for several minutes, occasionally muttering "Buzuluk" and "Gori," apparently unable to decide what to do. Finally, he picked up the document and disappeared into an adjoining office. Gene felt his palms grow sweaty. Half an hour ticked by. Could this be the moment his luck ran out? No, his guardian angel was with him. When the officer returned, he was smiling. He handed Gene a new document and a small wad of banknotes. The document authorized 15 men to travel to the Polish army in Buzuluk by way of Gori. The officer had swallowed their cover story. But that was not all. Outside the office Gene found a neatly stacked pile of boxes, sacks, and cans full of provisions.

"Is this all for us?" he asked.

"It's for 15 fighting men," said the officer beaming. "And remember not to spare any Nazi bandits when you get to the front."

Gene stammered his thanks. "It's nothing, my friend. It's a mark of solidarity between our two nations," the officer declaimed.

"The Polish nation will never forget the support it has received from its Soviet brothers," Gene responded, knowing how addicted the Russians were to such phrases. A buggy was provided to carry the load to the station, where Mark and Henek waited. They quickly bought tickets with the money and loaded the food onto the next train. It was too much for them to carry, so they discreetly gave most of it away to other passengers, keeping only what they could carry in their packs. And so began the final stage of their journey through Asia.

CHAPTER 12

A Case of Typhoid, a Game of Chess

The last leg of their train ride was uneventful. They passed the city of Askhabad and embarked on a final 24-hour stretch to the Caspian Sea, cutting through an unrelenting desert landscape. Occasionally they glimpsed camels ridden by menacing-looking tribesmen wearing heavy black capes and shaggy wool hats. That was the only sign of life they saw. Henek said he did not feel well and slept the entire way.

As they neared the port city of Krasnavodsk, they caught sight of the choppy, blue-gray waters of the Caspian Sea. The next hurdle would be boarding a ship to get to the other side. Gene looked at Mark and Henek. They seemed tired and dejected after the long ride across the desert. "Come on vagabonds, shape up! Smell that glorious sea air," he said, trying to rally their spirits.

"I'm hungry," Mark complained. "I want some real food. I'm sick of this dry stuff that they gave us at Mary." Gene rubbed his brother's stubbly face affectionately. "You're always hungry, and you're also filthy," he said. Mark had been a smooth-skinned 16-year-old when all this had started. Now he was a few days away from nineteen. His mother would scarcely recognize the disheveled, unshaven bandit her baby had become.

"And you're clean, I suppose," Mark retorted.

"I could do with a wash and a shave," Gene conceded.

They looked at Henek, waiting for him to say something. But Henek was silent. His eyes protruded in a face that had turned quite pale. "Are you all right?" Gene asked him.

"I don't know, I feel a little sick," Henek replied in a shaky voice. "I have this splitting headache, and I'm a bit dizzy."

"Maybe a bowl of borscht will help. Let's find some food," said Mark.

Krasnavodsk was a dreary town squashed against the sea by rolling hills. There was a nervous air about the place. As soon as the three turned out of the station, they were accosted by a man in uniform. "Who are you? Let's see your papers," he ordered. Gene pulled out their travel documents and release papers. The man examined them suspiciously. "Foreigners, are you? Don't you know this is a closed city? You're in a restricted military zone. You have no right to stay here. Have you registered with the authorities?"

"We were just going to do that," said Gene. "We only just got here."

"Well, do it right away. You can only stay here three days."

For all its small size, Krasnavodsk was of key strategic significance. The main port on the eastern shore of the Caspian, the town had significant oil drilling and storage facilities and was the main transit point between the Caucasus and central Asia. The place swarmed with the military and security men, whose main function, it seemed, was to run refugees and other undesirables out of town. Even the locals were wary. Gene approached some townspeople to ask where he could buy food. They hurried to the other side of the street without answering. Eventually the boys found a rough eating-house. The manager was abrupt and surly.

"What have you got?" asked Mark.

"Fish," said the man, pointing to a barrel in the corner. Mark peered into it and saw a few herring pickling in brine.

"That's it?" he asked, disappointed.

"What did you expect? Caviar?"

"We'll take three of the fish," said Gene.

Henek did not want to eat, but Mark told him he would feel better if he did. The salty food left them intensely thirsty.

"Can we have some water?" Mark asked.

"Water's rationed," came the curt reply. "If you want to drink, line up like the rest of us." The man pointed out to the street, where people carrying containers were lined up at a public water tank, waiting for the authorities to switch on the supply.

By the time they quenched their thirst, it was late morning, and Henek was feeling worse. Mark felt his forehead. "I think you've got a fever," he said. "Gene, what are we going to do?"

"We'll have to find a doctor if it gets worse. Meantime, I'd better go down to the port and see when there will be a ship. You two wait here." Henek promptly fell asleep on a bench, anxiously watched over by Mark.

There were two officials in the security office by the harbor, a plump middle-aged man dressed in civilian clothes and a uniformed NKVD officer who wore a suspicious expression matching his occupation. This was the third time Gene had presented the travel warrant since leaving Tashkent and each time had been an ordeal. In Samarkand and Mary the document had passed inspection, but Gene had an uncomfortable feeling the examination here would be more thorough. Taking a deep breath, he approached the counter and said he had been directed to apply for a passage to the Caucasus. "Papers," said the civilian, in an uninterested voice. Gene handed over the warrant. As the man inspected it, his bored expression gave way to a distrustful look. Obviously he had never seen a document like this before. He called over to his uniformed colleague. "Take a look at this."

The NKVD man surveyed the paper and looked at Gene. "Do you have any other credentials?" Gene gave him his release papers. The man read them carefully, his skepticism deepening. "It says here you are 15 men. Where are the others?"

"Some are here in Krasnavodsk. The others are on the way. They should get here in a day or two," Gene replied, trying to keep his voice matter-of-fact.

"How will they get here?" the officer asked.

"We left them money in Mary to buy train tickets."

"Why aren't they with you now?"

"There was no room on the train."

"That's unusual. Where are you going?"

"Like it says on the paper, we're going to Gori."

The officer examined the papers again, frowning. "Nobody is permitted to cross the sea except returning residents, military personnel, and others performing official duties," he said.

"We are military personnel," replied Gene, not missing a beat. "We're Polish draftees on our way to join our unit so we can fight the Germans." The officer plainly did not know what to make of this. His training told him that the thing to do in such situations was to consult a superior, push the responsibility onto someone higher up the chain of command. "Well, I don't know anything about any Polish army in Buzuluk. I never heard of such a thing. Anyway, why do you have to go to Gori?"

"For technical training. After the course, we'll proceed to Buzuluk," said Gene.

"Technical training, eh?" repeated the officer, his voice oozing doubt. "Well, we'll see about that. I'm keeping your papers so we can verify these things."

"But how can we stay in town without papers?" asked Gene, anxiety creeping into his voice.

"That's your problem," said the officer. He disappeared into the next office, the precious papers in his hand.

Even worse news awaited Gene when he rejoined his brother and cousin. "Henek's getting really bad," Mark said. "I think his fever is going up; he's been tossing and turning on the bench and muttering all kinds of nonsense."

"Maybe it was that stinking fish we had," said Gene.

"I don't think it's the fish. He was complaining all day, long before we ate. And he slept for nearly 24 hours on the train," said Mark.

"It's too late to do much about it today. We need to get to the station to find a place to sleep. He'll probably be better in the morning."

"I don't know," said Mark. "I'm really worried. I've never seen him like this before."

They spent the night huddled in the waiting room. There were no thieves, but militiamen kept stomping around, roughly waking people to check their documents. They were obviously recording how long each individual had been in town. They were particularly suspicious of Caucasians and Asians, who were notoriously lacking in enthusiasm for the war and had deserted the Red Army in droves. When the guards reached Gene, he told them that the NKVD had their papers.

"Be sure you get them back if you want to stay here tomorrow," an officer told them. They slept little the rest of the night. Henek's condition was becoming more alarming by the minute. He was clearly running a high fever, his shirt was drenched in sweat, yet his teeth were chattering. He had a severe headache and a raging thirst. He shivered uncontrollably on the hard floor and kept moaning, "I feel bad; I feel very bad."

"We've got to get him to a doctor," Mark said, as dawn came.

"I know," said Gene. "Let's get him on his feet and find out where there is a clinic or a hospital." Hoisting Henek up, they stumbled slowly into the street. The hospital, they discovered, was about three miles outside town. It took a long time to get there. They had to support and at times half carry Henek, stopping every few minutes for a rest. When they arrived, a doctor took one look at Henek and had him hustled away. Gene and Mark waited nervously until the doctor reappeared.

"Well, my lads, your friend will have to stay with us. It looks like typhoid. We need to keep him here for observation."

"Typhoid, my God, what will happen to him?" Mark asked.

"What will happen to him? What happens to anybody. Either he'll get better or he won't," the doctor said wearily, but seeing the look of horror on Mark's face, his tone softened. "Don't worry lad. We'll take care of him. I've seen a lot worse than your friend who pulled through."

"Is it catching? Does that mean we might get it too?" Gene wanted to know.

"You usually catch it from contaminated food or water," the doctor said. "Where have you come from? You're not from around here."

"We traveled from Mary. Before that we were in Samarkand and Bukhara," said Gene. "That's where he must have caught it. They said there was an epidemic there."

"Can we see him?" Mark asked.

"You can see him, but you can't go near him," said the doctor. When they saw Henek, he was asleep.

Henek's illness changed their situation. Now they needed to find a way to stay in Krasnavodsk long enough for him to recover. First, they had to get their papers back. Returning to town, Gene and Mark tried to trade their remaining supplies for something to eat. There were few takers among the sullen townspeople, but they eventually managed to exchange a bag of green Uzbek tea for a hunk of dried meat, which they tore into ravenously. Then Gene left Mark and hurried back to the port to check on their papers.

Entering the office, he was relieved to see the NKVD man was not there. The civilian, his sleeves rolled up, was studying a chessboard. Gene greeted him politely and asked for his papers back. "Sorry, can't do that, investigation still in progress," said the man, not looking up, absorbed in the chess game. He kept muttering, "It doesn't look good. It doesn't look good."

"But we need papers. Otherwise, how can we stay here?" asked Gene.

"You need papers, young man, and I need to do something about this knight attacking my queen before the chief comes back to make his move," said the official, mopping his brow with a grubby handkerchief.

In the absence of his superior, the man seemed more human. He was simply another bureaucrat, Gene concluded, sometimes harassed, sometimes bored, and, like all Soviet officials, deadly afraid to make a wrong decision. Any mistake could be costly and he obviously had not survived this long by showing personal initiative. Thinking what to say next, Gene glanced at the chessboard. The man was playing black. Gene instantly saw he was in a rotten position, his pieces bunched together.

"What about moving your bishop here?" Gene suggested diffidently, trying to establish some human connection. The man considered the move and immediately brightened. "That's good, that's quite good," he said. "I see you're a chess player. We must have a game. Come back tomorrow. We'll play then."

"Tomorrow? How long are we going to be here?"

"The chief is still checking your papers. He couldn't get through by telephone so he sent out a telegram. We'll have the answer soon enough. You'll just have to wait."

Gene's heart sank. That was what he had feared. The travel document was good enough to pass a spot check, but would it hold up under real scrutiny? There was no Polish unit in Gori and, although Gene did not know it at the time, the one in Buzuluk would soon be gone. It was transferring to a location near Tashkent. With Henek hospitalized and no papers, Gene felt he was walking on thin ice. The one hope was to keep bluffing. The Soviet bureaucracy was slow moving at the best of times and now, with everything disrupted by war, it was likely to be even less efficient. This might allow them to stay in town long enough for Henek to recover. But he had to get some kind of document that would satisfy the militiamen at the station.

He told the official, "I'd like to play you tomorrow very much, but how can we stay in town without papers?"

The man looked down at the chessboard, staring at the bishop now protecting his position. "I wouldn't do this for everybody," he muttered. Then, he picked up a pen and wrote a short note stating that Gene's documents were with the port authorities and that he and his companions were permitted to remain in town for the prescribed period. Looking around to make sure the two of them were still alone, he slid it across his desk to Gene. "Don't disappoint me. Ten o'clock tomorrow morning. We'll see how you play," he said. Gene thanked him, put the paper in his pocket, and left, feeling that he had gained a little breathing space.

The night passed uneventfully, though neither Gene nor Mark slept well. The next day would be the last they could legally remain in Krasnavodsk. If they had to leave, a horrible decision awaited. Where would they go? For the first time in weeks, Gene found himself thinking about their parents and brother back in Poland. He wondered how they were surviving. He knew they had been forced to leave their home and were imprisoned in a ghetto, probably struggling to make ends meet in the face of daily humiliations. Gene wished he could reach them with word that he and Mark had survived the camps. That knowledge might strengthen his mother and father in their own ordeal. But, of course, there was no way to contact them.

Mark was thinking of Henek, his constant companion and best friend. What if they had to leave him behind? "We can't. We'll find a way to stick together," he told himself. But the worry would not go away.

When Gene returned to the port the next day, his friendly official had already set up his chessboard. He offered Gene his hand with a broad smile. "I've been looking forward to this all morning," he said. "Dmitri Antonovich is the name."

"Yevgeny Adolfovich," Gene replied. "I was hoping that today we could get our proper papers back."

"Papers, papers," the official fussed. "First things first. We're here to play chess. The papers can wait 'til afterwards." He moved his king's pawn forward and the game began. For all his enthusiasm, it soon became clear that Dmitri was a mediocre player. He played slowly, muttering to himself as he tried to decide his next move. Gene had been a fierce competitor in his school days, when he hated to lose at anything. But now he was playing for higher stakes. He did not care about the game. What he needed was to somehow persuade the official to issue new papers so they could stay in town until Henek recovered.

Gene set his mind to turning the game into a drawn-out struggle, ignoring the official's errors or countering with mistakes of his own. As they played, they began talking. When the conversation touched on Gene's release from labor camps the man visibly stiffened. "Were you prisoners of war?" he asked nervously.

"That's right, prisoners of war," Gene replied. "But now we Poles and you Russians are allies, fighting the same enemy. That's why they want to train us, so we can fight the Germans." The man relaxed slightly. By then, half the morning was gone, and the game was approaching its bumbling climax. The official had stumbled into a winning attack. He sacrificed his knight with a flourish. Gene pretended to be astounded, then accepted the sacrifice. The white queen bore down on his king. "Checkmate," said the delighted official. "My word, that was quite a game." His chubby face was wreathed with smiles, his tired eyes shone with enthusiasm. Gene knocked over his king in surrender and looked up, a rueful expression on his face. "You certainly surprised me with that sacrifice," he said. "I didn't see that coming at all."

"So I did, so I did. But you had me worried earlier on. You play pretty well for a non-Russian. But that maneuver with the bishop, that caught you napping, didn't it? You see Yevgeny, what they say is right. There is no substitute for daring at the right time. Well, cheer up lad! We'll play again tomorrow."

At this rate, Gene thought, we'll be here for weeks. "What about our passage across the sea?" he asked casually.

"Your passage? Ah yes, your passage. Well, I've nothing to tell you about that today. But perhaps we'll have some news tomorrow and you can try to get your revenge," said Dmitri, still flushed with victory. Gene shook hands with his new friend, congratulated him again on his win, and rejoined Mark in town. "No news," he said, "but I managed to lose to him at chess."

"It took you long enough," Mark said. "You had me worried waiting here so long. Half the day's gone. Come on, we have to go to the hospital to see Henek."

When they arrived the doctor was not available, and the nurse in charge refused to let them see the patient. "He's got typhoid. He's in isolation. Now go," she said, waving them out of the room.

"Let's see if we can find him through the window," suggested Mark. So they circled the building peering into each window until they spotted Henek lying in bed. He was awake but when they motioned for him to come to the window, he looked back without a glimmer of recognition. They returned to town in a somber mood.

That night, Gene and Mark did not dare sleep in the railway station. They had already overstayed the permitted three days. They walked to a beach outside the town and found a place in the dunes. Fortunately, it was warm. They lay side by side, each sunk in his own thoughts. They had virtually no possessions, little money, no work, no friends, and no roof over their heads. All they had was each other and their freedom. And how long would they keep even that?

The next day, Gene retraced his footsteps to the port. He found Dmitri Antonovich studying a thick file. The official waved Gene into the office and gave him a glass of Russian tea while he waited. Gene saw that his own documents were on top of the desk. Finally, Dmitri looked up. The jollity of the previous day was gone. His voice was serious. "Yevgeny Adolfovich, let us speak frankly. It's best to be open," he said.

"Absolutely, I've been open all along," Gene replied.

"Well, perhaps you have," said the official. He paused for a second, collecting his thoughts. "Yevgeny Adolfovich, I'm trying to be a friend to you. In my job, I don't often do favors to people. But I like you, young man. That's why I want to help you."

He paused again. "Look, we don't know really who you are," he continued. "We don't know where you came from or where you are going. But the chief is very suspicious. Let's face it, your story is fishy. You say there are 15 of you but nobody else from your party has arrived. My advice to you is to leave here as soon as possible. For your own good. Am I making myself clear?"

Gene swallowed hard. "That's what we came here for. To get tickets for the boat. There's nothing to keep us in Krasnavodsk," he said quietly.

"Listen to me, Yevgeny Adolfovich. The chief could have you arrested right now. But he would prefer it if you leave immediately. He likes a quiet life. He doesn't want the political commissars on his back. You do have a valid travel warrant, and your warrant says Gori on it, so he's covered if he lets you go. If you stay here, he'll be forced to act. There's a boat leaving tonight for the port of Makhachkala across the water. If I were you I would be on it. How many of you are there really?"

"Seven," said Gene, unwilling to admit that there were only three of them.

"I'll arrange places for you on the boat. The tickets and your papers will be waiting for you on the dock at ten tonight."

"Thank you, Dmitri Antonovich," said Gene, standing up to leave. "I won't forget it."

"Not so fast, young man," said the official sternly. "We still have one more piece of business to conduct."

"We do?" asked Gene.

"We do," said Dmitri, getting out the chess pieces. "It's your turn to be white, I think."

So the hammer had fallen. There was no putting off a decision any longer. Sitting through another tedious game with the official, Gene was deeply troubled. And as he and Mark trudged that afternoon to the hospital, both were thinking the same thing. They prayed that Henek would have recovered enough to go with them. But that hope died as soon as the doctor ushered them into a small room where Henek was lying. "Don't get too close to him," he warned.

Henek thrashed in his bed, mumbling half-phrases in a mix of Polish and Russian. Sweat ran down his face. He looked at them without recognition. "Henek, Henek, we've got to talk to you," said Mark urgently, trying to will him to understand. But Henek was in another world.

"He's delirious," said the doctor. "You won't be able to talk to him."

"How bad is he?" Gene asked the doctor.

"Hard to tell. His fever is very high right now," said the doctor. "But that's rather normal in these cases. How do the two of you feel?"

"We're fine," Gene said.

"That's good," said the doctor. "With every day, your chances of catching the disease are falling."

"What about our cousin? How quickly can he be out of here?"

"It's much too early to say. Maybe two to three weeks if he's very strong, but possibly longer," said the doctor. He stood up to leave, telling them, "I'll be in the next room if you need me."

They sat in silence for a while. What could they do? They could not stay without documents, and the only way to get their documents back was to board the ship. "What about going back the way we came and finding somewhere to wait until he gets better?" Mark asked eventually.

"Find somewhere where? For hundreds of miles on the train journey we saw nothing but desert. You can't hide there. And how will we travel? We have no papers," Gene said.

"I know," Mark murmured. They lapsed into silence, both choked with emotion. "We have no choice, do we? We have to take the ship," Mark said.

"I hate to do it; I just hate it," Gene said, his voice cracking. "I never thought I'd be talking about leaving him. But what else can we do? The NKVD man in the port gave us an ultimatum. We either get out or we get arrested."

"Goddamn it, why did he have to get sick here of all places?" Mark shouted.

"I don't know."

"You always said we must keep together at all costs."

"I did say that. I still believe it. But who could have imagined a situation like this?" said Gene. "If we stay here and get arrested, how would that make Henek feel, knowing that he was the cause? We have to take that boat."

There was another long silence. "We must find a way of letting him know where we are," Mark said finally. "We've got to leave word for him."

"We'll leave him some money, too. Then he can join us as soon as he's well enough," said Gene.

"Poor Henek," said Mark. "He'll think we abandoned him."

"Not if we leave him a letter. We'll give it to the doctor. He seems like a decent man. He'll pass it on, I'm sure." So Gene wrote a short note explaining why they had left and where they were heading. He promised to write again as soon as they found a place to stay so Henek would know where to rejoin them. And he told him to see Dmitri Antonovich at the port regarding his sea passage to the Caucasus. They stuffed most of their remaining money in an envelope with the letter and gave it to the doctor, who promised to give it to Henek as soon as he was well enough. As they left the hospital, both were near despair. For years, neither of them could look back on that moment without a twinge of guilt.

That night, a man met the brothers at the harbor with tickets and their documents. He asked no questions when only two of the expected seven travelers showed up. They boarded the ship and sailed away.

Henek never received their letter or the money.

CHAPTER 13

Arrested Again

It was a rough crossing; waves lashed the ship all night. Shut in a small cabin, Gene and Mark were soon violently ill. They tried to reach the deck to breathe some fresh air, but the storm drove them back. So they wallowed in their bunks, feeling sorry for themselves, until the boat pulled into port the following afternoon.

They had arrived at Makhachkala in the autonomous Soviet republic of Dagestan, one of the mainly Muslim regions of the Caucasus. It was a picturesque town of white clay houses built on terraces hewn out of a mountainside. The brothers immediately started to shiver. It had been warm in Central Asia, and they had traded some of their heavy clothing for food. Most of the rest had been stolen. Here, it was still winter, not the hellish winter of Russia's heart, but cold nonetheless. A shallow layer of snow covered the ground, and a sharp wind whistled off the sea. Opening the door of her house, a woman caught sight of them and asked why they were not wearing winter clothing. "Because we don't have any," Mark said through chattering teeth. "Poor boys, come in for a few minutes," she said kindly.

She let them warm themselves by her fire and gave them hot tea. They gazed around the small room. Photographs of men dressed in uniforms stood on a sideboard under the baleful stare of Josef Stalin, whose portrait occupied the place of honor. Rummaging in a cupboard, the woman pulled out a hat with earflaps that she said had belonged to her husband. "Here, take this," she said, putting it over Mark's head. It was much too big, reaching down to his eyes. Gene laughed. "Now you look like a real Russian," he said. The woman was immediately offended. "Is there something wrong with that?" she asked.

"No, no, of course not," the brothers answered together. "We're very touched by your generosity," said Gene. "Giving us this hat is the nicest thing anybody has done for us since we arrived in the Soviet Union." The woman's eyes brimmed with tears. "Perhaps someone will show the same kindness to my sons if they need help in a distant place," she said, crossing herself. The boys left the house cheered by the thought that perhaps this part of the Soviet Union was different and that here they would find a safe place to live.

The nearest large town was the oil city of Grozny, capital of Chechnia. The brothers boarded a train in that direction without difficulty. They got off at the first stop, a small town called Kizijurt. They had decided to stay close to the coast so that Henek could easily rejoin them when he recovered. Because it was still light, they immediately went to the local government building to seek work.

"Who are you?" asked the clerk. "We're released Polish prisoners," said Gene. For once, this reply produced no reaction. The man seemed unconcerned. He said that there was a shortage of young men in the area, and they could work in a local collective village. "That sounds good," said Gene. "How much will they pay us?"

"You'll get enough to live on," said the clerk. "There's a truck going out to the village in half an hour. You can ride with him."

After their past troubles, this seemed almost too good to be true. A few minutes later, a man driving a battered vehicle pulled up and waved them aboard. He took them on a bone-shaking 12-mile ride over an unpaved road. The light was fading, but the driver hurtled through the gloom at breakneck speed, throwing them from one side of the cab to the other. At one point, the track dipped down to a frozen stream. The truck rattled to a stop and the man climbed out, apparently trying to decide whether the ice would bear their weight. Concluding that it would, he clambered back and drove on. The ice promptly broke. But the water was shallow, and he was able to plow through to the other side. Eventually, they reached a village. The driver pulled up outside a flat-roofed house that seemed to be built of mud. He honked the horn and a fiercely mustachioed man with wiry black hair emerged.

The driver, who had not said a single word to the brothers, held an animated conversation with the villager in a language they did not recognize. He kept waving his arms in the brothers' direction. Eventually, the two men shook hands, and in broken Russian the villager invited the boys to come inside. They entered a dimly lit room and were immediately assailed by a pungent animal odor mixed with smoke from an open fire. Could it be that they were to live in a stable with the man's animals? But no, he ushered them to a corner of the room, where shadowy figures sat around a great iron cauldron. In the flickering light they saw an old woman dressed in black. A younger woman sitting cross-legged on the floor and two children gaping open-mouthed at the strangers completed the circle. This side of the room was slightly elevated, with a wooden plank floor. There was no furniture apart from a low table and a carpet covering the floor. The family apparently slept on rugs laid out in a corner of the room.

Rubbing his stinging eyes and trying not to cough, Mark surveyed the other half of the house, where something was moving, making a strange snuffling sound. Then it spoke. "Moo," it said plaintively. Gene swung around. In the half-light he made out the shapes of a cow, two sheep, and some chickens that shared the building with the family. He could not take his eyes off the sheep. They were strange, shorthaired animals with spindly legs, scarcely able to waddle about the bare earth floor due to the weight of their huge tails. He nudged Mark to look. The sheep had little trolleys with wheels attached behind them to support their tails.

The entire room, including living quarters for humans and animals, was about 40 feet long and 20 feet wide. The brothers' eyes swung back to their host, who in turn, was examining them through half-closed eyes. "You stay in this house, you get good food," he said finally.

"Good food, it sounds wonderful," said Mark.

"You get good food, pay rubles," the man added. Surprised, Gene and Mark looked at each other. They had very little money, certainly not enough to pay for lodgings. "We thought we were to work for our keep," Gene said slowly, trying to make the man understand his Russian. But he did not seem to get through.

"We give you good food. Now we make tea," the man said, gesturing them to sit by the fire with the family.

The man spoke to the old woman, who reached up to a shelf and took down a block of some dark substance. Breaking off a piece, she tossed it into the bubbling water. It was Uzbek tea, compressed into a hard, square cake. The water immediately took on the color of pondweed. Meanwhile, the younger woman grabbed a broom, went to the animals' side of the room, and began sweeping their dung into a pile. Mark wondered if this was a display of tidiness to impress the guests. Later, they learned that it was a regular part of housekeeping performed at regular intervals. The dung was carefully stored and used for fuel or as building material.

The old woman had not finished with the tea. She dropped in a few scrawny vegetables, then reached for the main delicacy—a lump of sheep fat about the size of a tennis ball. She waved it under Mark's nose, then pitched it into the pot. The fat was extracted from those massive sheep tails and was considered a great treat. The family watched with anticipation as the lump melted, forming eyes of grease that floated on the surface.

"Very good tea," the man said, rubbing his belly. Gene and Mark exchanged anxious glances as the grandmother stirred the bubbling cauldron. Soon the meal was ready. With great ceremony, the man dipped a ladle into the brew and filled a tin bowl, which he offered to Gene. A moment later Mark was also staring at his supper. The man quickly served the rest of the family, and they immediately began to devour their portions, slurping with pleasure. Mark and Gene looked at each other again, then back at the dark green soup. "Go on, drink it, or they'll get upset," Mark whispered in Polish.

"You drink it first," Gene hissed. "You're the one who's always complaining about being hungry."

One by the one the family members finished, looking up to see that Gene and Mark had still not touched their tea. Gene was watching, fascinated, as tiny droplets of fat formed on the man's mustache. He forced his attention back to his own soup. Aware that the entire family was watching expectantly, Gene brought the bowl to his mouth. Pieces of something floated in the shiny liquid, but whether they were tealeaves, vegetables, or gobs of lard, he could not tell. He drank as much as he could manage, swallowing the lumps whole, smacking his lips in appreciation. "Very good tea," he gasped. The man guffawed with satisfaction, displaying a magnificent set of metal dentures. He looked expectantly at Mark.

"Very, very good tea," said Gene, smirking at his brother. "Drink it up; it will make you big and strong." Seeing that he was trapped, Mark closed his eyes, raised his bowl, and drank. "Agh," he sputtered as it slipped down his throat. The man clapped him on the shoulder with delight. "You want more?" he asked.

That night, lying under a smelly sheep pelt that the man had given them, the brothers discussed what to do next. "I don't think we can stay here," said Mark.

"We haven't seen the place yet. Can't judge it after one meal. We need to see if they have work," Gene whispered back.

"But they're so primitive. That's not how I imagined the Caucasus at all. We won't be getting any white bread here."

"This wasn't what I had in mind either, but let's see what happens tomorrow."

"They don't even speak Russian. Besides, they want money. The man said he wanted rubles," Mark objected.

"If we work for them, they'll have to pay us. Then we'll have money," Gene replied. Neither of the brothers knew much about a collective farm—a kolkhoz—but Gene assumed that as hired laborers they would be paid enough for food and lodgings.

Over the next two days, the brothers quickly learned that there was little or no work for strangers in the middle of winter. There were only a few maintenance jobs, handled mainly by women and the elderly. The village was very backward. The mud houses had neither running water nor electricity, to say nothing of modern toilet facilities. In summer, conditions probably eased. But summer was months away. Their host also kept asking them for money. The brothers had a hurried conference.

"You were right," said Gene. "We have to move on. But I'm afraid to travel any more with the papers we have. It's too dangerous pretending there are 15 of us. Every time I present that warrant, I'm afraid I'm going to get arrested. Before we move on, we have to get new papers just for the two of us."

"Where will we get them?" asked Mark.

"In Grozny. I'll go there tomorrow. Maybe I'll be able to get some rations and money too. You'd better stay here until I get back." They told their host that Gene was going to town and would return next day with money. Gene also persuaded the man to lend him a *kufaika*, a thigh-length coat padded with cotton wool. He promised to pay for it when he returned.

A villager drove Gene back to Kizijurt. To his dismay, the train station was crowded with soldiers, and the police were out in force searching for deserters. Gene was too scared to show his travel warrant. He thought about buying a ticket to Grozny, but the ticket office was closed. As he turned away, a burly policeman stopped him. "What do you think you're doing here?" he demanded.

"I need to get to Grozny," Gene replied. "When will they open the ticket office?"

"What's it to you? You have no right to be here. This part of the station is only for military personnel."

"All I want to do is buy a ticket," Gene said, trying to sound reasonable.

"The office will open when there's room on a train. Now move along," the man barked, grabbing Gene by the arm and pulling him away. Gene's face reddened. For a second, all his accumulated frustrations threatened to boil over. Furiously, he brushed off the policeman's arm, realizing in the same instant that he was behaving like a fool. Anxious to get away before he was arrested, Gene turned on his heel. He felt the policeman's eyes boring into his back as he melted into the crowd.

Gene waited outside the station until it was dark. Then, taking care not to be seen, he crept across the tracks and boarded a stationary train. Eventually, it started moving and pulled into Grozny two hours later. Gene spent the night in the station. As usual, it was jammed with a motley crowd of civilians, soldiers, and military police prowling for deserters. The streets around the station were full of men drowning their sorrows in vodka. As daylight came, Gene ventured into the town.

The capital of the Chechen autonomous Soviet republic, Grozny was an important administrative and industrial city and the second most important oil center in the Soviet Union after Baku on the Caspian Sea. It was surrounded by derricks, refineries, and factories. The smell of fuel hung over the city. Turning out of the station, Gene found himself on a boulevard lined with sorry-looking poplar trees. He was directed to one of the grandest buildings in town, a four-story structure with mock Roman columns. Inside, it bustled with assorted functionaries, attendants, and uniformed military and NKVD officers.

None of the officials knew what to do with Gene. He was sent from one department to the next, from one blank-faced clerk to another. Eventually he was ushered into a high-ceilinged office. A stony official sat behind a grille in a small cubicle at one end of the room. Gene gave him his papers.

"I need a new travel warrant," he explained. "This one is for fifteen people, but there are only two of us left." The man studied the papers, then disappeared through a door at the back of his cubicle, taking the papers with him. A minute later, a more senior official appeared. Gene repeated his story. "What happened to the others in your group?" the official asked.

"We got separated from them in various places," said Gene. "It's been hard to travel on the trains in a large group." The official scrutinized the papers as if searching for a secret message. "These will have to go to the first secretary himself," he said. "Come back this afternoon."

Gene bought some food in a neighboring cafeteria, but spent most of the time skulking in shadows, avoiding men in uniform. In the afternoon, he returned to the paneled room. After a few minutes, the second official came out of the back office. "The secretary is still looking at your papers. Stay here," he ordered. Gene tried to convince himself it was good that a high official was working on the matter. Unlike most Soviet bureaucrats, he reasoned, a senior functionary had the authority to issue new documents. On the other hand, such a man also could order arrests.

Gene sat there for two hours, increasingly nervous. New applicants filtered into the chamber, and a line formed. When he was not dealing with the people in line, the clerk in the cubicle stared at Gene with open curiosity but he never said a word. Gene wanted a glass of water but did not dare ask.

Once an NKVD man stuck his head around the door, examined Gene, then disappeared. Half an hour later, a uniformed woman opened the door and eyed him curiously for a minute. Gene felt helpless. Were these people casually wandering into the room or were they deliberately scrutinizing him? Finally, the official returned. "The first secretary has approved your application," he said. "Your new papers are being written. They will be ready soon."

Gene was elated. His luck had held. Now, he and Mark would have a proper document that listed just the two of them instead of fifteen phantom soldiers. Half an hour later, the clerk behind the grille beckoned him forward. The man counted out nine brand-new 100-ruble notes and slid them under the grille. Gene could smell the fresh ink on them and felt like planting a kiss on Lenin's face, which was stamped in the middle of each banknote. A few minutes later, the official returned with a new travel warrant, emblazoned with a ministerial stamp of approval.

"Here you are, everything's in order. You can now join the just struggle against the barbaric occupier," he announced in the Soviet manner. Gene eagerly began to decipher the document. Halfway through, he stopped, his good humor seeping away. It was a masterpiece of Soviet bureaucracy. The document stated that a group of released Polish prisoners, numbering 15, was authorized to travel on the railway system to Buzuluk, where they would join the Polish army. Gene did not know whether to laugh or cry. The hours of uncertainty, tension and fear had all been in vain. He had exchanged one document for another identical one. But Gene was in no mood to argue. He felt lucky not to have been arrested. If he had to travel with an imaginary band of 15 men, then that is what he would do.

When he returned to the station, it was dark, and the ticket office was closed. Gene was determined to return to the village that night, knowing that Mark would be anxious. He walked down one of the tracks until he saw a train pull in and stop. Unlike the others in the station, its windows were blacked out with blinds. But it was heading in the right direction. Gene waited for the train to start moving again. As it lurched into motion, he swung himself aboard the back of a car. Inside it was dark, and there was a smell of disinfectant. The car was lined with bunks of wounded soldiers, some groaning in pain. At the other end of the carriage, two nurses talked quietly.

Gene realized that he had boarded a military hospital train. If discovered, he would be immediately arrested. He quickly retreated to the space between two carriages, trying to recollect how many stations there were to Kizijurt. The train was not stopping at any of the small towns along the way, but it did slow down whenever it passed through a station. Eventually, he thought he recognized Kizijurt and prepared to jump. He launched himself from the car, but the train was moving quite fast. The platform rushed at him more quickly than he had anticipated. Stumbling as he landed, he reached out to steady himself and was caught by someone standing there. "Thank you very much," he gasped gratefully, looking up at his rescuer.

It was the burly militiaman from the previous day. They recognized one another at the same moment. Gene tried to break free, but the man held him tightly. "Oh no you don't, not this time," the man said. "You're under arrest."

CHAPTER 14

Interrogation

After less than three months of freedom, Gene was back in the clutches of the NKVD. Armed guards put him on another train to Makhachkala. He was not handcuffed but a guard sat opposite in an empty compartment, revolver on his lap, silent and watchful. Gene was surprised at his own calmness now that the worst had happened. His initial thoughts had been about his brother, who would be wondering what had happened to him. But he forced Mark out of his mind. First, he had to help himself. "Think," he urged himself. "Stupidity got you into this. Only cool thinking can get you out."

To begin with, he had to hide those brand-new ruble bills. Their discovery would be sure to lead to hard questions about the missing 15 men and whether he had made them up to steal money from the Soviet state. He asked the guard for permission to use the toilet, hoping to conceal the money. But the man insisted on going with him and would not let him close the door. Returning to his seat, Gene began stealthily crumbling the notes into small balls with one hand and stuffing them into the lining of his *kufaika*. He ripped a hole in the lining and laboriously worked each note around to his back where it would less easily be found. It gave him something to do but the fact was that even if the money escaped detection by the authorities, it would not be hidden for long if he were thrown into a cell with criminals. However, that was one of his lesser worries at the moment.

He was also thinking furiously about the charges he might face. How could he explain that he had been traveling in the opposite direction from the destination on his travel warrant? In the Soviet Union, all foreigners were distrusted at the best of times. But this was wartime and he was an alien, caught jumping off a military hospital train in highly suspicious circumstances. He could be charged as a saboteur or enemy agent. For that there was only one punishment—a bullet in the back of his head.

Arriving in Makhachkala, Gene was marched to the prison. Somewhat to his surprise, he received only a superficial body search. Instead, he was immediately taken down a long whitewashed corridor to a small cell meant for three or four prisoners. The guard flung open the door. Gene counted five bodies on the stone floor, with two more men lying on a wooden bunk in the corner. All the men seemed to be dozing, but a couple looked up as the door opened. From his camp experience, Gene knew that this was a dangerous moment. He had to assert himself at once, to appear strong, better still to seem violently unstable. As soon as the door clanged behind him, Gene strode straight for the bed, seized the nearest prisoner who was half asleep, and heaved him onto the floor. The second man he shoved toward the wall. "I am Zjenka from the camps," Gene snarled. Unwashed, unshaven, and frowning ferociously, he thought himself a fearsome sight. He waited for the other prisoners to react. None did. The man Gene had displaced made no attempt to reclaim his position on the bed. Gene glared at each of his cellmates until he was sure they would not challenge him. Privately, he permitted himself a smile. "Round one to me," he thought.

Far from being dangerous criminals, Gene's cellmates were a sorry crew. They were deserters or soldiers from units that no longer existed—a mixed bunch of central Asians, Chechens, and Kalmucks, half-starved, filthy, and scared. One of them had only one leg. Gangsters would have stolen Gene's money within a few hours. This crew was too downtrodden even to try. After a while they began talking to Gene. One told how his unit had been surrounded by the Germans somewhere in the Ukraine. Planes strafed them, and artillery pounded them mercilessly. Half the unit was wiped out. Somehow, the man had managed to slip through enemy lines. Not knowing what to do, he had headed for home. It had taken him three months. Instead of congratulating him for surviving, the authorities arrested him and threw him in jail. Now, he was awaiting trial.

The prisoners were fed twice daily. It was the usual convict diet of black bread and watery soup, but there was more of it than in the camps. There was a latrine bucket in the corner for personal needs. The prisoners were never allowed out of their cells for fresh air or exercise. The air was thick with the smell of unwashed men, but one got used to it.

Interrogations and trials took place nearly every day; "justice" was swift and certain. A prisoner taken away for questioning would usually return to the cell less than half an hour later. "What did you get?" the others would ask. The answer was always the same—ten years. A few hours later or the next day, the guards would call his name again, telling him to bring his bundle of possessions. His cellmates would stand up, slap him on the back, and wish him luck. And the man would be on his way to the gulag.

For Gene, being sent back to the camps seemed almost more terrifying than being shot. He knew there was little chance of surviving a ten-year sentence. He also worried about Mark and Henek. "So much for the three musketeers," he thought bitterly. "One in a hospital with typhoid, one in prison waiting for a bullet, and a third on his own without any money in a village of strangers." But he tried to keep his hopes up. Perhaps he could still talk his way out of this mess. It all depended on how he handled his interrogation. In his mind, he reviewed possible questions and answers. He decided to stick as close to the truth as he could without mentioning Mark's existence. He also dare not mention the fact that he had run away from the Polish army in Buzuluk. If that became known, he would be accused of desertion. Gene knew there were big holes in his story.

Back in the village, Mark knew something had gone terribly wrong. When three days passed with no sign of Gene, he began to panic. But he could do little but sit tight and pray. He kept busy every day, going out to the fields to pick cotton that had been missed during the harvest. His host occasionally badgered him for money, and Mark put him off as best he could. What other choices did he have? If he left the village, Gene might never find him. Besides, he had no money and no papers. But how long could he stay before the family threw him out? "I'll give him one more week," he told himself, not daring to think what he might do when the time was up.

On his fourth day in jail, Gene's name was called. He was led into a large room on the first floor. Two officers sat behind a single desk: an army colonel and an NKVD major. To his right, a stenographer prepared to take notes. Gene told himself to take his time and remember his prepared answers. His mind jumped back to high school exams. He had the same feeling—shaky hands, butterflies in his stomach, dry mouth, pounding heart. The major pointed to a chair in front of the desk. Gene sat.

The questioning began with routine biographical details: Gene's name, his father's name, his date and place of birth, his education. Gene was careful to say that he had been born in Poland. He did not want to complicate matters by telling them he had been born on Russian soil. The major's tone was colorless. He appeared bored by the entire business. The second officer listened to the questions through half-closed eyes, tapping on the table with a pen, occasionally making a note. Eventually, the major got to the point.

"You were arrested in Kizijurt. What were you doing there?"

"I was in a group of released prisoners. We were on our way to Buzuluk to join the Polish army," Gene said, telling the story yet again.

"You had travel documents, I see," the major said, referring to the file in front of him. "Where were they originally issued?"

"In Tashkent," Gene replied. "Then we got new ones in Mary and again in Grozny." This was his first prepared answer. The papers had originally been issued in Vologda. But there was no way to explain how he could have been traveling from Vologda to Buzuluk via the Caspian Sea. This answer brought the colonel to life. He leaned forward, opening his eyes.

"In Tashkent? You've certainly seen many parts of our great country," he said sardonically. Gene kept his mouth shut.

"So you were in Tashkent and you were heading for Buzuluk. So what were you doing here?" the colonel asked.

"We were chosen for a special unit to be trained as political activists. The training was going to be in Gori and from there we would proceed to Buzuluk," said Gene, using another prepared response.

"Political activists?" The major did not hide his disbelief. "And why were you chosen for this exalted task?"

"I suppose because we all had a higher education."

"And where are the other 14 of this highly educated group now?" the colonel asked, motioning to the major to let him continue the questioning. Gene said

that some had been left in Tashkent to catch a later train and three had caught typhoid in Uzbekistan.

"So only seven of us crossed on the ferry, and since we couldn't all find room on the same train, four of us went on to Grozny, and the other three were left behind," he concluded. It sounded thin, even to him.

"In that case, why were you arrested on the train coming from Grozny?" the colonel asked.

"I got worried because the other three hadn't arrived. So I thought I would go back along the line to look for them," Gene said.

There was a brief silence. Then the major changed tack and started asking about Gene's time in the camps. "Where and when were you arrested?"

"In Lwów, in June 1940," Gene replied, relaxing a notch.

"And what were you charged with?" the major asked.

"I was never charged with anything and received no sentence," Gene replied. The major almost seemed pleased at this response and offered Gene a cigarette. He took it happily, and the major gave him a light.

"Take that damn thing out of your mouth," the colonel suddenly shouted, slapping the desk. "Rubbish like you don't smoke here."

From conversations with political prisoners, Gene was familiar with this good cop/bad cop interrogation technique. He stubbed out the cigarette and asked the major whether he could keep it.

"Keep it, keep it," the major said, as if the colonel had never spoken. Gene put it in his pocket. The questioning resumed, this time the colonel taking the lead. "Tell me, comrade Polish patriot, what is your attitude to the Soviet Union?"

Gene was not ready for that one. He considered a moment. "We both are in this war together against the Nazis," he said at last. "I admire the Soviet soldiers who are bravely sacrificing their lives to defeat the fascist enemy. We are allies and we need to fight together."

"What were your political affiliations in the former Poland?"

"I had none."

"And you say you got your travel warrant in Samarkand?" the major interjected. They are trying to trip me up, find inconsistencies, Gene thought.

"We were issued the warrant in Tashkent," he answered. The pace picked up, one question following another without pause.

"And two of your supposed comrades were left in Krasnavodsk?"

"No, only one."

"Why were you on the hospital train?"

"I didn't know it was a hospital train."

"Where did you get on?"

"Grozny."

"What were you doing in Kizijurt?"

"I thought the train had reached Makhachkala station and I jumped off because I had no ticket to show at the gate."

After about two hours, the officers stood up and walked over to the window to talk between themselves. They called a guard to escort Gene into the corridor. He felt exhausted. He had not allowed the investigators to trip him up but he was not sure he had convinced them he was telling the truth either. After what seemed a long time, the major stepped out and ordered the guard to return Gene to his cell.

"How much, how much did you get?" his fellow prisoners asked. "I don't know," Gene said. The others said that was a good sign. "If they haven't sentenced you right away, that means they don't know what to do with you," the one-legged man said.

Two days later, he was called again. The colonel was not present. Another officer had replaced him sitting next to the major. He must have been some kind of witness, as he did not say a word during the whole proceeding. The major resumed the questioning.

"Let's go back to when you were released from the camp. Where did you go from there?" the major asked.

"I told you, Tashkent," Gene replied.

"True. You told me Tashkent. But I ask myself, why Tashkent when the Polish army was in Buzuluk?"

"I didn't know there was a Polish army until I reached Tashkent. I had just been released from the camp."

"How did you find out?"

"I heard about it from some Polish refugees."

"What were their names?"

"I don't remember. I didn't know them."

"How did your group of 15 form?"

"We all signed up for the army at the same time."

"Did you know the others before?"

"No."

"When were you selected for this special unit in Gori?"

"When we signed up for the army in Tashkent."

"Why did you go to Tashkent in the first place?"

"That's what it said on the travel warrant I was given when I was released from the camp."

Suddenly the major's beefy hand slammed the table. "Do you think I can't see through you? I've got better things to do than listen to this garbage. Now let's go back again. What were you doing on the hospital train?"

"I told you, I was looking for my comrades."

"What comrades? Where were these comrades? Do you really expect me to believe that?" the major shouted.

"It's the truth," Gene said, trying to sound calm. "Otherwise, how would I have gotten hold of a travel warrant for 15, which was renewed by a first secretary in Grozny just last week?"

As quickly as it had blown up, the major's anger subsided. He looked at Gene and sighed wearily. "Let's ignore the more incredible aspects of this ridiculous story and consider the facts," he said. "The facts are these: we find you wandering where you have no right to be. You say you are going to Buzuluk, but in fact you are traveling in the wrong direction. You say you are one of 15 men, but there is no sign of any of the others. What do you expect me to believe?"

"I've told you the truth."

"It's clear you had no intention of going to Buzuluk."

"No," cried Gene.

"You had no intention of joining the Polish army."

"No."

"Or any other army."

"No, no, it's not true," Gene shouted desperately.

"In fact, at best you are a coward and a deserter, if you're not a foreign saboteur."

Gene gathered his wits. Looking the major in the eye, he mustered as much dignity as possible. "I'm not a deserter because I haven't yet joined the army and I'll fight the Germans as soon as I get the chance. All I did wrong was to travel on a train without a ticket," he said. The major sighed. "Guard," he called, "take him back to his cell."

On his eighth day of captivity, Gene was brought before the major for a third time. The man looked at him thoughtfully. "You still stick to your story?" he asked.

"It's the truth," Gene said.

"You were on your way to Buzuluk."

"Yes."

"You were separated from your comrades."

"Yes, I was."

"And you're sticking to that?"

"It's the truth."

"Well, no doubt we could sit here for months going around in circles. But I don't have the time. I've spent too much time on you as it is. The prison is full of shit like you and you're making me fall behind schedule."

"I'm not shit, and I'm not a deserter," Gene protested.

"No, what you are is a fucking headache. I'm inclined just to send you along to some people who can worm the truth out of you."

Gene felt bile rise in his throat. He searched for words that would convince the major not to transfer him. "You've got to listen to me," he shouted wildly. "I really do want to fight the Nazis. We Poles and Russians, we're on the same side now. Comrade Stalin himself has declared Soviet-Polish friendship. Why are you treating me like an enemy when Comrade Stalin has said we are friends?"

The door opened, and the colonel entered. Gene had not seen him since the first interrogation. "What's all the fuss about?" the colonel said.

"I'm telling the truth but he won't believe me. I'm a Polish patriot and an ally of the Soviet Union. Comrade Stalin released me from the camps to fight the fascists but he wants to send me back again," Gene sobbed.

The colonel looked at him thoughtfully for a moment, then cocked his head at the major. They strolled to the window and began talking, their backs toward

Gene. The colonel returned to the desk and picked up Gene's file. Gene knew his fate was being decided. There seemed to be disagreement. Finally, the colonel waved in the guard. "Take him back to the cell for his things," he said. Addressing nobody in particular, he added, "There is a typhoid epidemic in Uzbekistan."

Walking back to the cell, Gene still did not know what they had decided. "What did they tell you this time?" his cellmates asked. "They said to bring my things," he said.

"They're going to let you go," said one. Standing up, he wrapped his arms around Gene in a smelly embrace. The others also gathered around slapping him on the back, hugging him with real affection.

"Good old Yevgeny, at least one of us is getting out," the one-legged man said. Gene was numb. He still feared the worst as the guards escorted him out of the building and hustled him into a car. "Where are we going?" he asked the driver.

"To the military headquarters."

"What for?"

"To get your new papers, colonel's orders."

So it really was true. His luck had held yet again. Gene closed his eyes in silent thanks. He had no idea why they were letting him go. He was too relieved to care. He remembered what Adsum the priest had said. Perhaps there really was a guardian angel watching over him.

In the village, another day was drawing to a close for Mark. For more than a week, he had wrestled with what to do. He had nearly given up hope that Gene would return, but he could not bring himself to leave the village. As he trudged back to the mud house, he tormented himself with the same thoughts. Where the hell was he? Why had he not come back? Mark flung the door of the hovel open, his senses assaulted again by the smell.

"Ugh, I hate it here," he muttered in Polish.

"Don't say that. It's not as bad as all that," a familiar voice responded through the gloom. Mark could not believe it. He rushed across the room, flinging his arms around his brother, nearly crying in relief.

"Where were you? Where on earth were you? You've no idea. I was so terrified. Where were you, for God's sake?"

"Hey, calm down," Gene said. "I just had a minor delay and a few days of rest, courtesy of the NKVD, that's all."

"I was so scared. I didn't know what to do. I was going to leave here, but I decided to stick it out and wait for you."

"You did the right thing, you did the right thing," Gene kept on repeating. He hugged Mark again and tousled his hair. "I had a close call," he said softly.

CHAPTER 15

The Cossack Village

Gene and Mark paid their debts to the Dagestan family and left early the next morning. Armed with their new documents, they boarded a westbound train and passed through Grozny without stopping. They had only a vague sense of their destination. Any place where people spoke a language they could understand and where they could find work would do.

The train skirted snowcapped mountains; the air was thin and pure. Although their future was still uncertain, their spirits were high. They caught glimpses of deep gorges and silver ribbons of water flowing below. Gene was still elated by his narrow escape. Mark was overjoyed to be reunited with his brother and to have seen the last of the village. The world seemed much less daunting when there were two of them.

About 150 miles west of Grozny, the train stopped at the small town of Georgievsk. The name was pure Russian, so they decided to get off. They were just a few miles from Pyatigorsk, the mineral spa where the great romantic poet Mikhail Lermontov was killed in a duel in 1841. But it was February 1942, and the age of empty romantic gestures was long gone.

The hungry brothers found a small eating house on the main street. As they began their meal, Mark nudged Gene. "There's a man over there staring at us," he said. Across the room, a tall, well-built man with graying hair was examining them. "Take no notice. Our papers are in order," Gene told Mark.

"He's coming over," Mark said anxiously.

The man arrived. "May I join you?" he asked.

"Please yourself," Gene said cautiously.

"I couldn't help noticing you—two strong young men. May I ask what you're doing here?"

"Look comrade, we have papers, and everything is in order. Who are you anyway and what do you want?" Gene snapped defensively.

"Excuse me; I didn't mean to alarm you. I am the agronomist at a village near here, and I was wondering if you were looking for work. We could use some strong young bodies."

"Do you have work even in the winter?" Mark asked.

"We have jobs all year round," said the man, smiling. There was something appealing about him. He held himself erect like the former solider they later discovered him to be and spoke with an old-world courtliness. "Are you interested?" he asked. They were.

The man introduced himself as Efim Vasilevich, offered each of them a firm handshake, and marched them to the local government building where they were issued with work permits and a letter to the village secretary. The village was called Nezlobnaya and was about three miles away. They began walking down an empty country lane bordered by immense fields of stubble. Then they rounded a corner, and Mark caught his breath. In the distance, he saw a white shape in the sky, suspended above the horizon. "What's that?" he asked in awe.

"That? Oh that's Mount Elbrus, said Efim. "It's the highest mountain in Russia by far. Look how it towers over everything in sight."

"How far away is it?" Mark asked.

"Maybe 80 or 90 miles. You can see it clearly today. It has its moods. Sometimes, it shines at our *stanitsa* like a half-moon, as it's doing now. Sometimes it's angry, covered in black clouds. Sometimes it pretends to be a cloud itself. Other times, it's completely hidden in dust and haze."

"Excuse me, what is a *stanitsa*?" Mark asked.

"It's a Cossack village. We're Cossacks here, you know. Or at least we used to be," said Efim, with a melancholy smile.

The word *Cossack* gave the brothers pause. For Jews, the very mention of Cossacks evoked images of terror. Generations had deeply rooted memories of wild drunken horsemen sweeping down on Jewish communities to rob, burn, rape, and murder. Could they find refuge among such people? On the other hand, Gene thought, nobody knew that they were Jewish, and no one need know. The agronomist seemed friendly, and they were desperate.

Soon they entered the village, walking down a wide main street lined by small wooden cottages with red-tiled roofs. Each had a tiny garden behind a neat picket fence, where the villagers kept chickens and grew vegetables. They passed two large brick buildings several stories high. "What are those?" Mark asked.

"They are our flour mills. They need workers there, too," said Efim. They crossed a river. The shallow water ran bright and clear; the air was fresh. Gene already liked the place. "This might be what we were looking for," he whispered to Mark.

Efim took the brothers to the village council and they were given lodgings with an old couple, Pavel and Yekaterina Lebedev, whose three sons were all in the army. Efim Vasilevich also boarded with them. The villagers were friendly, and although they were curious about the two foreigners, they did not ask too many questions. For the first time since leaving the camps, the brothers felt almost safe, although they never completely lowered their guard. By Soviet standards, the village was quite prosperous—meals were regular, and the houses had electricity. They were issued new clothes—Red Army fatigues that made them look like soldiers. Now that they had an address, they wrote to Henek at the hospital, telling him where they were. If only he could join them, everything would be perfect.

Several weeks went by without a reply. They wrote again, then a third time. "Why doesn't he answer?" Mark kept asking

"Maybe he has. Maybe his letter is on its way right now," Gene said. "The postal service isn't exactly dazzling in this part of the world right now. He could just turn up one day."

But Henek did not. What came instead after several weeks was a letter from the hospital saying that Henek had recovered and discharged himself. "He couldn't have received our letters," said Gene.

"I bet he never got the money either. He probably thinks we abandoned him," Mark lamented.

"No, Henek knows we would never have left unless we had no choice. And we didn't have a choice."

"I know that; you don't have to keep reminding me. But I thought we might see him as soon as he got better. Now he's on his own," Mark said.

"At least we know he's alive," Gene said. They asked themselves where Henek might have headed for after he left the hospital. The only addresses they knew in the entire Soviet Union were Nusia's in Siberia and Max's in Bukhara. So they wrote to them, explaining where they were and asking if they had heard from Henek. Neither one wrote back. As weeks passed, they were forced to accept the fact that they would not see their cousin until the war was over, whenever that might be.

In the village, Mark first worked as assistant to the blacksmith, and Gene was assigned to the carpentry shop. Mark quickly developed muscles from hammering the hot metal from the forge. He liked the work. It felt good to be earning an honest keep. While waiting for Gene at the Dagestani village, Mark had turned nineteen. Alone and sick with worry, there had been precious little to celebrate. But now, he began to feel like his old self again. In normal times, he would have been starting university. Instead, he was already a graduate of a far tougher school, Stalin's university of the gulag.

After a while, Mark changed jobs and joined Gene in the carpentry shop. They repaired window frames, made wheelbarrows, and built coffins. Mark had always been good with his hands. He enjoyed handling tools, the smell of fresh wood shavings, and the thought that he was constructing something useful, even if, in the case of the caskets, the users would not be in a position to appreciate his craftsmanship.

On one side of the village, next to the river, were peach, apricot, apple, and cherry orchards. Spring brought an explosion of color, and the air grew heady with the smell of blossoms. They were almost dizzy inhaling it, strolling among the wrinkled trees, catching glimpses of Elbrus between the branches. Midmorning, as the sun began to climb, was the best time to see the mountain, before it was swallowed by the afternoon haze. Even in the early morning, its lower slopes were almost always obscured in a light blue mist that rose over fields dappled with clumps of yellow wildflowers.

In early spring, Gene and Mark moved into a single-room cottage down the road from the Lebedevs. Now they had some privacy. They even had two beds, an added luxury. But before they got too comfortable, Gene suddenly fell ill. He was running a high fever but complained of feeling cold, and he shivered uncontrollably. Mark rushed to the doctor who told him that it was malaria. This attack would pass, the doctor said, but the disease would plague Gene on and off for years.

When Gene returned to work, he was transferred to a small farm about ten miles away that belonged to the village. He rode out in a horse and cart, enjoying the sight of the countryside awakening from winter. Birds were singing, insects buzzed, and Gene felt as though his own body was also emerging from a long hibernation. Then, as the cart rolled into the farmyard, he met his new supervisor.

She was smiling. The sun danced in her blond hair. Gene was dazzled as the cart stopped unsteadily before her. She grabbed the reins, patted the horse, and looked at him for a couple of heartbeats. Bending her face to the horse, she murmured, "Well, well, and who might you be?"

"My name is Yevgeny, Yevgeny Adolfovich to be exact," Gene stammered. The woman surveyed him, taking her time about it, while he blushed and shifted awkwardly, trying not to stare at her breasts rising and falling beneath her work shirt.

"Yevgeny Adolfovich," she repeated. "A young man. A rare gift from heaven. One sees them so rarely these days. Are you the one they're sending to work here?"

Seeing her smile, Gene lost his shyness. "Yes, I've come to work here. Who are you?"

"I'm Marusia." She seemed so alive, so normal. He imagined her tasting of peaches and apricots.

"Marusia," he repeated, "I'm very happy to meet you. Are you my boss?"

"That's right," she said, returning his look. "You do what I say and you'll be all right."

The brothers' best friend in the village was Efim Vasilevich. From the beginning he took them under his wing. As the weather warmed, they spent more time with him. Efim liked to tell stories about Cossack history and folklore. He seemed lonely. Few in the village shared his interests in literature and history. His stories usually harked back several centuries and implied a longing for a bygone time before communism destroyed the traditional Cossack life. He also seemed quite interested in their lives in Poland. Gene and Mark were careful what they told him. They never revealed that they were Jewish.

About 2,000 souls lived in the village, the majority Russian. Most families were Cossack, but there were also some refugees and a few Armenians and Persians. At one end of the village were two flourmills, their silos full of flour. After all the boys' dreams of white bread, here it was. It could not be any nearer. But they never got any to eat. The flour was reserved for the State. Villagers ate yellow loaves made from millet—not very appetizing. Gene and Mark also received food rations from the village collective. In the winter, when they first arrived, there was little variety. Later, as fruit and vegetables ripened, their diet improved.

Each day, Gene made his way to Marusia's farm. She was Efim's assistant and in charge of eight workers, but she always chose Gene to accompany her on her rounds. For two years, he had not thought about women. Now he brimmed with desire. Every day he rode out to parts of the farm with Marusia to inspect the crops and feed the livestock. She rode a lively chestnut filly; Gene, who had never ridden a horse, trundled along in his cart, watching her rise and fall in the saddle, rise and fall.

"Here, let me help," she would say, as he struggled with a bale of hay. "One, two, three, lift," and they would fling it into the cart. They stood, panting from the exertion, close enough to reach out and … hoist the next bale.

"I want you; I want you," Gene yelled silently, trying to summon the courage to tell her how beautiful she was. "One more," she would cry, "here we go, one, two, three, lift." Up it went and down it crashed into the cart. And on to the next one. And then one day, as she hoisted a bale, she stumbled and lost her balance. Gene reached out and grabbed her and without thinking more about it pulled her against him and they were kissing and sighing and laughing all at the same time. Finally, they fell in a heap on the ground.

"Well it took you long enough," Marusia said lazily when it was over, poking him with a piece of straw.

"What did?" Gene asked.

"To make a move. How long did you expect me to throw myself at you, you stupid dolt? I was beginning to wonder whether you were a man at all."

"Now that you know the answer, you'd better beware."

Now that the dam was broken, they could not get enough of each other. Marusia shared her house with another girl, and Gene sneaked in occasionally to spend the night. But most of their lovemaking was in barns, on haystacks, or out in the fields. They never spoke of feelings or love. Gene knew Marusia had a two-year-old daughter back in the village and an absent husband whom she never mentioned. Gene did not know if he was away in the war or even if he was still alive. "Oh, he's out of my life," she would say, when Gene asked about him. "Never mind, let's make love."

The war seemed distant and unreal, but that was an illusion. The Soviets suffered new disasters in that spring of 1942. The Red Army was driven from the Crimea and routed in Kharkov, losing hundreds of thousands in the process. The details were kept secret from the public, but people read between the lines of newspaper and radio reports. When a dispatch spoke of "fighting in the Rostov direction," it usually meant a city had been lost. If Soviet forces were said to be in "heavy defensive battles against superior enemy forces" that meant they were probably in disorderly retreat. The latter phrase came more into use as spring turned to summer and Hitler and his staff began planning their knockout blow, which they intended to deliver in the Caucasus. This was also the time when the Nazis began implementing the "Final Solution," which began with a drive to exterminate all the Jews of Poland.

The village heard news through loudspeakers that blared out Moscow Radio. Gene and Mark listened for glimmers of information about Poland, where their parents and Nunek were trapped. They also scoured copies of *Pravda*, the official Communist party newspaper that occasionally made their way to the village. They did not suspect the horrible truth.

One day, Marusia decided that Gene should learn to ride. "After all," she said, "you're among Cossacks, so I need to make a Cossack of you." She put him on her horse, slapped it on its rump, and Gene was away, careering across the meadow for dear life. "This is great," he bellowed, until the horse swerved to avoid a bush and pitched him headlong. Over time, Gene's riding skills improved a little, though he was never going to be much of a Cossack.

Horses had always been at the center of Cossack life, but little was left of that life by this time. Stalin had seen to that. The communists had even banned the use of the word *Cossack*. Forced collectivization in the 1920s had been followed by famine, purges, and executions. Nezlobnaya had become a collectivized farm like any other.

As a special privilege from the state, each family could own a cow and a few chickens and was allowed to tend a small private plot in their spare time. Every morning, the women brought their cows to the bridge at the edge of the village where a cowherd was waiting to take them out to the fields. At dusk, the cowherd brought the animals back to the bridge and released them. Bellowing loudly, the herd paraded down the main street in a stately procession, each animal knowing where to turn into its own yard. Women stood ready to open the gates for their animals, greeting them with affectionate slaps on the neck.

Gene and Mark's cottage was down a slight hill below street level. As they looked out the window, they could see only the legs of people passing. That is how Gene first saw Galia. She definitely had the shapeliest legs in the village. The first time he saw those legs walk by, he rushed out of the house to see who owned them. A girl turned around to look at him, and he caught his breath. She had a pale and expressive oval face with high cheekbones. Her first backward glance caught him like a hook.

Marusia had fulfilled Gene physically but left him emotionally hungry. He was ripe for love. Over the next few weeks, Galia filled his dreams, even though he had not yet spoken to her. He learned that she and her mother, Raisa Pavlova Voznesenskaya, were refugees from Leningrad. The mother worked in the flourmill; the daughter looked after the children of the mill directors, and the two of them lived in a cottage a few houses down the street from the brothers. They never stopped to pass the time of day with the village women and kept themselves to themselves.

Gene learned their routine and began intercepting them to say hello and draw them into conversation. After a while, the mother unbent enough to engage in polite chats about the weather. They exchanged names, but that was as far as it went. Galia would stand there silently, looking at the ground, avoiding his gaze. Her indifference—or was it shyness—made her even more alluring. At night, her soft features haunted him. He felt foolish, callow. Was this love? Gene thought it must be; he had never felt this way before. He wanted to hear her voice, hear her pronounce his name. Her coldness was driving him crazy. He was not used to being ignored, but she seemed entirely unresponsive to his charms. It took the arrival of the German army to change that.

CHAPTER 16

Invasion

At the beginning of July 1942, Gene was laid low with his worst bout of malaria yet. When he recovered enough to leave the cottage, he immediately bumped into Raisa Pavlova and Galia on the street corner. For once, Raisa was eager to talk. Skipping the usual pleasantries, she grabbed Gene's arm. "Yevgeny Adolfovich, have you heard that Vishnayev has left and taken his family with him?"

"Vishnayev? Who's he?"

"You know, the manager of the flour mill. He disappeared early this morning before anyone else was up. What can it mean?"

"Has anybody else left?" asked Gene.

"I don't know Yevgeny Adolfovich, but it worries me. It's ominous."

"Maybe he knows something we don't," said Gene.

"That's what worries me," said Raisa.

Next day it became known that Vishnayev was not the only one to flee. Other prominent officials were also hurriedly clearing out. Fear spread through the village. Vishnayev had left orders to open the mill's flour stores to the people. A notice went up directing all citizens to take as much flour as they could and hide it so that it could be returned to the State when the emergency was over. Instantly, the mill was besieged by people with carts, wagons, trolleys, horses, and oxen. Young and old staggered from the mill with sacks of precious flour. The ground was sprinkled white. Gene and Mark carried a couple of sacks home on their backs. At last they could eat the white bread they had dreamed about in the prison camp. But there were more important things to worry about. The Germans were coming.

Hitler had launched his Caucasian offensive the previous month. His armies swept south and east, aiming to seize control of the oil fields around Baku and Grozny. On July 23, the Germans overran Rostov, gateway to the Caucasus. Two weeks later they were on the outskirts of Pyatigorsk, less than 30 miles from the village. A large part of the town was on fire.

Even in out-of-the-way Nezlobnaya, the signs of the German advance became impossible to ignore. Citizens were mobilized to dig antitank trenches to defend the nearby town of Georgievsk. Truckloads of grim-faced Soviet troops and the occasional tank kept passing through moving east. Civilians, primarily communist officials in commandeered trucks, joined the exodus. After a few days, the trucks gave way to wagons and rickety carts drawn by horses or oxen. The quiet main street was suddenly streaming with traffic.

Gene and Mark had to decide what to do. Their instincts were to flee. They knew enough about the Nazis to realize that they would be in mortal danger if they were identified as Jews. But Gene was still recovering from malaria, they had little money, and if they left it would have to be on foot. There would be small chance of boarding the packed trains. Even if they managed to stay ahead of the Nazis, which was doubtful, the Soviets could easily arrest them as suspected spies, or simply as foreigners, and return them to the gulag.

The discussion continued intermittently for several evenings but always returned to the same point: there was nowhere to run. "I don't want us to be refugees again," Gene said one night. "The train stations and the roads must be swamped with hundreds of thousands of them. It was bad enough before. It must be hell now."

"I'm tired of running and you're still weak from malaria," Mark agreed. "At least here we have a place to work and a place to live. We are among people that know us."

"Do you think any of them suspects we're Jewish?"

"Not that I know of. I've kept my mouth shut. As far as I know, they all think we're Catholic Poles."

"We need to keep it that way."

"That's it then? We stay here?" asked Mark.

"I think it's our best hope. Let's take our chances with the rest of the people," Gene said.

The refugee torrent flooding past their door continued to swell. One morning Gene and Mark woke up to an amazing sight. The village was engulfed by cattle driven by men on horseback. The collective farms in the area had been ordered to evacuate their livestock so that it would not fall into German hands. It was a scene from a Wild West movie, transported to a bizarre Russian setting. Animals were crammed together, filling the grass verges on either side of the road, pressed up against the villagers' fences, moving slowly forward. After a while, a column of sheep straggled through. Next came an undisciplined parade of pigs. The air was full of baaing and bleating, grunting and squealing, and the smell of scared animals, as the herders whipped the compressed mass onward.

Other villagers were also watching, some spitting contemptuously at the retreating men and beasts. Gene caught the eye of Andrei Sonim, his next-door neighbor, and gestured as if to catch one. Sonim nodded and drew his thumb across his throat. So Gene opened his garden gate and politely ushered in a fat pig while the nearest herder was not looking. Mark quickly manhandled the squealing animal around the back of the cottage. Sonim slaughtered the animal. The meat and sausages would help feed them in the days ahead.

The stampede ended, and an unnatural silence fell over the village. Everyone stayed indoors, waiting. No one wanted to risk being caught in the open when the Germans finally arrived. Those could be dangerous moments of indiscriminate shooting and unpredictable violence. But as darkness came, people began venturing out, looking for somewhere to spend the night in the safety of numbers. Nobody wanted to be stuck in bed when the enemy entered the village.

Most people headed for the fruit orchards. Gene and Mark decided to go to the carpentry workshop. When they reached the deserted building, Mark's eye fell on one of the coffins they had made in their early weeks in the village.

"How about trying out one of these for size? It seems like a good resting place, and nobody needs it yet," he said. Given the circumstances, the joke fell somewhat flat.

"The Germans will soon make sure someone does," said Gene. "But it's not a bad idea if you're not superstitious." They each slipped into a suitable-sized casket and pulled the lid three-quarters shut.

"I've always wanted to know what this felt like," Gene said. "Now I know. Rest in peace, little brother." The coffins were surprisingly comfortable, the night was dark and silent, and they both quickly fell asleep. When they woke up the Germans still had not come.

The next day passed like the previous one, only slower. Insects buzzed over the piles of droppings left by the horde of animals, but nothing else moved. As darkness came, there was a knock on the cottage door. Gene opened it to find Raisa Pavlova outside, Galia a few paces behind. Raisa was agitated. "Yevgeny Adolfovich, excuse me for bursting in on you like this," she began.

Gene invited them in. She hesitated, then walked quickly into the cottage, nodding at Mark in the corner. "Yevgeny Adolfovich, I have come to request your help," she said. "I hesitate to ask you this, but we simply have no one else to ask. We are two women alone here, without family, without friends. We are defenseless. To be very frank with you, we are frightened. Last night we were in the orchard, and it was terrible. Every sound, every whisper, made us shake. One hears such hideous stories about the Germans, such horrible things."

"I'm glad you've come. Everybody is frightened. Of course my brother and I would be happy to help you any way we can," Gene said.

"May I ask where you slept last night? We looked for you in the orchard but we couldn't see you."

"We slept in the workshop, in coffins."

"That doesn't sound so comfortable," Raisa replied with a slight smile, while Galia could not suppress a giggle. "Surely it must be more pleasant sleeping under the stars in the orchard than in a dirty workshop."

"I suppose so. Comfort wasn't the first consideration."

"Yevgeny Adolfovich, since we first met you, my daughter and I have seen that you seem to be a well-mannered young man. I feel we can trust you. We have two blankets to spare. We would feel so much better if you and your brother were with us tonight."

So it was that Gene found himself sitting on a blanket under the stars with Galia. When they reached the orchard, Mark hoisted himself into an apricot tree and began devouring the fruit, spitting the pits in the direction of imaginary

Germans. He appeared ready to spend the entire night that way, but after half an hour he reluctantly climbed down, grabbed a blanket and went to sleep. Raisa Pavlova also lay down and closed her eyes. From her breathing, Gene could tell that she was wide awake and listening intently. He looked at Galia, and for the first time she returned his gaze. Both of them were slightly trembling. He took her hand, raised it to his lips, and kissed it. She made no attempt to stop him and gave a tiny smile.

For a while they sat without talking. Gene put his arm around Galia's shoulders and pulled her closer. They lay down together under the blanket. Gene could scarcely believe it was happening. At first, he was nervous and tentative. But whether from fear or desire, Galia was responsive. Gene was aware of everything: the girl; her smooth, warm skin reacting to his touch; her silent but attentive mother lying alongside; the other villagers quietly speculating on the arrival of the Germans; his own physical arousal. "Galia," he whispered, "why did you ignore me all this time? I thought you didn't like me."

"No, it wasn't that. I was just a little scared to talk to a foreign citizen," she whispered back. "Besides, I have a jealous boyfriend. His name is Alexander."

"Where is he?"

"In the army somewhere; I haven't heard from him for months." Her voice was low and melodious. Gene decided to forget about Alexander and concentrate on the here and now. "But Galia, is it really true that you like me a little?"

"Of course I do. And it was funny watching the way you would rush out of your house to talk to my mother about the weather every time we passed by. I started looking forward to it, wondering if you would say a word to me."

"Galia," he whispered again.

"What is it, Zjenya?" she asked, using the Russian diminutive of his name for the first time.

"I don't know. I just can't believe that we're here together like this. I just like saying your name."

"You can keep saying it all night. Maybe that way the night will never end, and the Germans will never come."

"No, they'll come. But hopefully not until tomorrow."

The following day was hot and muggy. After a whole morning in their airless cottage, the strain of waiting inside became too much. Mark and Gene decided to go out for a breath of air; it seemed safe enough. The village was still as they sat barefoot on a log, eating sunflower seeds. They felt as if they had been waiting so long that the Germans might indeed never come. The hush was punctured only by the sounds of birds and insects, the nuts cracking between their teeth, and the distant throb of an engine. Suddenly a lone command car skidded around the corner. There was no time to move. It halted in front of them.

"You two, are you soldiers?" shouted a man from the back seat.

"No, we're not soldiers," Gene called back. An officer sat beside the driver in the front of the vehicle. In the back, two soldiers flanked the man who had spoken, evidently an interpreter. All wore helmets and steel-gray Wehrmacht uniforms. Gene and Mark realized they were wearing Red Army trousers issued by the village. They wished they had waited inside their cottage like the other villagers.

"Soldiers, you're soldiers," the interpreter yelled. "Where is your unit? Get your hands in the air fast."

"We're not soldiers, we're Polish laborers," said Gene, hastily broadening his Polish accent. The soldiers pointed their weapons at them while the officer demanded a translation.

"Where are your papers? Show us your documents!"

"They're in the house."

"Get them, quick," said the interpreter. The guns swung to cover Mark as Gene went into the cottage. As he took out the papers, another thought struck him. Their name, Elsner!

It could be German, it could be Jewish, but it was not Polish. With all their talking about whether to stay or run, how did they forget that? Gene realized he must not present these papers to the Germans.

He called out. "I can't find the documents. Can my brother come in and help me look for them?" There was a pause for translation. If the officer refused, what would Gene do next? He did not know. Then the interpreter spoke to Mark: "Yes, yes, go and get them but be quick. We haven't got all day."

As Mark came in, Gene whispered, "We're not showing them these papers. Come on, we've got to get out of here." Grabbing their shoes and the papers, they slipped out the back door. There was a steep bank behind the cottage. They slid down it and ran, half-crouching on the steppe, ignoring the thistles stabbing their bare feet. They zigzagged across the rough field, for 200 yards and threw themselves behind a bush, listening for signs of pursuit. None came. The Germans apparently had more important things to do than chase stray fugitives.

They stayed in the field for about an hour, keeping a nervous lookout. "That was probably just an advance patrol. The main body of the Germans can't be far behind. They'll probably be here by nightfall. We have to change the papers immediately, that's obvious," said Gene. "You'll have to do it, Mark. You're the artist."

As dusk gathered, they returned cautiously to the cottage. Mark sat down at the table and surveyed the Cyrillic characters of the documents. His only tools were a sharp knife borrowed from the carpentry workshop and pen and ink. He held his hands out until they were still, thinking what he might do to change the names, knowing their lives might depend on how well he did it.

"Well, what do you think?" Gene asked.

"I think it can be done," said Mark. He decided to start at the end of the name. Using the knife, Mark gently scratched away the tail of the final letter, adding careful pen strokes to make the r into a *k*. Then, he examined the next two letters. Joining one loop to make a circle, he turned the *n* into an *iu* sound. He stopped again and dried his sweaty palms while he considered what might be done next.

"Let me see, let me see," Gene said as Mark scratched away, painstakingly calculating each pen stroke, refusing to be hurried. "What have you got?"

"Elesiuk. It doesn't sound bad, does it?"

"It's better than Elsner, that's for sure. But what kind of name is Elesiuk? It doesn't sound quite right. Is there anything else you can do?" Gene asked.

"Hold on a minute. I think there is." Mark picked up the pen and scratched away at the first letter of the name. It became an *o*.

"Olesiuk," said Gene. "That's good. Not exactly Polish but it should work. It sounds sort of Ukrainian."

"It is good, isn't it." Mark chuckled, delighted with his work. "I'm pleased to meet you, Eugene Olesiuk."

"And I to meet you, Mark Olesiuk." They shook hands. "But the name isn't enough on its own," Gene said. "We need a story to go with it. You know, birthplace, address, father's name, all of that. We may be asked."

"Also, we both need to tell exactly the same story in case someone tries to trip us up," Mark agreed.

"How about this? We're Poles from Lwów. That's good because Lwów is surrounded by Ukrainians, which would explain the name, and we know the place well enough to sound convincing if we're asked about it."

"And for our address we can give that building where we lived, the one that was demolished. That way, if they take the trouble to check, there won't be anyone to ask if they know us," said Mark.

So they became the brothers Olesiuk. Mark's heart would always skip a beat whenever they had to produce those papers. He feared that anyone who examined them closely would see the scratch marks and added pen strokes. They both thought about where in the village there might be documents with their original names. They were registered in the local council, of course, but they remembered that in the absence of the village secretary at the time, the formality had been done in a perfunctory way. They were told to report at a later date to fill out the papers, but somehow they never did.

None of the villagers knew their family name. To them, the brothers were Yevgeny Adolfovich and Mark Adolfovich. Then Gene remembered that the doctor had his name on file because of his malaria treatment. A few nights later, with Mark standing guard, he broke into the clinic, stole some files, including his own, and trashed the office to cover his intentions. Casually encountering the doctor a few days later, he asked jokingly, "Hey, I bet you don't even remember my name."

"Of course I do. It's Yevgeny Adolfovich," the doctor replied.

"Yevgeny Adolfovich Olesiuk," Gene told him firmly.

CHAPTER 17

Under the Nazis

Now, the swastika fluttered over the flourmill and adjoining building. German soldiers strutted down the main street. The Nazis lost no time rounding up all the Jews they could find in the area. On August 27, about 700 Jews from Georgievsk were loaded on trucks, taken to the antitank ditches outside the town, and shot. Unknown to Gene and Mark, a Cossack family living across the road from them had been sheltering Jews. Someone denounced them to the Nazis. The Jews were taken away and killed.

The Nazis left the structure of the *kolhoz* intact for the time being but set up a new local council. To the brothers' surprise and dismay, its head was Efim Vasilevich, the agronomist, now revealed as a German sympathizer. Under the communists, Efim had kept his background a secret. He now let it be known that he had been a Cossack military leader before the Communist revolution and an officer in one of the anti-Bolshevik armies in the Russian Civil War. He called on the villagers to rally to the Germans, promising they would destroy the evils of communism, restore Cossack rights, and reestablish the old way of life. Gene and Mark ran into him when they filed into village council office to register for German identity papers. As they had hoped, no one had questioned their new family name. But they were nervous when they came face to face with Efim.

He was all smiles. "Ah, Yevgeny Adolfovich, my friend, and Mark, how are you?" he greeted them. The brothers nodded uncomfortably. They remembered their debt to him and certainly did not want him as an enemy, but once he had gone over to the Germans he could no longer be their friend. "Yevgeny Adolfovich, I've been meaning to talk to you," Efim continued, seemingly unaware of their unease. "I remember you once telling me you spoke good German. How would you like to work with me? I need an interpreter in my daily dealings with the Germans and you would be doing me a favor."

"I couldn't do it, Efim Vasilevich," Gene replied. "It wouldn't be right. We have not forgotten how much we owe you. But we are strangers in this country and we shouldn't get involved. The villagers would think we repaid the kindness they've shown us by siding with the Germans."

"But the Germans will be good for us here, Yevgeny Adolfovich. They'll restore the Cossack to what he once was. They'll give land back to our people. We're well rid of Stalin and his damned commissars."

"It may be the right thing for you Efim Vasilevich, but this is just not our fight." Gene motioned to Mark and they left the office. They saw Efim rarely after that and avoided him whenever they could. It soon became clear the local self-government he had hoped to lead was a sham. Efim had no real authority. He was nothing more than a figurehead following German orders.

The Germans tried hard to win the Cossacks to their side. They announced that Cossacks would not be categorized as *Untermenschen*, or sub humans, like other Slavs; they recruited a local police force and announced they would soon dissolve the collective farms, a promise they never kept. They also appealed to historic Cossack antisemitism, urging them to join the fight against "Jewish Bolshevism." Some responded. But the majority saw the Germans for what they were—a ruthless invader and enemy of Mother Russia.

A few days after their encounter with Efim, two German soldiers burst into the cottage looking for Gene. Their jackboots and carbines with fixed bayonets instantly reminded him of Jasło. "Come with us. Hurry, hurry," one shouted.

"Where to?" Gene asked in alarm.

"You'll see. Hurry, hurry." Gene obeyed, trying to think who could have denounced him and how he could warn Mark. Before he could think of a plan, they reached German headquarters in the flourmill. Ten minutes later, Gene was in the office of the commandant. To Gene's slight relief, he wore the uniform and insignia of a captain in the Wehrmacht rather than the SS or Gestapo. He was in his fifties with blond, graying hair and an air of authority. The other person present was a young lieutenant, his blond clean-cut features the classic newsreel picture of a Nazi. "I'm told by our new village headman that you speak German," the captain addressed Gene. "Is that correct?"

"Yes." There seemed no point in lying.

"Have you ever served in the Soviet armed forces?"

"No."

"Why not? You appear fit enough."

"I'm not a Soviet citizen."

"Then tell us your name and where you come from." Gene gave the answers he and Mark had rehearsed. The lieutenant wrote them down, occasionally asking for the spelling of Polish names.

"Where did you learn German?"

"At school. Also at one time my family lived near some *Volksdeutsche*, and some of my childhood friends were Germans."

"Where is your family now?"

"Still there, in Lwów."

"In Lemberg, you mean," the captain said, referring to the city by its German name.

"Yes."

"Good. They are living under the jurisdiction of the Reich and all the information you've given us can be verified. Are there any brothers and sisters?"

"Yes, a younger brother."

"Still in Lemberg?"

"As far as I know."

"How did you get here?"

"I was deported by the Soviets in 1940. I and some others were eventually released from prison and we traveled through different parts of the country until we found work."

"Where are the others you traveled with?"

"They found work in various places. I don't know where they are now."

The captain leaned forward. "Tell me," he said, "why, in your opinion, did Poland start this war with Germany in 1939?" Gene was surprised by the question and unsure how to answer.

"That's not how I remember it," he said finally.

"But didn't the Poles persecute the Germans in Danzig and Pomerania? Didn't Polish forces cross the border and violate our territory?"

"Poland was weak. How could we have dared to attack a mighty power like Germany? We Poles may be stupid but we're not crazy," Gene replied. The lieutenant nearly jumped at such impudence, but the captain smiled. "Very well," he said. "You have nerve. That's good. I'm all in favor of honesty and frankness. So let me ask you this: If you were to be employed by the German army, who would you favor, the Germans or the Russians?"

Again, Gene searched for words. "I'd try to mind my own business," he said.

The captain seemed satisfied. "Very well," he said. "We will verify everything you've told us. Meantime, I need interpreters in the field. You will report here tomorrow morning at seven o'clock."

Gene left the office, relieved he had survived the interview but bewildered by this new twist. His position was even shakier than before. Surrounded by Germans, he would have to watch every word and control every emotion. He also worried that their cover story would not stand up to a thorough German investigation.

Next morning, Gene reported for duty. The man in charge introduced himself as Sergeant Mueller and told Gene to board a truck. He found a seat on a bench, surrounded by German soldiers. They were in high spirits, sure they would soon win the war and joking about making out with the local girls. They ignored Gene. He could reach out and touch them; they were men just like him. But if they knew he was Jewish, they would arrest him and kill him.

Eventually the truck pulled up at the Georgievsk railroad station. The soldiers belonged to a technical engineering unit. Their job was to transform the wide-gauge Soviet railroad system to the narrower gauge used by the rest of Europe, so that after the Nazis had conquered the Caucasian oil fields, they could ship the oil back to Germany to fuel their war machine. The unit had about 90 soldiers. Each day, they broke into groups, fanning out to work with captured Russian engineers converting the signals and points. Other soldiers kept watch over Russian forced laborers who were pulling up sections of track and laying new rails.

The first day, Sergeant Mueller ordered Gene to come with him. They drove deep into the steppe until they reached a signal post. Inside, Russian technicians were working at a control board. Mueller told Gene to translate as he questioned the Russians. Gene had difficulty with some of the technical language. "Don't worry," said Mueller. "Do the best you can for now. I'll get you a dictionary of engineering terms from headquarters."

Gradually, Gene got to know the soldiers in his unit. They came from all over Germany and spoke in a blend of regional accents. Some were reservists—older men with spreading waistlines and families back home. Others were young recruits away from home for the first time. Mueller, who was in charge of supplies and logistics, was a stout man with thick glasses, plump cheeks, a bull neck, and a bulging uniform. He was constantly harassed and spent much of his time trying to reach regional headquarters on the telephone to plead for materials and equipment.

An Austrian soldier, Otto Bauer, tried to make friends with Gene. He spoke a clipped Austrian dialect and was an ardent Catholic who had little in common with the rest of the unit. Otto was constantly talking about the farm he had inherited from his father, about his mother left alone to take care of it, and about the girlfriend he hoped to marry. He kept asking Gene about his supposed family in Lwów. "Now that you're in German territory, you can contact them again. You could even send them parcels by military mail, same as we do. I assure you they don't take too long," he said. Gene said he would.

The others in the unit soon grew used to Gene. They Germanized his name, calling him Eugen with a hard G. He learned their songs, admired photographs of their sweethearts, played football, and drank their German beer. But he never relaxed his guard. He learned to control his face and sometimes woke up in the morning with aching jaws, having clenched them as tight as a mousetrap in his sleep. He was plagued by nightmares that he could not fully remember after they had jerked him awake. The tension gnawed at him. Some days when he went to work, he wondered how long he could keep up the pretense without making a slip that would give him away, or when an innocent conversation might suddenly take a dangerous turn and threaten to expose him.

Occasionally he managed to visit Galia's cottage in the evening. He had convinced himself that he was in love with her. But he could not confide in her without endangering both of them. There was no privacy in the two-room cottage, and they seemed unable to recapture the magic of their night under the stars. Her mother rarely left them alone. When they did grab five minutes by themselves, Galia was shy. She seemed guilty about being with Gene and often spoke of her boyfriend. Gene also occasionally ran into Marusia in the village. She was friendly but they both knew their relationship was over. In any case, it was no longer the season for lovemaking under the sun.

All Gene could think about was how to survive the next day. Simple tasks like urinating were dangerous. He never relieved himself by the sides of fields or roads like the soldiers did and took care not to drink too much so as not to be caught short. If a German saw that he was circumcised it would mean death.

Some mornings on the way to work, the unit would take one or two prisoners in the truck to turn over to the Gestapo in Georgievsk. Most were young teenagers denounced by spies and collaborators as members of the resistance. They would sprawl on the floor between the two lines of German soldiers, their eyes wide with fear. Some of the soldiers taunted them. "Stalin's kaput, Stalin's kaput," they would jeer, drawing their fingers across their throats. Usually the captives seemed too paralyzed by terror to pay much attention. They knew what was waiting for them. Once, a young boy raised himself to his elbow and shouted in defiance "Hitler kaput." Two of the older Germans restrained the others from bayoneting him.

A few times the unit took Jewish prisoners to town. The captives were dropped off at an elegant brick building in the center of Georgievsk with iron bars across its windows. Few of those who entered for interrogation ever emerged alive. Townspeople often heard gunfire from the courtyard at night or early in the morning. Sometimes the Germans dumped tortured bodies on the platform of the railroad station for their families to claim and as a warning to others. Hundreds were shot against that courtyard wall or beaten to death in the months of Nazi occupation.

One day Gene's unit brought a young Jewish woman to Georgievsk. She was in her early twenties and once had been pretty. Now she was bedraggled, her dark hair matted, her face filthy and bruised. The men amused themselves, calling her a damned Jewish bitch and promising her an unpleasant fate. Gene felt as if he would break in two, but there was nothing he could do. He tried to hold himself rigid and keep his face expressionless. Then one of the German soldiers noticed that the girl was staring at Gene. "Hey Eugen, the Jewish trash has taken a shine to you," he called out.

"Won't do you much good with your girlfriend in the village," another guffawed. They kept up the banter for a while. Gene did not respond. He tried to avoid the girl's eyes but found himself drawn to meet them. What the soldiers said was true; she stared at him for the entire journey. Toward the end, tears welled silently and tracked their way slowly down her face. She still gazed at Gene but never spoke. What was she trying to tell him? She was there in his head, mutely crying for help, when he closed his eyes that night and for years to come.

In Georgievsk there was a sunflower-oil factory where German soldiers bought cans of oil to send home to their families. Otto kept urging Gene to send some to his parents in Lwów. "They can use it, I'm sure. Cooking oil is scarce even in Germany, and it's bound to be even more precious in Lemberg," he said. After a while, Gene decided it would look suspicious if he did not do so, so he mailed a few cans to his fictitious family, hoping that they would not return marked address unknown.

Once the Germans brought a film crew to Georgievsk to make a propaganda movie. Some of the actors and technicians were stationed in the village for a few days. Gene joined some soldiers who took a truck into town one afternoon to watch. The director had rounded up scores of hapless townspeople at gunpoint and dressed them in Russian uniforms. The crew was filming an attack by German forces on the railroad station. At the director's command, the Russian extras keeled over and played dead as soon as the Germans opened fire. Fake bombs exploded while smoke and noise filled the air. Then came German actresses dressed as German nurses to minister to the wounded—the German wounded, that is.

In October, streams of German units drove through the village on the way to the front, yelling "to Baku, to Baku," as they passed. The Nazis seemed unstoppable. They were enveloping the strategic city of Stalingrad on the Volga River and were expected to capture it any day. A few miles to the east, a major battle was developing around Grozny. Out on the steppe, soldiers would gather around the radio once or twice a day to listen to broadcasts, which always reported triumphant advances and new victories. They would slap each other on the back and in the evening would hurry to the bar, stand each other drinks and shout "Sieg heil, sieg heil, hoch, hoch, hoch—hurrah, hurrah, hurrah!" Gene would drink with them and occasionally pay for a round.

Sometimes the troops passing through would stop in the village for a night or two. These units terrified the villagers. A reception area had been set up for them where they could spend the evening downing beers. Then, randy and belligerent, they would swagger down the street, shoving residents off the sidewalks and hunting for young women. The soldiers were billeted in the villagers' houses, where they made free with people's possessions as well as their women. One day, an unusually large unit stopped at the village. That afternoon, Raisa Pavlova rushed to Gene's house in a panic. "They've stationed three German soldiers in our house for the night. What are we to do? What are we to do?" she cried, nearly hysterical.

"Calm yourself Raisa Pavlova," said Gene, appalled by the thought of Galia with the Germans. "You could come here."

"We cannot come, Yevgeny Adolfovich. They'll destroy everything we own out of spite and frustration if we're not there, like others of their kind did in people's houses. We are defenseless. You are the only person I can turn to."

"Yes, I see, Raisa Pavlova. Of course I'll help. Just give me a little time. I'll think of something."

But what? Obviously the women must not be left alone. But how could he defend them against three armed Germans who might well be roaring drunk by the time they came back to the cottage late at night? He decided to confide in his Austrian friend, Otto Bauer. "What can I do? Should I tell the captain about it?"

"No, I wouldn't do that. The captain can't take your side against the German army. He has to defend the army's honor, no matter what. And it's not as if these boys have done anything yet," Otto told him.

"If I wait until they do something, it'll be too late."

"Obviously. We need to think of something else." He thought for a moment, then said, "I have an idea. You're about the same size as me. I could let you have my spare uniform. They may not want to mess with a fellow in a German uniform."

Gene wasn't sure. The idea of wearing a Nazi uniform was repugnant. He did not want to be identified in the village as a collaborator, and he was not sure the plan would work, since he obviously was not German. On the other hand, he couldn't think of anything else. Reluctantly, Gene nodded. It felt very strange putting on the uniform. When he pulled on the jackboots, he almost recoiled.

Otto was grinning; he viewed the whole thing as a lark. "Do you want to see how you look?" he asked, shoving a cracked shaving mirror in front of Gene's face. A clean-cut, grim-faced Nazi trooper stared out of it. Otto swung him around and inspected him from head to foot. Then he clicked his heels and thrust his right arm into the air. "Heil Hitler," he barked. Gene could not bring himself to respond. "Come on, Eugen. You have to enter into the spirit of it," Otto said. He tried again. "Heil Hitler!"

"I haven't got time for this," Gene said. "I have to get over there before it's too late."

"Oh very well. I'll come with you. Wouldn't want to miss the fun," Otto said. They knocked on the door, and a white-faced Galia opened it. She jumped when she saw Gene standing there in uniform accompanied by another German soldier. "Hush," he whispered, putting a finger to his lips. "Not a word."

The three Germans had just arrived and were in the bedroom trying out the beds. Otto quickly took charge. He introduced Gene as an important member of the unit and a friend of the commandant. Then he apologized that as guests the Germans would have to sleep in the kitchen on the floor, since one bed was reserved for the mother and the other for Eugen and his betrothed, commandant's orders. Then, winking at Gene, he left. The Germans retreated to the kitchen, complaining under their breaths.

Raisa Pavlova looked at Gene gratefully, but he shook his head, gesturing to her to keep quiet. She lay down on one of the beds and closed her eyes. Galia led him by the hand to the second bed and undid the top buttons of his shirt. They could hear the Germans through the thin partition, grumbling, coughing, and belching. Galia giggled. He kissed her to prevent her from laughing out aloud and they collapsed on the bed.

"What a circus," Gene thought. Here he was, a Jew masquerading as a Nazi, lying on a bed with a beautiful Russian girl, her mother barely five feet away, and three real Nazis in the next room. One of them grunted. Galia giggled again. "*Mein* hero," she whispered in his ear, her breath hot against his neck. Suddenly they both forgot about the Germans. What was it about danger that was so arousing? They were under the covers, her hands tearing off his shirt. "Be careful with the uniform," he tried to say.

"Never mind the uniform," she said kissing him.

"What about your mother?" But there was no time to answer. They tried to move together without moving, stifling half cries, rocking softly while one of the Germans in the next room snored like a steam engine.

Some days, Gene had to stay behind at headquarters to work with the commandant, Captain Peters, or to give him his full title, Herr Hauptman Herbert Peters. Without ever saying anything, the captain gave the impression of a man uncomfortable with his duties, although he was determined to carry them out to the letter. In civilian life, he had been a company director and an army reservist, called up when the war began. A chess player, he was soon inviting Gene to stay after work for a game. "I must seem ancient to you," he said to Gene one evening.

"You must be about the same age as my father," Gene replied.

"How old is he?"

"About 50."

"You aren't far off. I'm 54. Did he fight in the last war, your father?"

"He fought on your side, in the Austrian army."

"Really? Where?"

"He fought right here in Russia."

"How strange. We were comrades. I was here too. We came as far as Kiev. This time we've come much farther." Gene said nothing. Peters sighed. His face was almost lost in darkness. The room was very still. "Tell me," the captain said, "do you have a girlfriend here?"

"Yes, I do," Gene replied.

"Is she very pretty?"

"She's beautiful."

"And do you think you have a future together?"

"Who knows? At the moment, we scarcely even have a present. Maybe after the war..."

"I had a love affair in Russia," the captain said softly. Gene could hardly hear him; he almost seemed to be talking to himself. "I fell in love but she was..." He lowered his voice even further although there was no one else in the room, "...she was Jewish. I wanted to marry her. Imagine, me with a Jewess. What would have become of us and our children if I had married her?" His voice trailed off.

After that, a cautious rapport grew between the captain and Gene. The captain had a son about Gene's age. Perhaps that explained it. They talked about literature, art—anything but politics and the war. Once, the captain asked Gene which books he had read in German. Gene said that as a boy he had enjoyed books about the Wild West written by the famous German author Karl May.

"Is that so? He's the Führer's favorite writer," the captain said.

Once, the captain even asked Gene about how his troops were behaving in the village. Gene said that in general they conducted themselves correctly; the problem was with the units that passed through and spent a night or two in Nezlobnaya.

"Well, men are in short supply here and I understand there are a lot of women who don't mind having some enjoyment with our German boys," the captain said.

"They may be willing, but they don't want to be forced," Gene said.

"Have you heard of rapes?"

"I have."

"Well, there's a war on. I don't approve, but it happens. The peasants here may not be as finicky about these things as you or I."

"I don't know about that. You understand that these are not ordinary Russians. They are Cossacks, and they have their pride. They value their women very highly. They would not hesitate to kill anyone, even a German soldier, if he offended their honor."

"The Cossacks are no strangers to raping; they have done quite a bit of it themselves in their time, I understand. And I wouldn't advise anyone to try to harm one of our soldiers. Once we were in another place and there was such an incident."

"And what happened?" Gene asked.

"We ended up having to take hostages to force them to give up the criminals. When that didn't work, we shot the hostages." There was silence.

"I hope and pray that won't happen here, Herr Hauptman," Gene said.

"It won't if things stay quiet. But I keep hearing stories that something's brewing in this village. The Gestapo tells me there is an illegal transmitter operating here. You wouldn't know anything about it, would you?"

"No," Gene replied truthfully. But he thought, if this was true, he should try to warn these people, whoever they were.

Sometimes when work took them far from their base, Gene's unit stayed in the field for two or three days at a time, sleeping in tents. By now, autumn had come and clouds of brown dust raised by a chill wind shrouded the mountains. One November day found Gene with a group of six soldiers and an officer camped by the side of a vast field. A deep anti tank ditch dug by the Russians in a vain effort to slow the German advance slashed across it. Some soldiers were working inside a signal box. The others, including Gene, were outside warming their hands by the fire. Suddenly, two trucks pulled into the field some distance yards away. A dozen German soldiers jumped from one vehicle and took up positions behind the second, weapons ready. Then they opened the rear flap and hustled out a crowd of civilians. There were about 25 of them, mostly women and children.

The men around the fire stopped talking and watched the soldiers prod and shove the civilians to the edge of the antitank trench. The soldiers formed a line; the officer stood to one side. They heard him bark an order. There was a prolonged crackle of gunfire, muffled shouts and screams, and some of the figures toppled into the crevice. The soldiers kicked the rest into the pit and fired another long burst to make sure everyone was dead. Then, they climbed back aboard their trucks and drove away. Around the fire, no one said anything. Perhaps they had seen such things before. Some men lit cigarettes, a few stood up to get back to work; they all avoided each other's eyes.

An hour later, the trucks returned with a new batch of victims. Dead bodies lay atop each other, out of sight, but Gene saw them anyway in his mind. He was numb with horror. What was going through their minds, these men standing next to him? Did they retain any human compassion? Any guilt? Or were they telling themselves it didn't matter because they were all Jews anyway, or Communists, the dead children and their dead mothers. But they all saw it all, and they all knew. They were all accessories to murder, every last one of them. They were all guilty.

The soldiers came back the next day for more executions and again two days later. By now, Gene's unit was getting used to it. Some did not even stop working while the victims were lined up by the ditch and shot. When it was over, the officer in charge of the execution squad strolled across the field. "Hello there," he called cheerily as he drew near. "Mind if I warm my hands by your fire?"

"Please, please, be our guest," said the lieutenant in charge of Gene's group.

"Hell of a cold day. I've got another lot coming in a while, so I thought I might as well be warm with you while I'm waiting," said the executioner.

"By all means, any time."

Gene shrunk into the background, hoping not to be noticed. He was the only one present not wearing a uniform. The two officers quickly fell into an animated conversation. They discovered that they came from neighboring towns and began exchanging news from home. The newcomer pulled out a letter from his wife and began reading it aloud. There were shortages everywhere, she complained, and she was having problems with the oldest girl, who didn't want to go to school in the morning. She knew her dearest husband was doing important work for the Fatherland and she adored him for it and could he send home some cans of honey and cooking oil? The man, a loving husband and proud father, appeared unconcerned by what he had done less than half an hour before and what he would soon do again.

"It's all girls?" the lieutenant asked.

"That's right, two of them." The officer brought out a photograph, and the men passed it around. Then the officer saw the truck in the distance, heading back to the execution ground. "Well, it's been very pleasant," he said, shaking hands with the lieutenant, "but duty calls. Back to work, you know." And off he went, clumping across the field to supervise the next firing squad.*

Gene looked at his workmates, men who now accepted him, traded jokes with him, and occasionally bought him beers. He hated them, every one of them who wore the uniform of child murderers. From that moment, he became obsessed with the idea of fighting the Germans. There had to be a way.

---

* Documents in the Georgievsk museum viewed by the author indicate that the Nazis carried out mass executions in the town's area on August 27, 1942; September 8, 18, and 27; October 6, 14, and 26; November 5, 6, and 21; December 6, 11, 19, and 27; and January 6 and 7, 1943. Mass graves were uncovered in various places. For example, between the Georgievsk and Vinogradia railroad stations, 858 corpses were discovered, including approximately 400 women and children of seven or younger. The rest were Red Army soldiers. In antitank ditches between Nezlobnaya and Georgievsk, 351 bodies were found; 126 were soldiers, the rest women and children.

He got a chance a few days later after the unit returned to the village. Otto had a date with a Russian girl. He was supposed to meet her at a friend's house. He asked Gene to come along to make it a double date and wear the German uniform again. Gene would be able to understand what the girls were saying to one another and tell Otto if he had any chance to get lucky. Gene did not want to wear the uniform but he owed Otto a favor and felt unable to refuse him.

Soon they were sitting around the table in a cozy, half-dim room with the two girls. Otto had brought along two packets of cigarettes, a bottle of vodka, and a bar of chocolate to help his campaign and was whispering endearments to one girl, who would giggle and comment sarcastically to the second. When the Austrian worked his hand under the girl's skirt, murmuring soft coaxing words, Gene heard her complaining to her friend about the things she had to suffer for the cause.

"What did she say?" Otto asked Gene in German.

"She said you're a dare devil, a real lady-killer."

As the evening wore on, Otto became progressively drunker. He started singing folk songs, at which point one of the girls asked her friend in Russian, "What's the point of all this if we can't understand a word they are saying? How are we going to get any information out of him?" Soon it was time to go. As they left, Gene wished them good night in Russian. Their faces blanched. "Don't worry, I'm a friend," he quickly added. "I'll ask a friend of mine to come to see you and explain. She lives in the village and she knows me."

When Gene asked Galia if she would be willing to act as a go-between, she immediately agreed. He warned her they would both be taking a risk. If the Nazis suspected them of helping the resistance, they would both be tortured and killed. But Galia saw a positive side. "It could be a lifesaver for both of us if the communists come back," she said.

She visited the girls the next day and explained that Gene was not German and why he had been wearing the uniform. She told them that the Germans knew about their radio transmitter and were searching for it. The resistance was just trying to get organized and planning sabotage operations. Its leaders needed to know the identity of village informers and collaborators. That's where Gene could help. Working with the Germans, he often overheard valuable intelligence that he was able to pass along. But working for the resistance added a new layer of danger to his life.

CHAPTER 18

The Gestapo

It was the fourth winter of the war. Gene's routine had changed. The captain found a new interpreter and no longer needed him. The interpreter, Sonia Mayevska, had moved into the village with her *Volksdeutsche* sister-in-law and their three young children. They said they had fled from the Volga German region to avoid deportation. The captain immediately recruited Sonia to work in his office. She claimed to be a native German speaker but Gene thought some of her expressions sounded more Yiddish than German.

He still went to the office occasionally to translate written texts, but now mainly to play chess with the captain. One day Gene was there when a Russian came asking for a job. He had a letter of recommendation from the German high command in Kiev and a story to tell. The man was a Nezlobnaya native who had been stationed in Kiev at the time of the Russian invasion. He was part of a Red Army unit that had laid explosives in key buildings. But the German advance had been so swift that the Soviets fled before detonating the charges. The man had hidden during the retreat and went over to the Germans as soon as they arrived. He immediately led them to the explosives and helped dismantle them. In return, the grateful German commander promised to make him headman of his home village if and when it fell under Nazi control. The letter asked the German authorities in Nezlobnaya to make good on that pledge.

Captain Peters explained that the post of headman was already occupied by Efim Vasilevich. There was, however, a vacant position as chief of police. His first task, the captain instructed, was to find the illegal radio transmitter hidden in the village and break up the resistance cell that operated it.

Gene passed on the information to his resistance contacts. As a native, the new police chief was well placed to win the villagers' confidence. He started putting together a network of informants, but his recruits were shunned by most villagers. The chief soon realized that people knew what he was up to. He immediately suspected that the young Pole, who had been sitting in the captain's office and who had heard him tell his story, had given him away.

One evening after work, the captain sent for Gene. "The Gestapo want to see you tomorrow in Georgievsk," he said. Gene felt as though he had fallen through a trapdoor. "Why, what have I done?" he made himself ask.

"I don't know yet. Perhaps you should tell me."

"Nothing, I've done nothing."

"Eugen, you remember our first conversation?" the captain asked.

"Of course."

"I asked you whether you would side with the Russians or the Germans."

"Yes, I remember."

"And you said you would mind your own business."

"Yes."

"Have you done so?"

"Yes, I have. I've reported for work every day and I have done my work conscientiously. I doubt if the Soviets would think I've been neutral."

"How well do you know the Ukrainian language?"

"I can understand a bit, but I can't speak it," Gene answered baffled.

"Very well." The captain leaned back, his fingers drumming the desk. Gene tried to contain his agitation.

"Unfortunately, the inquiries I tried to make about your background have not turned up any answers," the captain continued. "I asked Mueller about it today when I learned that the Gestapo want to see you. It would have helped to have had some corroboration."

"That's not my fault," Gene said.

"Indeed. But we still know nothing about you that can be verified. Not that you've ever given me any real reason to disbelieve you." The captain sighed heavily. "This is a bad business. The Gestapo have their own logic in these matters. My influence is limited, but I'll do what I can for you. I've asked Sergeant Mueller to go along with you tomorrow. He'll testify to your valuable services to our unit."

Gene went straight to Sonia Mayevska, the captain's new interpreter. She opened her door as if she had been expecting him. "It's that police chief who's behind it," she said immediately. "He's the one who's denounced you, I'm sure of it."

"Denounced me for what?"

"He doesn't think you're really Polish, and he suspects you of passing information to the resistance. He and the captain had a long talk about it this afternoon. I could hear snatches from the next room."

"What do you mean not Polish? What does he think I am?"

"He thinks you're a Ukrainian and that you were planted by the Soviets."

A Ukrainian? What a joke! But in the end it made no difference what one got shot for. Sonia stepped forward and put her arms around him. "I know how hard this must be for you. Believe me, I do. You and I have a lot in common, more than you think. Your secret is safe with me," she whispered.

"What secret? I don't have a secret," Gene said, trying to pull away. "I don't want to know anything you're trying to tell me. Don't you realize how dangerous it could be for you to be grilled by the Gestapo if I am arrested? You don't know anything about me, do you hear?"

"Yes, of course you're right. Forgive me for my moment of weakness. I'll pray for your safe return tomorrow."

Gene went home to tell his brother.

"What did that Mayevska woman say?"

"She thought it was the damned police chief who informed on me. She thinks he may even have denounced me as a Soviet spy. She's Jewish, as well you know. She all but told me so."

"Oh God," Mark groaned.

"I know. It could be bad."

"But they didn't arrest you. Maybe that's a good sign. They would have come for you right away if they thought you were a spy," Mark said.

"They know I can't escape. They may be waiting for me to try, or maybe they expected me to lead them to others if I panicked."

"Well at least the captain's still on your side."

"I think he is. But Mark, listen. If I don't come back at the usual time tomorrow, you've got to disappear quickly. Don't waste any time. Just do it. If they get me, they'll come after you as well."

"Where would I go?"

"Ask the girls, the ones I pass messages to. Ask them to hide you until they can put you in touch with the partisans, and tell Galia to run, too."

"I don't even want to think about that."

"You must," Gene answered fiercely. "I don't know what the Gestapo wants, but I do know that once they get hold of you, they seldom let go." He shuddered.

Neither of them slept much that night. Gene wanted to tell Mark how much he loved him and a thousand other things but he couldn't bring himself to speak. He wondered if he could bear torture and thought about the young Jewish woman he had seen transported to the Gestapo a few weeks before. He parted from Mark after a breakfast that neither of them touched. Mark headed for the carpentry shop, and Gene went to board the morning truck to Georgievsk. While he was waiting, he saw the captain's car pull out of the gate and turn in the direction of town. Then Sergeant Mueller arrived to accompany him to the Gestapo. "Cheer up Eugen," he said breezily. "I'm carrying the highest references for you from the captain. We'll have a beer tonight, you'll see."

The others on the truck knew about Gene's summons and teased him during the trip. "It's been nice knowing you, Eugen," one joked. "Any messages for your next of kin?"

"Don't look so worried. They probably just want to recruit you," another snickered.

"Give the poor lad a rest. He's obviously scared out of his wits," said a third. "You don't want to believe everything you hear about the Gestapo, Eugen. They're not as bad as all that. They're much worse."

By the time they arrived, Gene's nerves were at the breaking point. He fought to preserve a poker face as the sergeant escorted him through the gate and into the main building. The place was teeming with jeeps and trucks pulling in and out of the gate and uniformed men hustling handcuffed detainees inside. Ahead was the pockmarked wall where they did their killing.

Mueller seemed to know his way around. This was where he handed over the prisoners they transported from the village. He led the way up the stairs and knocked on a door. Gene waited outside. It was like any office building. Uniformed Gestapo officers bustled past him carrying files, their boots slapping on the scrubbed wooden floor. The place smelled of polish and disinfectant. It all seemed so ordinary; one could almost forget that the business this place dealt in was mass murder. Eventually Mueller emerged with a faint smile. "Good news. Captain Peters is inside," he announced. "He's trying to sort everything out."

Gene felt a flicker of hope. Perhaps the captain could save his hide. Then the door opened and Peters came out with a Gestapo officer. The two Germans strolled down the corridor without acknowledging him. Gene tried to appear nonchalant, although inside he felt like jelly. The Gestapo man seemed to be doing most of the talking, while the captain nodded. Once they both laughed at something, and the officer clapped Peters on the shoulder.

After what seemed like an age, the captain beckoned Gene. He approached, bowed his head in the approved Nazi way, and stood to attention. "Captain Peters tells me good things about you. He says you're a loyal member of his unit," the officer said. "In light of that, I'm going to assume that what was reported to us was done out of spite. I'm prepared to give you the benefit of the doubt, but we need your cooperation in return."

"Of course," Gene managed to say through dry lips.

"We know for sure there's a partisan group operating a radio transmitter in your village. It's absolutely imperative that we find the transmitter quickly. You have local contacts, don't you?"

"I know a few people."

"You are to go back and use those contacts to find out what we need to know. This ridiculous matter has defied us for far too long and has now become quite pressing."

"I'll try my best."

"Very well. It's irregular, but so is the very strong recommendation we have from your captain, so we'll let it go at that." He shook hands with Peters, turned on his heel, and disappeared. Gene resisted the urge to throw his arms around the captain and followed him out of the building in silence. Apparently the captain did not want to talk.

For Mark, that day seemed endless. He tried to imagine what Gene might be going through and kept telling himself that everything would be fine. He later remembered it as one of the longest days of his life. He could do nothing but wait. Afternoon came. He finished work and went home, wondering whether he should pack some things in case he had to flee. He decided not to; it would be tempting fate. Well before the time Gene usually returned, Mark was out in the street waiting for him. Finally the truck carrying German soldiers arrived and pulled into the mill compound. It was impossible to see who was inside. Another 15 minutes crawled by; then he saw Gene walk out of the gate. Mark rushed to meet him and threw his arms around him. "You're back, you're back, thank God," he cried.

"Not in the middle of the street, it looks suspicious," Gene hissed at him. Mark backed off and they hurried back to the cottage. "The captain saved me," Gene said. "There's no doubt about it. I don't know quite why he did it, but he did."

In mid-November, the tone of German radio broadcasts began to change. They became less bombastic. Fewer victories were reported. To the southeast, German forces were bogged down, unable to break through to Grozny. More important, the battle had swung the other way at Stalingrad. A massive Soviet counteroffensive had trapped a quarter of a million German troops in and around the city. The broadcasts did not mention the huge battle that was raging around the city, but rumors were flying and soldiers in the village could sense that things were not going as planned.

Gene felt the change in his work. His unit had finished converting much of the railway system around Georgievsk to the German gauge. Every day they went deeper into the steppe to more remote signal points, but the work pace had slackened as if the Germans no longer believed there was any point in completing the job. They were only working three or four hours a day. But he was not out of the woods yet. One evening, Gene was sitting in the German reception center drinking a beer when a group of soldiers passing through the village entered. A drunken German asked Gene where he was from.

"Lemberg," Gene replied.

"You don't sound like you're from Lemberg," the soldier said, suddenly more alert. "I'm from Jarosław, so I know Lemberg well. You're not from there. You don't have the accent, I can tell."

"What nonsense. There're plenty of Poles in Lemberg."

"It's not nonsense. You don't smell of pork either. All Lemberg people smell of pork. You've got black hair so you must be a Jew. You're a bloody Jew, aren't you?"

Gene pulled away, trying to appear insulted. "You're either drunk or crazy," he said.

"I may be drunk, but you're still a Jew. That will be easy to prove, won't it?" The man picked up his drink and waved over to his buddies on the other side of the room. "Guess what I found!" he shouted. Luckily, his voice was lost in the general hubbub. Gene looked around to see who else was in the bar. No one from his unit was there. He slipped out of the room and into the street, terrified that he might be followed or that the man might describe him to someone in his unit. He spent the night waiting for a knock on the door. None came. He was still nervous the next morning as he left for work. By the time he returned, the man's unit had pulled out. That evening he asked Sonia if she had heard any reports denouncing him as a Jew; she had not.

Strangely enough, a few days later, a beaming Sergeant Mueller summoned Gene. "Remember when you first arrived the captain asked me to check on your family? Well, I've finally heard back from headquarters. I think you'll agree it was worth waiting, Olesiuk," Mueller said. "They tell me your parents are alive and well in Lemberg."

"That's wonderful, thank you so much," Gene said, trying to sound delighted.

"Wait, there's more. Your younger brother has volunteered for the German army and even now may be fighting for the Fatherland. Come on, that deserves a drink, doesn't it?" Mueller said. So much for German efficiency, Gene thought.

At Christmas, Otto received a four-week furlough. He offered to stop in Lwów and deliver a package to Gene's parents. "You don't have to do that," Gene protested. "You need every minute of free time with your mother and your girlfriend."

"No, it's nothing, Lemberg is right on my way. I'll only lose a day. I'm happy to do it for you. After all, we're friends, aren't we? You'd do the same for me."

"Not if I had a girlfriend as beautiful as you say yours is," said Gene.

"Of course you would. I keep thinking about your parents. It's terrible for them, not hearing from you for so long."

"I write them. I even sent them packages."

"Maybe they didn't get the letters. Anyway, a letter isn't as good as firsthand news. Really Eugen, I insist."

So Gene put together a small package with some cans of cooking oil and a letter. He wrote about how happy he was to be serving with the German army and how delighted he was to hear that his youngest brother had enlisted. He wondered what Otto would find when he arrived in Lwów and what he would say when he returned to the village. It was yet another worry. Ironically, Nowy Sącz was not so far out of Otto's way. He could have easily dropped off the package with Gene's real parents if circumstances had been different. As it was, there was no way to get news either to or from them. Otto left early one morning; Gene never saw him again.

On Christmas Day, there was a special radio broadcast from the far extremities of the Third Reich. It included a broadcast from Stalingrad assuring the German people that all was well on the banks of the Volga. In reality, the German position was about to cave in. Even as they closed the jaw of the trap on Stalingrad, Soviet forces were poised to break through in the Caucasus as well. As 1943 arrived, the mood in the German camp turned sober. There was talk of imminent withdrawal. But the order was not given, even though a steady stream of units started moving through the village to the north. Then, on February 2 the Germans surrendered at Stalingrad. It was stunning news. Somber music droned from the radio for three solid days. The Germans could scarcely believe their defeat. Meanwhile, the Russians in Nezlobnaya celebrated silently, not daring to show their feelings with so much as a smile.

A week later, a special train arrived in Georgievsk. Gene's unit and other detachments worked around the clock loading it with equipment and documents. Sergeant Mueller was in a panic, banging his telephone with his fist in an effort to reach division command, which also was preparing to evacuate. At German headquarters in the flourmill compound, soldiers rushed in all directions getting ready for withdrawal. As he sped across the courtyard to the captain's office, Sergeant Mueller caught sight of Gene. "Hey, Eugen," he yelled, "evacuation is at five sharp tomorrow morning. You're on the list to come with us. Be here with all your things ready to board the train."

Gene was jubilant; he thought this day would never come. It was wonderful to see the Germans running around in a panic. But the danger was not quite over. He had to find Mark. It would be safest to hide until the Germans left. As he made his way toward the street, he saw Captain Peters walking slowly across the compound. He was immaculately dressed, the creases on his uniform as sharp as ever. But the captain looked old and tired; his eyes were bloodshot from lack of sleep and the lines on his face had deepened. As their path crossed, the captain stopped Gene and clasped his hand. "Auf Wiedersehen Eugen," he said. He released Gene's hand, patted him on the shoulder and walked away. He obviously did not expect to see Gene on the evacuation train. How much did the captain suspect? Gene would never know.

That night, February 9, 1943, Gene and Mark put on their warmest clothes, took some blankets, and crept away from the village and out to the steppe. They found a hollow and settled down. No one would come looking for them out there. It felt good. For the first time the Nazis were on the run. Perhaps the war had reached a turning point. "I keep thinking of Adsum," Gene said.

"Who?" asked Mark.

"You remember—Adsum, the Polish priest who was with us in the camps."

"Oh yes, I remember. He was tall and skinny. What about him?" Mark asked.

"He once told me that there was a guardian angel watching over me. Sometimes I think he must have been right."

"One angel couldn't do the job. There must be a whole squad of them up there trying to keep up with you," said Mark.

Apart from sporadic animal noises, the steppe was quiet. Gene could not fall asleep. Not a single day in the last six months had been free of danger, not one moment really, he reflected with a shudder. A jumble of faces and events crowded his mind. Some he had even grown to like in a way, even if they were German. Now, they were all leaving.

The Germans departed before sunrise the next morning. When the brothers returned to the silent village, the swastika no longer hung from the local council building. Efim Vasilevich was gone; so, too, was the police chief. For the rest of the day, truckloads of stragglers rolled down the main street, frantically trying to catch up with the main body of the retreating army. No one seemed to know exactly where the Soviets were, but they were not far away. In the early afternoon, Soviet prisoners of war were marched through under German guard.

They seemed to be mostly Caucasian or central Asians, rather than Russians. As they trudged out of the village, two German trucks, loaded with looted furniture and stolen chickens in cages, drove around the corner in the opposite direction.

"What idiots," cried Mark. "They're heading the wrong way."

The brothers were sitting outside their cottage on a log, just as they had been when the Germans first arrived. Gene glanced in the direction in which the trucks were heading and caught his breath. Two tanks appeared at the top of the slope beyond the flourmill. "They're Soviet," he shouted. "Quick, get back." They retreated behind the fence into their front yard.

The tanks froze as the German trucks, unaware of the danger, continued driving toward them. Then one by one the tanks began rolling down the slope, their gun muzzles dipping into a horizontal firing position. The truck drivers must have seen the tanks in that same instant. Tires squealing, engines gunning, the Germans tried desperately to turn around. There was a numbing blast as a tank shell slammed into the back of the lead truck. It was tossed like a broken toy, wheels spinning in the air, one side completely shorn away. Soldiers' bodies tumbled into the street. One soldier was sliced in half. The lower part of his body came to rest on the road, a lump of raw meat, pouring blood. The other truck managed to get a few yards farther before a second shell smashed into it. The explosion shook the ground. Gene and Mark's ears were ringing as the tanks rumbled through the village, not stopping to inspect what remained of the trucks.

As the tank engines died away, silence hung over the street, broken only by the sound of squawking chickens released from their cages. The two destroyed trucks lay by the side of the road, engines smoking. It seemed there were no survivors. A few minutes later, a swarm of village women rushed out of their cottages and dragged the bodies free of the wreckage. They methodically stripped the clothes from the dead Germans. One old woman squatted over the lower part of the soldier who had been sliced in half, pulling off his leather boots. "Vultures," Mark said, turning away.

"It makes you want to throw up," said Gene. "These can't be the same people we've been living with. Look at them!"

Soon the dead Germans were naked, their carcasses littering the roadside, as the women made their way home with their trophies.

The drama was not yet over. Gene and Mark did not actually witness what happened next. They saw the results. The tanks kept rolling and soon came upon the column of Soviet prisoners who had been marched through the village an hour before. Their German guards, realizing the Red Army was just behind, had abandoned them and fled. The confused prisoners milled around in the middle of the road not knowing what to do. The way the survivors described it, the tanks simply bulldozed their way through the crowd, crushing some men to death. Dazed stragglers limped back to the village, many injured. They made a makeshift camp outside the flourmill and tried to tend their wounds. Many were in shock. The crushed bodies of their dead comrades were left where they lay a couple of miles outside the village.

Gene, Mark, and some other villagers brought the survivors food and water. How could the tank drivers have done such a thing? The prisoners were their countrymen. They were all wearing Red Army uniforms, so there could have been no confusion. But that was not how the Soviets saw it. A cursory glance must have told the tank crews that most of the prisoners were not ethnic Russians; they belonged to nationalities they believed had betrayed them by siding with the enemy. The incident reminded the brothers that although they had survived the Nazis, they still had to deal with communists. They should have celebrated that night of liberation, but their mood was subdued.

Next day, the communists returned to the village to start settling accounts. There were many to settle. The extent of Nazi atrocities emerged as the communists discovered one mass grave after another. The NKVD moved into the former Gestapo building in Georgievsk, and arrests and interrogations of alleged spies and collaborators began. Everyone who had lived under Nazi occupation was suspect. Anyone who assisted the Germans in any way was a traitor. Gene was called to the old Gestapo headquarters one day in March. He approached the building in dread. The memory of his last visit was still fresh. He faced a three-man team, who demanded to know every detail of his work with the Germans. Luckily, the NKVD had also received "positive" testimonials from the resistance describing Gene's contributions. This, and a directive recovered from the files of the departed police chief, ordering close surveillance of "the Polish Ukrainian Y. Olesiuk, a suspected Soviet agent," cleared Gene of suspicion. He was dismissed and sent back to the village.

Adolf Elsner,
date unknown

Bertha Elsner,
1940–41

Nunek Elsner, younger
brother, killed in 1942

RIGHT: Gene, 1938

Nowy Sącz. Mark on the right, Henek on the left, and an unknown person in the center.

Gene as soldier, approximately 1944

2 soldiers, Gene and an unknown person. Date and place unknown

LEFT: Gene,
date and place unknown

RIGHT: Mark, 1937

RIGHT: Mark, 1940

LEFT: In Piening,
Carpathian Mountains,
Poland 1934–1935.
Gene is on the right.

RIGHT: Mark, Lublin, 1944

Mark, 1945

Mark, 1946

Mark, 1947

Group of soldiers, Kostroma, late 1943/early 1944.
Seventh from left, standing, is Gene.

The battery trained and commanded by Gene, Luck, Poland, 1944.
Circled is Gene.

Gene (left), Mark (center), and Henek (right) taken in
Israel in 1990, a year before Henek's death.

CHAPTER 19

The Artillery College

Normal life slowly resumed in the village, but distant political events were again shaping the brothers' fate. In mid-April, the Nazis discovered the mass graves of thousands of Polish officers in a forest near the Russian village of Katyn. The Germans and the Soviets accused each other of the crime. When the Polish government-in-exile asked for an impartial inquiry by the Red Cross, Stalin seized the request as an excuse to break off diplomatic relations with the Poles.* Stalin then formed his own Soviet-based Polish committee, whose obedient communist members would eventually grow into a puppet Polish government that would enable the Kremlin to rule postwar Poland by proxy.

Soon after this, the Soviets announced the creation of a new Polish army; the first division was named after Tadeusz Kościuszko, a hero of the eighteenth century Polish national uprising as well as of the American Revolutionary War. Stalin conceived of the new force as the future instrument of his will in Poland. It would be Polish in form but under the firm control of the Red Army. The authorities began scouring the country for suitable recruits. Thousands of refugees were tracked down in distant places of exile and enlisted. At the end of April, Gene and Mark received conscription papers, informing them that they had "volunteered" to join the new patriotic Polish army and directing them to

---

* In 1990, Soviet authorities finally admitted that the NKVD had carried out the massacre.

travel without delay to a locality near Moscow. Their days in the Cossack village were over.

Gene said a tearful farewell to Galia and her mother. If anything, he felt that the mother was the sorrier to see him go. She clasped his hand tightly, choking back tears. Then she left him alone with Galia. He knew it was unlikely that he would ever return. Gene put his arms around her, not knowing what to say. After all that they had shared he still did not know how Galia really felt about him. Throughout their relationship she had been mystifying and maddening by turns, sometimes passionate and yielding, other times remote and evasive. Now, she flung her arms around him. "Don't forget me, Zjenya," she cried histrionically.

"Of course not. We'll write to each other. How could I forget what we've been through together?"

"Ah, you say that now, but you'll soon find other women while I'll be stuck here in this dead place for ever."

"You won't be here forever. Some day the war will end, and we'll all be able to go back to our homes."

"Oh Zjenya, what will I do without you? Life will be so dreary. It's all very well for you men, going off to war. What about the women who are left behind?"

"I don't know what to tell you, Galia. The war brought us together. Now, the war is parting us. Who knows what our future holds." He kissed her for the last time.

Gene and Mark left Nezlobnaya with mixed feelings. The village had offered them shelter and friendship when they most needed it, but they both felt it was time to go. Ever since the war had started they had been on the run. Now they would get a chance to fight back.

Their journey started badly. As they boarded the train, Gene began to feel sick again. His temperature shot up. It was another malaria attack, and there was no way to get medical treatment or drugs until they arrived at their destination. He sweated and shivered as the train traveled northward through a war-ravaged countryside, littered by burnt-out tanks, artillery and trucks. After many hours, they pulled into a station. The passengers piled out in great excitement. "Where are we?" Mark called out the window. "Stalingrad," several voices replied.

Already the name had an epic ring. There was enough time for a quick tour. Everyone was eager to see the site of the Soviet victory.

"Do you want to come?" Mark asked Gene.

"I suppose I should," he shivered.

"Let's go. We won't ever see anything like it again."

Stalingrad was a vision of hell. The battle had ended only a few weeks before, and the work of clearing away the wreckage had just begun. Unexploded shells and mines littered much of the city, which had been almost entirely flattened. Great tangled piles of twisted steel girders lay where factories had once stood. Two massive chimneys somehow remained upright, towering drunkenly over the desolation. The Volga's banks were strewn with burnt-out hulks of barges and steamers. Smashed tramcars and splintered tree trunks marked the former path of the central avenue. The ground was honeycombed with dugouts, shell holes, and bomb craters. Hundreds of thousands of people had died; the destruction was almost incomprehensible. Mark and Gene were taken to see the underground bunker of the defeated German general, Friedrich von Paulus. Then they returned to the station and resumed their three-day journey north.

The new Polish brigade was located southeast of Moscow on a bank of the Oka River. The contrast with General Anders's Polish army was immediately apparent. The Soviets had deliberately starved the Anders army of food, weapons, and equipment. The new Polish corps enjoyed the best the Soviet Union could offer. Fortunately, Gene quickly recovered from his latest bout of malaria. He and Mark spent their time in the brigade headquarters, undergoing physical training and frequent political indoctrination sessions. The recruits were a mixed bag, dredged up from all corners of the Soviet Union, each with his own story of survival. Many deeply resented the Soviet Union, which had helped destroy their homeland and sent them into exile or labor camps.

The top commander was a Pole, Colonel Zygmunt Berling. But nearly all the other officers were Russians dressed in Polish uniforms. Many had Polish names and could have been of Polish extraction, but that fooled no one since they could not speak the language. Still, the authorities worked to create the impression that it was a truly independent Polish army. Red and white banners emblazoned with the Polish eagle flew over the camp. The facilities were festooned with Polish symbols, inscriptions, and nationalist slogans. The men wore prewar Polish uniforms, their square caps inscribed with the eagle. The old Polish army salute was preserved. There were even a few priests to serve as chaplains, and soldiers were allowed to attend mass. On joining, recruits were required to swear allegiance to the flag of the new democratic Poland and pledge fidelity to their Soviet allies.

After two weeks at headquarters, Gene, Mark, and about 30 others were sent to an artillery school in Kostroma, about 200 miles northeast of Moscow. Discipline was strict. The men lived in barracks and slept on army cots. The food was adequate. All in all, they were treated like human beings. For the first time, the brothers were living without fear and were happy to fall into a blessedly dull routine.

The day began before breakfast with physical drills. Then came several hours of lectures. There were sessions devoted to Marxism, Leninism, and Stalinism, as well as more exacting fare: topography, map reading, target ranging and trajectories, the role of artillery in attack and defense, organization and techniques of movement and fire, and cooperation with infantry. The course was demanding; the Red Army prided itself on its artillery and expected the recruits to apply themselves. The barracks became Gene and Mark's world. Except for field exercises, they were rarely let outside. In their six months in Kostroma, they never managed to see the fourteenth century monastery that is the city's claim to fame.

Gene and Mark took naturally to military life. After some weeks Gene was promoted to sergeant. He was in charge of unit discipline and acted as a liaison between the men and their Soviet officers. Slowly, the cadets were turning into effective artillerymen. The Polish contingent in Kostroma was assigned to operate the 152-mm cannon, one of the heaviest artillery pieces in the Soviet armory.

Mark specialized in reconnaissance. Eventually, he became a platoon commander in charge of four scouts, three field-telephone operators, two radio operators, and two topographers. Firing the massive guns accurately was a mixture of art and science. The reconnaissance platoon was usually deployed four or five miles ahead of the rest, in direct view of the front line. They would establish two observation posts at least a mile apart to take measurements. Triangulation enabled the battery commander get an accurate fix on the target.

The first two shots were used to establish range and direction. A good artillery commander was expected to score a hit by the third or fourth shot.

While Gene and Mark were in Kostroma, the war continued to turn against the Germans. In July 1943 the Soviets won the huge battle of the Kursk salient, smashing an attempted German counteroffensive. From that point on, the Germans were on the retreat. In November, the Russians recaptured Kiev. A few weeks later, Gene and Mark graduated from artillery school. Both were promoted to second lieutenant. Mark was sent to a frontline unit near Smolensk, while Gene was ordered to remain in Kostroma for a six-week course for battery commanders.

It was difficult for the brothers to part after so much time together, but they were at least able to exchange frequent letters. Mark wrote that his unit was being held back from combat for the time being. The first Polish units thrown into battle had been inexperienced and insufficiently trained and had suffered enormous losses. Because the brigade was created at least partly to ensure future communist control of Poland, the Soviets decided to hold it in reserve for a while. So for the first few months of 1944, Mark's unit moved through Belorussia and the Ukraine from village to village, always slightly behind the front, occasionally taking part in barrages to soften up the enemy, but rarely engaged in major battles. By the end of May 1944, the Red Army had advanced close to the old Polish border.

On May 26, two days before Gene's 26th birthday, Mark wrote to him:

> For the past four days I was away from my battery, digging an observation post. I had not heard any news from you for the past six weeks but after my return to the battery I found two postcards and two letters from you. As you see, I am now relatively close to our home. You can already meet lots of Poles and sometimes our pretty girls. Recently we have been quite close to the front line and no doubt we'll soon be involved in the fighting. That doesn't scare me. I miss you very much. I can't get used to the fact that you are not here and I would like very much for us to be together again. I was very intrigued by what you wrote about meeting two acquaintances. It made me think of home and of our brother Nunek. I'm sure you remember his last letter from home in which he wrote that he was working near the town,

doing manual labor. Being here we get a lot more detailed information about German activities. I have strong doubts whether our parents are still alive. Until now, I haven't met anyone from our hometown. I miss our home terribly. I hope it won't be long now until we can return. I have to close now. Your Mark.

By this time, Gene was no longer in Kostroma. At the end of his commanders' course, he was promoted to lieutenant and posted to Ryazan to serve as an instructor in an artillery school for Polish cadets. Ryazan, 115 miles south of Moscow, had once been an important regional center. When Gene arrived, it had the familiar, tired look of Soviet neglect. Dilapidated plaster buildings and decaying residences formerly occupied by the local aristocracy surrounded its cobbled squares.

Gene lodged with a woman whose husband had been away at the front for more than two years. Not long after he arrived, he woke up one night to find his landlady leaning over his bed. She was about ten years older than Gene, an attractive, dark-haired, dark-eyed woman with two young children. "What's the matter?" Gene sputtered. "I thought you might be cold," she whispered, climbing into his bed.

"You're married. What if your children hear? What if your husband finds out?"

"Nobody will hear," she said. "As for my husband, who knows if he's alive or dead? You can't expect me to be a saint forever. I'm a woman."

After that, she began to make increasingly frequent visits to his room. Gene was very uncomfortable, sleeping with another man's wife with his children a few feet away. Fortunately, he found an excuse to keep her at arm's length after he met a sweet young Russian girl called Katia, who worked in the artillery school's office. She was shy and inexperienced, but that attracted him. They started spending evenings together. It was an innocent, mostly platonic relationship but it served its purpose with Gene's landlady. He declared himself in love and said he had to be faithful to his new sweetheart. The landlady mostly left him alone after that.

Gene was in charge of about 40 officer cadets. They trained by day. In the evenings, Polish communist activists sent from Moscow and Russian commissars led political meetings These talks always emphasized past Polish capitalist misdeeds and how the future Polish state would be different. It would be a country where all nationalities would enjoy equal rights and nobody would be exploited, just like the Soviet Union. Gene kept his thoughts to himself.

Gene also tried to keep in contact with Galia, occasionally sending money to her mother. In August 1943, he received a letter from Raisa Pavlova:

> It was very pleasant for me to read your heartfelt, warm letter. I am very sorry for Galia. She is bored here. You know how dull it is here for young people. Knowing her, you know what she's going through. We want very much to leave here. We are thinking of moving to the Ukraine. Galia cannot stay in the village any longer. I don't know what to do. I keep on hoping that perhaps you'll get leave and come to see us one day soon. I kiss you.

Galia also wrote occasionally. Gene kept her letters and a few somehow survived the war. In December 1943 she wrote:

> Each time there's a gap in your letters I promise not to torment myself with memories. But I can't help it. I've had no letter for 14 days. I live for your letters. Life here is so difficult and colorless. The only bright spot in my life are my dreams of you. I hope you will feel what is in my heart. It could be my bad nature but all my thoughts swirl around one question: why is there no letter? But I'm sure one will arrive and all will be bright again. If I could be with you, I would gladly give a year of my life for a few days of happiness.

But Galia's tone had changed by the time of her last letter to Gene, dated July 9, 1944:

> I've been wanting to write to you for a long time but it's painful. You know I am always led by my heart. Therefore I want to tell you the absolute truth. I met again my Alexander and I understood at once that I love him and only him. I am happy with him in a perfect way. You always told me you wished only for my happiness and now I am happy. One cannot turn back the clock. You should understand that without happiness life is not worth living.

Forgive me! I don't think we can continue to be friends. But if you want to write to me, I will always reply. Zjenya, don't think it was easy for me to write this letter. Don't think about me, it's not worth it. Galia.

Soon after his arrival in Ryazan, Gene came down with his worst case of malaria yet. He took to his bed with a very high fever. Staring at a corner of the ceiling, half delirious, he saw that an unfortunate fly had stumbled into a spider's web. It writhed vainly to escape, its movements growing weaker. As the spider crept up on its prey, Gene was filled with terror. Somehow, in his jumbled thoughts, he had become the fly. Do spiders smile? This one did, looming before his eyes with the self-satisfied smirk of the German officer who had slaughtered the women and children in the Caucasus. The Germans had just been toying with him, biding their time while he blundered into their web. Now he was trapped. With a supreme effort, he reached for his revolver next to the bed, pointed it unsteadily, and emptied the entire magazine at the spider.

The shots were deafening in the small room. Plaster fell from the ceiling. People banged on the walls; they thought there must have been a murder. When the door opened, Gene tried to explain that the fly was safe, but no one seemed to understand. His landlady took one look at him and called the doctor. He spent the next few days recovering in the hospital. Curiously, that was Gene's final bout of malaria. He was never bothered by the disease again.

That winter, the artillery school ran short of fuel. Gene was ordered to take a company of soldiers to a village a few miles away to stock up on firewood. They spent about two weeks there, going out to the forest each day to cut down trees. He had plenty of experience chopping down trees but this was nothing like the camps. They only did a few hours of work each day. The village was little more than a row of primitive wooden shacks and there was nothing for the men to do. So Gene designed an exercise program. He had the men up early to wash in the freezing water. Then they all came together and said their Catholic prayers. The villagers observed this in wonder—it had been years since they had seen anyone openly worshipping God. But it was a morale booster for the unit. It made them feel as though they were in a real Polish army. Gene often asked himself what they would have thought had they known their officer was a Jew. But no one ever challenged him.

One evening a soldier made a fire in one of the huts. To get it to burn faster, he poured gasoline on the flames. There was an explosion, and the whole house caught flames. Gene was in the next hut. He quickly raised the alarm and roused the entire unit. They formed a human chain and started passing buckets of water from the village wells, soaking the neighboring huts to stop the fire burning down the entire village. They could not save the hut where the fire had started or the one next to it, but they managed to rescue the rest. Far from being resentful, the villagers were grateful. The men took up a collection for the villagers who had lost their homes. Gene reported the incident to his superiors and asked that the people be compensated. He had no idea if they were.

Gene occasionally received two-and three-day furloughs, which he was allowed to spend in Moscow. A Russian air force girl was detailed to act as his hostess. Once they saw a huge parade of captured Germans. Thousands of prisoners of war stumbled in ragged ranks down the streets, led by 20 generals, their heads bowed, their chests plastered with medals and campaign ribbons. The feeling in the Moscow air that day was that victory, although still distant, was certain. Some in the crowd cursed and spat at the captured troops. Most watched in silence. It was deeply gratifying for the long-suffering Russians to see their enemies humiliated. As usual, the ordinary soldiers suffered most. Many had no boots; they stumbled along, their feet wrapped in rags, with the abject shuffle of prisoners. It took hours for the long procession to wind past. As the parade ended, a row of trucks came by, hosing down the streets to wash away every last trace left by German feet.

In Ryazan, when time allowed, Gene spent his evenings in the mess with his fellow Soviet officers. He found their boisterous company enjoyable. Vodka flowed freely. The artillery officers held frequent competitions to see who could drink the most before passing out. Gene took part just once to show he was one of the boys. There was a wild atmosphere that night. After a few drinks, the officers were ready for anything. Life was cheap in the Soviet Union. The Red Army had suffered unimaginable casualties—of every 100 Soviet soldiers who went to the front, only three reached the end of the war physically unharmed. So why not live on the edge? One drunken officer staggered up to Gene with a revolver and spun the magazine.

"Come on Polish boy, let's see what you're made of," he slurred.

"No, thank you. I don't play this game," Gene said.

"If you want to be one of us, you play," the officer insisted.

"Then I don't want to be one of you."

"Do you hear that comrades?" the Soviet shouted to his friends. "The little Polish gentleman doesn't play our games. What are you anyway, a Yid?" Gene spun around and punched him in the face, knocking him to the ground. He was instantly surrounded by the man's friends, some of whom pulled out their own revolvers. Alerted by the hubbub, a senior officer intervened.

"Gun roulette is forbidden in the Soviet Union, don't you know that? Are you all crazy or what?" he shouted. Somewhat sheepishly they dispersed.

In June 1944, the artillery school was transferred to Łuck, about 80 miles northeast of Lwów within the prewar borders of Poland. It was a typical Polish provincial town dominated by a medieval castle and a Jesuit church. The town turned out to welcome the soldiers. They were the first men in Polish army uniforms the townspeople had seen since 1939. Gene, who had been recommended for promotion to captain, was the senior Polish officer in the school; all his superiors were Soviets. He was immediately besieged by invitations to christenings, weddings, parties, and dances. Everyone in town was fighting over who should have the honor of providing him and his fellow officers with lodgings.

On the first Sunday after arriving in town, Gene marched the entire body of 600 cadets to church. Drummers beat time as they paraded through the streets, each soldier perfectly turned out, head held high. The townspeople had come out in hundreds to cheer. Although Gene was thoroughly enjoying the situation, his expression was appropriately solemn. He would have loved to announce to all that he was a Jew and watch the expressions change on their smug, beaming faces. But he held himself stern and unsmiling as the column reached the gates of the church, where a priest was waiting to welcome him.

Gene was escorted to a place of honor in the front pew. Suddenly, his confidence evaporated. The service was about to begin, and he had no idea when to stand, sit, cross himself, or approach the altar, and how to behave once he reached it. And he realized that 600 men were sitting behind him, waiting for his cue. They would only stand when he stood and sit when he sat. Oh Lord, this was going to be a fiasco. But the occasion was too dignified to spoil with a scandal. The priest quickly realized that Gene needed help and dispatched an acolyte to sit beside him and show him what to do. "Forgive me, Father," Gene whispered to the priest at the end of the service. "I've been in the Soviet Union for five years with no way to attend a service." "No matter, my son," said the priest, "God has brought you back to us. Now we will bring God back to you."

By this time, Gene was impatient to get into combat. The war was approaching its climax, and he had yet to fire a shot at the Germans. More important, he wanted to be reunited with Mark. He applied for a transfer to a frontline unit and was ordered to take command of an artillery battery, train them in the use of heavy guns, and lead them into action. In November 1944, the unit finally received orders to link up with the First Polish Army, in which Mark was serving. After nearly a year of separation, the brothers would be together again.

CHAPTER 20

The Front

In late July 1944, Mark's unit approached Warsaw, the Polish capital. Inside the city, thousands of resistance fighters were preparing an uprising. With the Red Army nearby, the Poles launched their revolt on August 1. They had some initial success, but were unable to sustain their advantage. The Germans counterattacked five days later, under orders from a furious Hitler to destroy the city. The Red Army, now encamped on the east bank of the river Vistula, watched the struggle from its positions on the outskirts of the city for most of August but did not intervene. Stalin calculated that the Nazis would do his work for him by eliminating the anti-communist Polish Home Army, which had started the uprising, leaving him free to dominate Poland after the war. Stalin not only refused to help the Poles; he also turned down requests from the British and Americans to use Soviet-controlled airstrips so that their planes could drop supplies to the rebels.

By mid-September, much of Warsaw had been systematically flattened, but Stalin's policy remained unchanged. For the Polish soldiers attached to Soviet forces, it was an agonizing time. They were lodged outside the city, listening to the incessant gunfire, watching the German air force pound their capital. They knew the rebels were being ground to dust. Finally the commander of the Polish brigade, without waiting for Soviet consent, ordered some of his units to cross the Vistula River and link up with the rebels. Mark's commanding officer, Captain Wolski, was one of the first across. Within hours, they lost radio contact with him. He was replaced by one of Mark's best friends in the battery, Captain Raban. Then Mark himself was ordered to take a small unit across the river.

It was a dark moonless night. Laden with gear, Mark's men crept down the riverbank to board small boats in which they were supposed to slip across the Vistula. Mark tried to control his fear. As far as he could tell, they were embarking on a suicide mission. His orders were to establish a position on the other side of the river and direct artillery fire against the Germans. But without Soviet backing and air support, the operation seemed no more than a brave but futile gesture. How long would it be until the Germans pinned them down and wiped them out?

From Mark's position in the boat, the Vistula looked immense. The soldiers sat waiting for the order to push off but it never came. Then an officer from headquarters materialized by the boat. "Everybody out," he hissed. "New orders. The operation is canceled. There will be no crossing."

They later learned that the Polish commander, General Berling, had been relieved of his post and summoned to Moscow to face charges of insubordination. There was widespread anger in the Polish brigade, but Mark felt he had been reprieved. Without Soviet help, the uprising collapsed, and the Polish resistance fighters who were still alive surrendered. From Stalin's viewpoint, this was a major strategic success. The military strength of the Polish national movement had been destroyed, eliminating a powerful stumbling block to future communist rule in Poland.

For the next three months, the front stabilized and Mark's unit stayed where it was, peering across the river toward the city, wondering what its ruined streets concealed. During this period Mark made a powerful enemy—Major Sokolowsky, the Russian commander of the battalion.

Mark was stationed on the top floor of a three-story building manned by a handful of scouts and telephonists under his command. Captain Raban, the battery commander, was deployed in a similar post a mile away. One day Mark received a call from Raban to say that Sokolowsky was on his way to inspect the post. Sokolowsky was middle aged, with dull, bloodshot eyes and the red nose of a drinker. He had clearly been drinking that day. The cross belt of his uniform hung limply by his side, and some of the buttons on his tunic were undone.

"Where are the targets?" he barked belligerently in Russian as soon as he entered. Mark pointed them out on the map.

Immediately Sokolowsky was on edge. "Amateurs, amateurs," he fumed. "What's this one?" Mark tried to explain, looking at Raban for help. He realized none would be forthcoming; Sokolowsky intimidated everyone. "What's this here?" Sokolowsky asked again. Mark tried to explain. The Russian exploded. "This is all wrong. These targets are completely different from Raban's. What the hell do you think you're doing?"

"Excuse me, major. I think you'll find everything as it should be," said Mark.

"Don't contradict me, you caricature of an artilleryman. What the hell kind of army do you think you're in anyway?"

Mark could not understand why he was being humiliated in front of his subordinates. His back stiffened. Speaking quietly he said, "Major, I'm in the Polish army. I'm doing my duty and I don't deserve such abuse." Sokolowsky glared at him, his mouth snapping shut. Perhaps he realized that he had gone too far. He quickly ended the inspection and left the observation post, but from that day forward he seemed to have it in for Mark.

The Soviets finally launched their major offensive in January 1945. It began with a pulverizing artillery barrage from the south of the city. By the time the tanks went in, there was little resistance. Mark's unit entered the city a few days behind the tanks, driving their trucks across the frozen river. The once-proud Polish capital was in ruins. A few people emerged from cellars, but most of the population had long since fled, or been deported or killed. Warsaw was devastated. Few buildings were intact; nearly all were damaged. For his part in liberating the city, Mark received a certificate signed by Stalin.

Back in Łuck, Gene's battery had been reorganized and received the order to advance in late November. Their first stop was Lublin, where they were supposed to pick up equipment. Lublin was crowded with refugees, soldiers, and Communist party activists who were organizing the city's future Polish government. It was in Lublin that Gene began to realize the extent of Germany's crimes against the Jews. The extermination camp of Majdanek had been established only a few miles from the center of town. There, the Nazis had murdered more than 200,000 people, including more than 100,000 Jews. Gene heard that whenever the wind had blown from the east, the entire town had inhaled the stench of burning human flesh and that smoke from the crematoria had turned the sky brown. He feared for the fate of his family as never before.

On his second day in Lublin, Gene was driving down a crowded street with two of his soldiers when someone shouted "Elsner, Elsner." Gene jumped. No one had called him by his proper name in more than two years. He looked around and saw the smiling face of Bugosław Migacz, one of his best friends from high school in Nowy Sącz. Gene turned away and drove on. He was Olesiuk now, and this was no time to blow his cover. But he was sorry for the lost opportunity. He was desperate for news from home.

Two days later, Gene was walking down the street when someone grabbed him by the arm. It was Migacz. "Don't you know your friends any more?" he shouted.

"Migacz, I'm so happy to see you," Gene said.

"Are you? You didn't give me that feeling the other day."

"It's because you were calling me by a wrong name. I'm not Elsner anymore, not for the time being anyway, and I don't want anyone to know that name."

"Well who the hell are you?" Migacz asked.

"Olesiuk," said Gene, grinning. "Eugene Olesiuk. Sounds good, doesn't it?"

"You sound like some kind of Ukrainian."

"I am, 100 percent."

"At least you're alive. So many of our classmates are dead. How did you survive?" Migacz asked.

Gene gave an abbreviated account of his adventures. Migacz had not had it easy either. He was in the first group of prisoners sent to Auschwitz in June 1940. He showed Gene his tattooed number. It was the first time Gene had heard about the camp or seen a prisoner's tattoo. Of course, when Migacz had been there, Auschwitz was just another concentration camp where people suffered maltreatment and starvation. They did not start exterminating Jews there until almost two years later, by which time Migacz, a non-Jew, had been released. Gene asked his friend about news from Nowy Sącz, which was still under Nazi occupation. But Migacz did not know much. "All the Jews were deported, and nobody knows what happened to them," he said.

"All the Jews were deported, young and old?"

"That's right. They were loaded on trains and taken away."

"When did this happen?"

"It must have been over two years ago, in the summer of '42."

"And since then, not a letter, a postcard or a whisper from anyone?"

"No, not to my knowledge. No one knows what happened to them."

"Where were they taken?"

"I don't know. Somewhere in the east, so the rumors said."

"Were my parents with them?"

"I don't know for sure, but I'm afraid they must have been. All the Jews except a handful of young strong ones were taken. I don't know if your parents could have survived. You must've heard what the Germans were doing to the Jews here at Majdanek."

"I've heard about it."

"Majdanek wasn't the only such place. There were others and still are, all over Poland."

"What about my brother Nunek? He was young and strong. Maybe they didn't take him," Gene said, begging for a crumb of comfort.

"I don't know. I just don't know. I'm really sorry," said Migacz.

After eleven days in Lublin, Gene's battery set out for the front. They crossed the Vistula and joined the fighting south of Warsaw. Shortly after, they received their first test of fire, when the battery took part in an artillery barrage to soften up the German positions. They were trying to catch up with the rest of the army, including Mark's unit, but it was not easy. The front seemed to be moving faster than they were. The Germans were now in headlong retreat toward their own border.

The battery mainly traveled on secondary roads through small towns and villages. Progress was painful; they were in the middle of a mass of traffic streaming westward toward the German border. Thousands of German settlers, brought in by the occupiers to colonize parts of Poland, were also frantically trying to outrun the advancing Red Army, fleeing westward on snowbound roads. They had good reason to be terrified. The Soviets were intent on exacting revenge for all their country had suffered. Whenever they entered a German settlement, the Soviet soldiers went wild, raping, looting, and killing. The officers turned a blind eye and often encouraged their soldiers' excesses.

Often, Gene's battery became separated from their field kitchens. When that happened, Gene had to scrounge food and shelter for his men. Sometimes he left the main road to find farms where they could stay the night. Many were deserted, with unmilked cows mooing in distress and unfed animals wandering listlessly. One evening they reached a village whose Polish inhabitants had been entirely displaced by German settlers. When the terrified residents realized that Gene's men were Poles and not Soviets, they begged them to stay. Only old people were left in the village. The men had presumably been taken for military service, and the younger women had fled or were in hiding. Even so, an old man came forward to complain that his wife of over seventy had been raped by a detachment of Soviet troops who had passed through the previous day.

Gene gathered his men. "There's to be no drinking, no looting, and no raping tonight," he said. He instructed his officers to keep an eye on the men and ensure that his orders were followed. Gene himself stayed at a farm that night. By morning, his German hosts had regained their self-assurance. One woman even came to Gene to complain that someone had stolen her wash from the clothesline. Gene almost exploded in anger. "Do you know what you and your German countrymen have done to my country and half of Europe? And now you have the nerve to complain that somebody took some of your laundry. Just get out of my sight."

At this point, Mark's unit was only a short distance ahead of Gene's, trailing just behind the vanguard of the Soviet forces. The advance was moving so fast that Mark's men hardly had time to get their artillery into firing position before they were ordered to move forward again. The only resistance came from isolated German strongpoints. When they reached the town of Bydgoszcz, some in Mark's battery went on evening forays, breaking into abandoned apartments to see if there was anything worth having. Mark was not interested in loot, but he was looking for a violin. Somewhere along the way he had found a battered old instrument, but it was in such bad shape that he found it almost impossible to play. One night, a soldier told Mark that he had seen a violin in a German woman's apartment. Mark went there. A woman in her forties opened the door. Mark wasted little time on niceties. He asked in German if she had a violin. She nodded and went to get it. He lifted it out of its case and drew the bow across the strings. The sound was sweet and mellow. Mark wanted the violin, but he did not want to simply take it, although the Germans had stolen and destroyed virtually everything in his life that he held dear. He decided on a swap, reasoning that an exchange was not robbery. He took the violin and returned next day with his own battered instrument. From then on, Mark played wherever he could—in dugouts, in observation posts, even in the truck moving toward the ever-shifting front.

Gene's battery reached Bydgoszcz only a day after Mark had left. Soviet and Polish infantrymen were still clearing the town of German snipers. Gene's orders were to find accommodation for his men and contact the divisional commander. He quickly located a four-floor building suitable for the entire battery and sent in an armed detachment to ensure it was deserted. On the top floor they came upon a locked room. They were just about to shoot their way in when they heard a babble of voices appealing to them in an unfamiliar language. Then someone starting singing "O sole mio" at the top of his voice. "They're Italians," said one of Gene's men. "Spaghetti, macaroni?" he shouted. "Si, si, macaroni," came the excited response. There were six of them in the room, Hitler's reluctant former allies trying to make their way home. Gene made sure that they were unarmed and then left them alone.

Mark's main worry at this point was his divisional commander, Sokolowsky. Ever since the observation post incident, the man seemed obsessed with getting even. He kept arriving for unannounced inspections of Mark's platoon, obviously hoping to find something wrong. He never found anything, which made him even angrier. Then, one evening, Sokolowsky ordered Mark to take several men and link up with an infantry unit that was preparing to attack a village still in German hands. Ostensibly, Mark was to act as a liaison between the infantry and the artillery. Everybody knew the order was absurd, since artillery had no role in the attack. It was Sokolwsky's way of taking revenge.

The operation began at about ten o'clock that evening. The moon was out, and visibility was good. The men crept across a field toward the village, their bodies black against the snow. Mark was edgy. He was practically unarmed. As an artillery officer, the only weapon he carried was a revolver. "Spread out more," he whispered to the men beside him. He crossed a shallow ditch and stopped to take stock. He moved forward another 20 yards and stopped again. It was too quiet, some sixth sense told him. Two bewildered infantrymen were standing beside him. "Drop down," he ordered them sharply.

The instant they did so, an explosion of sound shattered the night. Bullets whined just over Mark's head. He flattened himself against the snow, cursing Sokolowsky. The Germans had obviously been waiting for them. For the next half hour he was pinned down. The Germans were so close that he could hear the clunks of metal as they changed magazines, but apparently they could not see him. There was no question of returning fire and drawing their attention. He lay as still as possible. Then he heard rumbling engines coming from the village. "God, they're going to send in tanks against us," he thought. Am I going to die for Sokolowsky in this God-forsaken field?"

Should he try to retreat, or stay where he was? He listened for more engine sounds, but it was difficult to hear anything above the sporadic gunfire. Still lying on the ground, he shifted in the direction of the soldier next to him. "Do you have a spade?" he hissed. The soldier nodded. It was standard infantry equipment. "We're going to dig a foxhole," Mark said.

They did not even dare sit up; bullets were whining overhead. But they managed to dig a shallow trench that offered a modicum of cover. Mark had lost track of how long they had been pinned down. After a while, perhaps an hour, perhaps more, the firing slackened. "We've got to try and get back," Mark told the other soldier.

He crawled out of the hole and began slithering back across the field, not waiting to see if the soldier was following him. Less than four yards from the trench he blundered into the body of a soldier. He felt for a pulse, but the man was dead. Making his way around the corpse, Mark kept going on all fours until he reached the ditch, passing several bodies along the way. He felt a bit safer. He began crawling through the ditch, hoping to put more distance between himself and the Germans. Half an hour later, soaked and exhausted, he reached the edge of the field.

There he blundered into a large infantry detachment, apparently forming for a frontal assault on the village. "Here, you," the commanding officer called. "Come over here."

"I'm an artillery officer. I shouldn't be here," Mark protested.

"I need every officer I can get. We're going to attack," the commander said. Mark had little choice but to obey the orders of a higher-ranking officer. A few seconds later, the charge began. The Germans opened up with machine-gun fire, and men began to fall. After 100 yards, Mark decided that enough was enough. He pitched forward. The charging troops disappeared into the darkness, and Mark was alone once more.

For a second time, with renewed determination, he began to crawl back out of the field. He had no intention of getting killed simply to gratify Sokolowsky. That was not what his war was about. It was four o'clock in the morning by the time he made his way back to his own unit. Everyone was awake, worrying about him. "Why didn't you obey the order?" someone asked.

"What order?" Mark shivered.

"Captain Raban realized right away that none of you had any business being out there and ordered all our men to withdraw."

"I never got the order. I lost contact with the others pretty early on," Mark said.

"Raban sent his orderly out to look for you. Did you see him?" Raban's orderly was an 18-year-old kid named Pachocki, blonde, handsome, and very popular with the entire unit. "No, I didn't see him," Mark said, "but it's total chaos out there. Our guys are charging around on foot." They found Pachocki the next day, lying in the field with a bullet in his head.

Gene finally joined up with Mark's unit about 30 miles short of the German border. They had a lot to catch up on. Foremost on their minds was the fate of their family, although they had independently concluded that there was little hope that their parents were alive. Nevertheless, they prayed for a miracle, and there was still a chance that Nunek had survived. He had been so young and healthy.

Soon after their units joined up, Gene's and Mark's batteries were ordered to establish a stationary position. There were a few days to drink and relax and time for Mark to play his violin. But it was a brief respite. A few days later, the order came to advance. They crossed the old German border and moved into the wooded country of Pomerania. Gene felt good. He was finally at the front and on German territory. If his luck held, he felt certain he would soon be able to witness the end of the Third Reich and take a small part in the fall of the monster who created it.

CHAPTER 21

Presumed Dead

It was February 7, 1945. Mark was to remember every detail: the dank weather, the shallow snow, the route he took and most of all the moment when he realized that Gene was probably dead. Yet the day began in an ordinary way.

Gene, we recall, left division headquarters early that morning with a truck full of soldiers to set up an observation point a few miles away. Mark was to follow on foot with a small detachment, laying down telephone lines to link the outpost to gun positions. The brothers never saw each other that day. Gene had already left by the time Mark gathered his group of four soldiers and set out on foot along the lane.

They found the first coil of telephone wire left by Gene on the roadside and began unrolling it, hanging the cable from tree branches. It was tedious work and Mark prodded his men to hurry. He was anxious to reach the observation posts before the light faded. After about an hour, they arrived at a crossroads and looked for the next coil of wire. They could not find it. "It should be somewhere over that way," Mark told his soldiers, pointing to the west. After a minute, one of the men shouted from across the road that he had found it.

Mark consulted the map. "He's gone the wrong way. Must've been for a reason," he thought. There were only a few sets of tracks on the road, so it was easy to follow Gene's route. After another mile, the tracks turned down a narrow road. Mark and his men followed across a bridge over a small stream. Half an hour later, they met the main road again, and Mark allowed himself to relax.

As morning turned to afternoon, a soft, wet snow began falling. Flakes clung to their faces like wet leaves and their progress slowed. They trudged on with heavy feet, patiently stringing the wires together. Eventually they reached a crossroads where an old German hunting lodge stood. The place was deserted, but a roll of cable waited on the ground. Mark looked at the map. "Nearly there boys," he shouted. "Turn right here." The soldiers began to work faster, eager to get out of the cold. Soon they reached the observation post, where soldiers were installing equipment and warming their hands over a fire. "Where's the battery boss?" Mark asked another officer.

"We haven't seen him. We're setting up the post without him," the man replied. Mark felt a first prick of anxiety. "What about the others who were with him?" he asked.

"We haven't seen any of them. We thought he'd gotten lost along the way and that maybe you'd seen him."

"No I haven't. They should have been here more than two hours ago," said Mark, now thoroughly alarmed.

Seeing a bicycle leaning against a wall, he grabbed it and rode back to the crossroads, slipping on the ice in his haste. He knew that Gene had reached the hunting lodge because he had left cable there. If Gene had taken a wrong turn, it had to have been there. "He must have gone on straight instead of turning right," Mark thought. "Why the hell did he do that?" At the crossroads, his fears were confirmed. A single set of tire marks led off down the lane in the wrong direction. Mark did not have his map with him, but he knew the tracks were heading directly toward the German lines.

He did not know how far he could go without running into the enemy. But he had to see what had happened to Gene. He dismounted and began to follow the tire tracks. After a while, the snow became thin and slushy. The road was deserted and silent, and it was getting dark. Every step he took in the snow seemed to reverberate. Mark told himself he would go another hundred paces and counted them off one by one. He stopped and listened. Nothing. Where were the Germans? Where was Gene?

He decided to go another 100 paces. One by one he paced them out, forcing himself to take long strides. Mark tried to remember where the German position was on the reconnaissance map. But that was 24 hours old, and things might have changed. He stopped to listen again but heard nothing, only the noises of the forest. He kept on walking, no longer counting his steps, but soon his legs refused to obey him. "This is nonsense. I'll get back to the post and find him there. And he'll call me a fool for blundering around in the dark in no-man's land," Mark thought. But back at the command post, there was still no sign of Gene or his men.

The next two days passed with no news. Mark's misery grew, but he refused to give up hope. His brother might have been wounded or taken prisoner. He might still be alive. On February 9, the Germans withdrew a few miles, and Mark decided to set out again on the bicycle. He soon reached the crossroads and turned right. This time, he had come equipped with a map. A mile beyond the hunting lodge, near the small village of Neuholz, he turned a corner and found a gray-green truck abandoned by the roadside. It was American, a Studebaker supplied to Soviet forces under the U.S. Lend-Lease Act. There was no doubt that it was Gene's. The doors on both sides were riddled with bullet holes, the windshield was shattered and the tires shredded.

Suddenly, it was very important not to break down. Obviously Gene's truck had been shot up. But that did not mean he was dead. He might only have been wounded. There were no bodies, no real evidence apart from the bullet holes and dried blood all over the seats. Mark climbed into the truck and sat in the passenger's seat to the right of the driver, where he knew that Gene, as the senior officer, would have been sitting. The truck doors were made of a double layer of steel, and he could see the entry and exit holes made by each bullet. The Germans must have been waiting in the ditches by the side of the road or hiding in the woods. They had opened fire at a range of five paces. It had been a massacre.

Mark's thoughts were jumbled. He wondered vaguely where his violin had gone. There was no sign of it or any of the men's belongings that would have been in the back of the truck. Then, looking at the bullet holes, he had an idea. With the double layers of steel, he might be able to measure the angle at which the bullets had hit the truck. Most of the bullets could have come in too high or too low to do real damage. Perhaps Gene had realized that he was trapped and had surrendered.

Mark stepped down and picked up a stick lying on the ground. Climbing back, he sat down again in Gene's seat, and carefully threaded the stick through two holes made by a single bullet. As the stick slipped into place, Mark saw that the bullet had taken a slight upward trajectory. The stick pointed directly at his chest. Another four or five bullet holes led in the same direction. Mark sighed. "Damn it, Gene," he muttered. "How could this have happened now, after all we've gone through?"

There was no more to be done. If he stayed longer, they would miss him at battery headquarters. He should go. But Mark was unable to tear himself away. As long as he stayed there, he and Gene were still connected. Leaving would be like letting go, severing the last link. He sat, thinking of nothing in particular, watching his breath dissolve in the air. Then, stiff with cold, Mark climbed out and walked slowly back to headquarters. His head told him his brother was dead. But his heart refused to accept the fact. "He's still alive, somewhere," he told himself. "He's lying wounded somewhere, hanging on."

Two days the Polish army newspaper *Życie Żołnierza* (The Soldier's Life) published a brief but lurid account of the ambush. Mark cut out the article and saved it with the few remnants he still had from home—a couple of photographs of his parents, some letters from Gene, two letters from Nunek. Where were they all now, the people he loved most in the world? Gone. He was the only one left. Sixty years later, the small newspaper clipping was yellow with age, the letters smudged, the paper creased, but it remained legible:

MURDERERS

A group of officers and men in one of our artillery units died in action. Their terribly mutilated bodies are one more proof of the bestial behavior of German soldiery. The body of Second Lieutenant Gardziel was found with all its limbs broken. The German bandits had cut out the man's heart and 16 slashes were found on his body. Also, the body of Lieutenant Olesiuk was terribly mutilated. The bodies of Sergeant Wandysz, Corporal Sadego, and bombardier Urban were found in a similar state. Our heroic comrades defended themselves to the last, as is proven by the spent cartridges and signs of hand-to-hand combat. They were subdued after falling into an ambush. The Hitlerite murderers did not spare the wounded and even mutilated the bodies of the dead, adding to the sum of our suffering. We will avenge the blood of our comrades!

For the rest of the day Mark was in a daze. That night, Captain Raban took him aside. "I'm really sorry about your brother, Olesiuk. He was a fine officer. Poland can ill afford to lose men like him," he said. Raban was a good friend but his words were of little comfort. He patted Mark on the back. "All that stuff about the bodies being mutilated—don't believe it. It's just army propaganda," he said. "It must have been over in a minute. He probably didn't feel a thing."

Gene's battery was in shock. The unit had lost more than one-third of its strength and was now operationally ineffective. In Mark's battery, soldiers gathered in a circle to mourn the men they knew. A vodka bottle began to make the rounds. They told stories about their fallen comrades. Many were about Gene, who had known some of the men as far back as the artillery college in Ryazan. The mood turned maudlin. "I'll tell you one thing about Olesiuk," one man slurred after a swig of vodka. "He could be a mean bastard when it came to discipline and equipment. But he knew what he was about and he was straight." Mark got up quietly and left the circle. He was in no mood for drunken eulogies.

The next day he decided to sketch a map of the ambush site. He wanted to keep a precise record, although he was not sure why. There was no one to tell about Gene's death, no next-of-kin to inform. Still, Mark worked carefully on his map, making sure all the distances were correct. He marked the site of the ambush with a single word: *Gene.*

A few days later, the unit moved on. Frequently, when some small incident happened during the day, Mark caught himself thinking that he would tell Gene about it later. Then he would remember.

Mark's unit was approaching the Oder River and he began to worry that Sokolowsky had some new plan in store for him. Mark felt sure the major would find a way to send him in the first wave across the river, hoping that he would be killed. They encamped near the Oder for two weeks as the Red Army gathered its strength. Mark was determined to survive. At least one member of the family had to make it through the war. He would not die just to satisfy Sokolowsky.

Then, a few days before the offensive, Mark was summoned to divisional headquarters and informed that he was being sent back to Moscow for advanced training in a military academy. He had been selected as suitable staff officer material for the Polish army of the future. The move meant Mark was out of Sokolowsky's clutches; it meant he would live.

He reached Moscow in late April, three weeks before the German surrender. Ever since the ambush he had been unable to grieve. In March he had written to the authorities in Nowy Sącz, which by then had been liberated, asking for information about his family. He received a terse note saying that they were not registered in the town and that their whereabouts were unknown. Both of his parents and both of his brothers had disappeared without a trace.

One night Mark was invited to a victory party. The mood was jubilant and the tables were heavy with food and liquor. Men and women were dancing, kissing, smashing glasses, hailing victory and toasting the future. The air was thick with cigarette smoke. Mark buried himself in a corner of the room with a bottle and downed vodka shots. Suddenly he was crying. No one paid attention. Great sobs forced themselves out of his body for an hour or more. Mark had survived. But he was alone. He had nobody with whom to share the past or face the future.

CHAPTER 22

Beyond Pain

It was night when Gene regained consciousness. At first, he could not think clearly. His body was awash with pain. Looking up, he saw a black sky and recognized Polaris, the North Star. He could not move his limbs but he realized he must be alive. He flicked his eyes from side to side, trying to see where he was. Wounded men were all around him, moaning and crying. The pain was like a blinding light inside him, radiating out of each nerve ending. He could hear himself gasping and moaning; then he heard German voices and knew this really was the end.

Hands lifted him onto a table and began stripping off his blood-soaked uniform. He was a rag doll in their hands, but his mind was still working, taking in the German, and translating it. "This one's a real mess," he heard one medic say. "The poor bastard must have stopped a whole magazine."

"Will you look at that?" another voice said. "He's circumcised. Looks like we found ourselves a Jew. What do we do with him now? Dump him?"

"I don't know, ask the doctor, that'll be the best."

"Doctor, doctor, come and have a look at this." Gene felt a new face peering down on him. "See that? He's a Jew."

"So I see." The doctor's voice was weary and indistinct. Gene was still following the conversation but now it seemed to come to him from a distance, barely penetrating his consciousness.

"What do we do with him?" the medic asked again.

"What uniform was he wearing when he came in? Soviet?" the doctor asked.

"No. He's Polish, and an officer as well." Another pause.

"Ah, to hell with it. We'll treat him. He'll probably die anyway," said the doctor.

Not that they could do much. They tried to clean him up a bit, then dumped him back on the ground, naked. The next thing he remembered was being loaded onto a train with other half-alive carcasses. They must have wrapped him in something because he was unaware of the winter cold. But every jolt of the train was agony. His entire body, his brain exploded with it. He drifted in and out of consciousness. When he finally came to, he was in a hospital ward. A nurse gave him a shot of morphine, and he sank into blessed oblivion.

Next morning a doctor came to look at him. Gene flinched as the man examined his wounds. His body was a bloody mess of mangled flesh and bone splinters. "Do you understand German? Can you hear me?" the doctor asked. Gene nodded. "You're in a German military hospital in Stettin, and you are very seriously wounded. As far as I can make out, you've got at least five bullets in you, which need removing, maybe more. The bullet in your neck is very near your spinal cord and is the most dangerous. You have wounds in your shoulder and right arm and left leg. Do you understand?" Gene nodded again.

"We have very limited capacity to treat you and we are short of pain-relieving drugs. Your leg doesn't look too terrible, although it'll need to be operated on, if you live long enough. But your arm is a disaster and will have to come off if you're to have any chance of pulling through. We'll operate tomorrow."

Gene tried to shake his head. He would not allow it. He did not want the Germans chopping his limbs off. He did not want them touching his body at all. With supreme effort, he opened his mouth. "No, no, leave my arm alone," he croaked.

"What did he say?" the doctor asked the nurse.

"Leave my arm alone. I refuse your operation," Gene gasped.

"Did you hear that? He refuses! Young man, I must warn you that you'll die from gangrene poisoning if you don't cooperate. It will be prolonged and painful. Do you want to die?" the doctor shouted. Gene closed his eyes to signal the end of the conversation. Perhaps he was not thinking clearly, but he knew that he did not want to go on a German operating table. He might well not survive another close examination. And he wanted to live as a whole man or not at all. After that, he would not allow the nurse to give him morphine, in case they operated on him against his will.

That night, Gene was taken out of the main ward into a dark little room. Later, they brought in another patient, a Soviet pilot with his stomach ripped apart and his guts hanging out. The man was calling for his mother. He looked around, his eyes wild and despairing. "Is there anyone here?" he cried.

"Over here," Gene gasped back. He could not tell whether the man heard him. "Mother, Mother, where are you?" the pilot kept moaning. Then he seemed to gather himself. "Tell her I died here," he whispered. "Let her know what became of me."

"What's your name?" Gene said, his own suffering put aside for a second.

"Sergei. Oh Mother, Mother, where are you?"

"Sergei who?" But the man was beyond comfort, slipping into his own private hell. "Help, help me," he howled over and over.

Toward morning, his cries became fainter. Finally he was quiet, his suffering behind him, leaving Gene drifting on his own private ocean of pain. In the morning they removed the pilot's body, and the nurse changed Gene's dressings. They had only paper bandages, which they tore from a roll. There was no more talk about amputating Gene's arm so he agreed to have a morphine injection and gained a few hours' reprieve.

That afternoon they brought in another badly wounded soldier. Gene realized that he was in a room for dying men and that they did not expect him to survive. He no longer cared. Death would be a merciful relief. As night fell, there was an Allied air raid over the city. While the sirens wailed, the patients in the main ward were hastily evacuated to a shelter in the basement. A nurse put her head into the doorway and asked Gene if he wanted to be taken down. He shook his head. She looked at him for a moment, then hurried away.

Bombs began falling, some nearby. One landed so close that the explosion shook the building. Gene closed his eyes and prayed for the next bomb to hit the hospital and put him out of his misery. There was a red glow outside the window. The city was burning; he was surrounded by death. But inexplicably, against all reason, he still lived. Gene barely noticed when the man in the next bed died. They took the body away after the all clear sounded. The next day they wheeled in another dying man to keep him company. The day after that, the doctor looked in. "Still alive, are we?" he said cheerily.

Another day, another night, another air raid; still he clung to life. Next morning a treat. The nurse washed him and changed his dressings. She was gentle and kind and tried to make him comfortable. He was developing bedsores and his wounds were infected and festering. He had not shaved in a week and the doctor took to calling him "Gypsy" because of his beard. But the pain never diminished and the morphine that in the beginning gave him five or six hours of sleep now wore off after two or three hours. They would give him only one injection a day, at six o'clock in the evening. He spent the entire day counting the minutes. Whenever the nurse passed the room, he begged for another shot. She was dressed in white like an angel. But rules were rules. "I'm sorry, I can't. It's no good for you anyway," she said.

"What harm could it do? I'm dying anyway," Gene whispered. She smiled as if he had made a joke and went on with her rounds.

Next morning the doctor returned with a group of dignitaries in white coats. Gene heard his voice in the corridor. "Let's stop here. Got an unusual case for you to see, a patient who refuses to die, although the gangrene should have killed him by now." The door opened and they all crowded around the bed. The doctor glanced at Gene's chart and inquired, "Well my Gypsy, still alive, are we?" Gene reached deep within him to where a small flame of defiance still burned. "I'll see you all hang before I die," he growled. The doctor looked at him for a second, then turned on his heel.

Perhaps that was the moment Gene made up his mind to live. He had endured so much that it would be a pity to let it go to waste. They had wheeled four dying men into his room, and he had outlasted them all. Another night passed, and next morning there was another body to be wheeled away. Some men died quietly, without ever regaining consciousness. Some struggled all night long before yielding. They always seemed to die just before dawn. But twelve dawns had come since the ambush and he was still here.

"Well, you've proved me wrong," said the doctor one morning. "By all rights the gangrene should have finished you off by now, but it didn't."

"I'm going to live, damn it," Gene muttered.

"I believe you might," said the doctor. "In any case we can't keep you here.

You're going to be moved to a place where you might get better treatment. You've earned your passage."

Later that day they wheeled him out of the hospital with a few other wounded men and loaded him on the back of a truck, on top of a layer of dead bodies. He still could not move and as the truck swung around a corner, the leg of a corpse fell against his own wounded leg. He shrieked in agony but could not shift it. The pain must have been too much to bear because he passed out. When he regained consciousness, he was lying on a stretcher with a railroad station crowd bustling around him. Eventually, they loaded him on a train. Nobody told him where he was going.

CHAPTER 23

When the Guns Fell Silent

In mid-June 1945, Mark received a letter from a member of his battery whom he had last seen at the front two months before:

> This is important news and I'm rushing to convey it to you at once. Your brother is alive! A few hours ago, Wandysz returned to our unit from a prisoner-of-war camp near Hamburg. Others who survived with him were Dubasiewicz, Jewosnik, and Wagnerski. All the others apparently perished. Your brother is still in an English hospital, address unknown. In detail, what happened that day was this: as they entered the forest, they were fired on from all sides. The first to be hit were your brother and the driver, Cukier, who was killed outright. Lieutenant Ostrycki gave the order to defend themselves and the boys opened fire. Then Ostrycki was hit in the head. His last words were "Boys, keep shooting, don't give in." When the shooting stopped (when our boys ran out of ammunition), the Germans collected six wounded. All the others were dead. They transported the wounded to the town of Deutsche Krone and from there to a camp in Hamburg, except your brother, who was taken to a hospital. They were all liberated by the British army. All this was told to us by Wandysz. The whole gang sends you greetings. Best wishes and write often, Henty.

Mark was still at the military academy in Moscow at the time. The news plunged him into turmoil. Suddenly there was new hope. But the letter did not say how badly wounded Gene was, and there was no way to get additional information while in Moscow. Germany had been divided into four occupation zones, and Gene was apparently in the British sector. For the next few weeks, Mark lived with uncertainty. Even before receiving the letter, he had decided to leave the Soviet Union. He had no wish to follow a military career in a Poland dominated by Stalin. His chance to escape arrived in November, when he was granted three weeks' leave. He headed straight for Poland. In early December he reached Nowy Sącz, his hometown, for the first time since 1939.

Hardly anyone Mark had known before the war was still alive. Nearly all the town's Jews had been killed; the only survivors were those like Mark and Gene who had escaped early in the war. Now they were returning in ones and twos, searching vainly for their loved ones. A Jewish committee had been established to try to answer their questions, although there were few answers.

The Nazis had subjected the Jews of Nowy Sącz to three years of cruel suffering and humiliation before exterminating them. First, they were expelled from their homes and packed into a tight, overcrowded ghetto, where many died in a series of epidemics. Thousands of Jews from surrounding towns and villages were rounded up and crammed into the same small area. There was hardly any food, and people slowly starved to death. Mark learned that Nunek was killed some time in late 1941 or early 1942 trying to smuggle food into the ghetto. According to a cousin who was there at the time, Nunek had managed to sneak in and out of the ghetto several times before he was caught. The cousin had warned Nunek repeatedly that his actions were too risky. But Nunek refused to listen. He was determined to get food for his family. One night a Nazi patrol arrested him. They took him to the Jewish cemetery and shot him. He was sixteen.

Life after that must have been hell for their parents. In the offices of the Jewish committee, Mark found a photograph of Bertha, apparently taken for an identification document. She stares blankly at the camera, her face old and martyred, scarcely recognizable as the beautiful and vital woman he kept in his memory. The end came in the summer of 1942. On August 23, about 12,000 Nowy Sącz Jews and thousands of refugees driven by the Nazis into the town from elsewhere were ordered to assemble near the railroad station. Townspeople gathered to watch, jeering and shouting insults. While they were waiting, the Nazis collected 250,000 złotys from the Jews, which they said was to cover transportation costs. The Jews were told they were being taken to the Ukraine, where they would be employed in agriculture. It is unlikely that many believed it; they must have known that they were doomed. The Nazis registered their names and selected about 800 young people for hard labor. The rest were hustled into a small, enclosed area, where they waited without food or water for 48 hours. With many people forced to stay outside in the streets, the Nazis amused themselves by occasionally firing into the crowd. Finally, the Jews were loaded on to trains and taken to the extermination camp of Bełżec in eastern Poland.

While he was in Nowy Sącz, Mark visited his old home. No trace remained of his family, but the man living there gave him a letter that had arrived from Henek several months before. It came from Tekele, in Soviet Kazakhstan. Dated March 4, 1945, the letter was the first confirmation that Henek had survived the war:

> Sir, I don't know if you received my earlier postcards. I wrote soon after the liberation of Nowy Sącz but have received no reply. I am terribly worried about the fate of my family. Can you imagine what I have gone through in exile, not knowing what happened to my loved ones? And so, I implore you to let me know as soon as possible their fate. I count the days for an answer.

The man had not bothered to reply. It was left to Mark to contact Henek with the news that his entire family had perished.

Mark's next task was to locate Gene. A friend told him that a former member of their Zionist youth group, Rezie Dreskin, had spent the entire war in London and might be able to help if Gene was indeed in a British hospital. Mark wrote her, asking her to check with the Red Cross and the British military whether Gene was still alive. Meantime, Mark's leave was nearly up and he had to decide what to do next. Poland held nothing but bitter memories. The townspeople, he could never forget, jeered and shouted insults at their Jewish neighbors in their hour of despair. He would head for the West and hope to build a better future there.

Some of his prewar classmates had gone into business smuggling goods and people to Czechoslovakia, and they agreed to take him across the frontier. On a December night, Mark left the country of his birth, never to return. He reached Germany by mid-December 1945 and headed for Munich in the American occupation zone. There, the news he had been waiting for arrived. Rezie Dreskin wrote:

> I managed to track down Gene within three days of receiving your letter and I sent his address to you by telegram. What a pity you never received it and are still worried about Gene. He feels quite well but as you correctly guess he was very badly wounded. He was hit by six bullets in his left leg and right arm. He must have suffered a lot but now he is quite comfortable. Yesterday I met a nurse from the hospital in Bad Rehrburg who is here on leave. She assured me he is feeling much better and is a favorite of the staff. Gene writes that soon he will be transferred, possibly to Britain to have his right arm operated on, but that's nothing compared to what he went through. One of the bullets grazed the back of his head. He is really happy to be alive.

Within days, a letter arrived from Gene himself:

> My Dearest Brother, I received from Rezie sensational news that you are in Munich though I can't understand how you got to Germany. In the time since the fatal day, a lot has changed. What happened was what we feared most—to be badly wounded. It was difficult to accept that it could have happened, so when I got the news that you at least got through in one piece I went quite crazy with joy. To bring you up to date, I was shot up by automatic fire from close range. The bullets were nearly fatal, but not too difficult to extract afterward. I was hit mainly in my right hand, shoulder, and left leg. The leg is back to normal (only one more little operation). I am walking with only a slight limp. The arm needs a complicated operation to implant an artificial joint that can be done only in a major hospital to which I will shortly be transferred. At the moment, I am working as a translator between the Poles, the Germans, and the English.

As soon as he received this news, Mark set off by train across Germany for

Gene's hospital. The journey took almost 24 hours. But when he arrived, Gene was not there. He had been evacuated to England the day before. It was another fifteen years before the brothers were reunited.

After he was taken from the hospital in Stettin in mid-February 1945, Gene had spent the final weeks of the war in a prisoner-of-war camp near Hamburg. It was called Sandbostel and housed about 20,000 prisoners—British, American, French, Italian, Polish, and others. Gene felt an enormous sense of relief to be among so many captives whom the Germans would not easily dare to mistreat and abuse. The doctors in the camp hospital were fellow prisoners rather than Germans. He was still in pain and could not move. A few days after his arrival, a Serbian surgeon performed the first of many operations, extracting a bullet from his neck that had lodged close to his spinal cord. The available anesthetic had lasted for only half of the surgery and Gene had to be held down by three men while the surgeon finished the operation. Later, the same surgeon removed splinters of bone from his arm and shoulder and sterilized the infected wounds. After that, the pain slowly receded. But his right arm still hung disabled and useless. His leg, too, would have to wait until after the war for proper treatment.

Life in the camp revolved around food and war news from at least two secret radio receivers. When news of President Franklin Roosevelt's death came, prisoners of every nationality assembled in the square in a spontaneous show of mourning. One day the prisoners received their first Red Cross parcels and Gene spent a sleepless night after drinking real coffee for the first time in many years. The Germans treated the Allied prisoners correctly, but the Russian prisoners were classified as sub humans. Isolated from the rest in a barbed wire enclosed compound, they were being deliberately starved to death. Gene heard them at night howling for food. He knew what real hunger was and their cries touched him deeply. There was nothing the other prisoners could do to help their suffering. To the last, the Nazis prevented anybody from throwing them a scrap of bread.

After a while, Gene was transferred to barracks for Polish officers. They were mostly veterans of the Warsaw uprising with a sprinkling of officers from the Anders Army. He was well regarded by the other prisoners until the day the orderlies took him to a shower and discovered he was a circumcised Jew. After that attitudes changed dramatically. Men who had come to Gene's bedside every day to talk to him and play cards stopped visiting. After all the Polish people had seen and suffered, it seemed they still hated the Jews. Gene made up his mind then and there to have nothing to do with Poland in the future. Whatever happened, he would not return to that benighted land with its hate-ridden people. So, lying in his bed, alone and without friends, Gene waited for liberation. When it came, it was almost anticlimactic. One day, a company of British soldiers arrived and took over the camp without firing a shot. Gene's war was over.

Peace came to Europe soon after that and the prisoners began to disperse. Gene was transferred for further treatment to a British military hospital in Bad Rehrburg, a small town near Hannover. The hospital became his home for several months. After a few weeks Gene was no longer bedridden. He picked up enough English to make himself useful as a translator between the British medical staff, German employees and tradesmen, and the British and Polish patients.

Now, when he was no longer in danger, Gene began to suffer frequent nightmares. He was visited nightly by familiar and unknown ghosts and demons. It would be many years before he could free himself of their presence. Nowadays, doctors would have diagnosed his condition as post-traumatic stress disorder. Then, the term did not even exist. Gene just had to struggle through the best he could.

In April 1946, Gene was transferred to a military hospital in the English city of Worcester, where he spent almost a year undergoing treatment. Gene was drawn to England from the first moment he saw its green fields from his aircraft window. It was a landscape that seemed to promise much-needed calm and tranquility. He found comfort and affinity in English moderation and tolerance, and learned to love its placid countryside. He felt a gratitude to England that he never lost.

It is difficult for me to imagine what it must have been like for Gene arriving in Britain in 1946. He was alone, penniless, semi-disabled, and spoke imperfect English. Initially, he applied to the University of London to finish his degree in chemistry. But the university was flooded with servicemen released from the army, and the only faculty that would accept him was the School of Slavonic

Studies. When Gene ran out of money he had to leave the university and find a job. To his eternal regret, he was never able to complete his studies.

He went into business, initially as an optical lens maker, eventually founding and managing a firm of ophthalmic opticians. He met my mother, Helen Farber, in 1950, and they married two years later. I was born in 1954 and my sister Gillian in 1955. My father is a strong and stubborn man. It was obvious that he found his job boring and unfulfilling, but he never complained. His war wounds occasionally caused him pain, but he never complained about them either. I do not remember him ever taking time off work, even when he was sick. He was an undemonstrative man, emotionally and physically. He clearly adored my mother and loved his children, but I cannot remember him ever telling us so. He emanated a sense of determination. He did not think of himself, and I never thought of him, as a Holocaust survivor. That was a label for the emotionally traumatized, those who had lived through Nazi concentration camps. My father did not view himself as a victim. He rarely spoke about the war. Growing up, I had only a vague idea of what he had endured.

After the war, Mark became an architect. He stayed in Munich for several years. There he met his wife Ela, a Polish Jew who survived Auschwitz. They had two daughters. In the early 1950s the family emigrated to Israel. Finally, in 1961, Mark and his family came to London, and the brothers were reunited.

What of Henek? We left him Krasnavodsk, sick with typhoid. He had his own dramatic story of survival. He was discharged from the hospital after three weeks, weighing barely 70 pounds, so weak he could hardly stand. Alone, scared, confused, and almost penniless, he had no idea what to do. He could not stay in Krasnavodsk, so he took a train back in the direction of Bukhara, thinking that Gene and Mark might have written to their Polish acquaintances there and he would be able to trace them. On the way, he fell ill again, and the train guard unceremoniously dumped him on the platform at a nondescript place called Kizyl-Arvat, in the middle of the Turkmen Republic.

Henek might have died there, but a Polish woman and her daughter happened to be at the station and took pity on him. They brought him to their home and nursed him back to health. They worked on a state farm, and after Henek recovered he began working there, too, as a night watchman. After four months, having saved enough money to pay his debts to the Polish woman and buy train tickets, he left. He headed north, where he knew there were large concentrations of Polish ex-prisoners and deportees. Henek ended up in Tekele, about 180 miles north of Alma Ata in Kazakhstan. There he found a small community of Poles and started working in a brick factory. His open manner and charm soon made him popular among his co-workers, and they elected him as their representative. He also became a potter, making plates and other bric-a-brac, which were soon in great demand, especially among the wives of Communist party officials and NKVD officers. Thus, he lived out the war.

In Tekele, Henek met and married Irena, who had been deported from Poland to the Soviet Union when she was only 16. After the war they moved back to Poland, where they had two children, a boy and a girl. Tragically, Irena died of leukemia at an early age. In 1956, Henek left Poland for the last time and arrived in Israel with his two small children. On the day he turned up at Mark's house, Mark was in the Israeli army. He had been called up as a reservist during the 1956 Sinai campaign. Fortunately, the war was over quickly and Mark was released after a few weeks. Mark and Henek's families grew up side-by-side and Henek eventually remarried to a wonderful woman called Mira.

Henek and Gene were not reunited until 1978, 28 years after they parted in Krasnavodsk. They spent hours that day talking, going over their experiences. Henek never complained to either Mark or Gene about their decision to leave him. Sadly, Henek died of a heart attack in 1991.

In 1986, Mark retired. He and Gene bought land in the town of Zichron Ya'acov in the foothills of Galilee overlooking the Mediterranean. Mark designed two houses, one for him and one for Gene. There the brothers live today, still side by side.

EPILOGUE

Two Bunches of Flowers

L ooking back, I am amazed how incurious I was about my father's childhood
and his family. I knew little about my father's adventures and how he had
been wounded. I remember as a small boy being both fascinated and
repelled by the huge pits gouged out of his leg and shoulder by the bullets. On
rare occasions he would tell stories about his hometown, but they were sunny
tales about swimming in the river and walking in the hills.

Of his parents, my father spoke so little that to me they were abstract figures
inhabiting an abstract world. I knew they had died in the Holocaust, but I did
not know how or when or where. Nor did I miss their presence. How can you
miss people when there is no tangible evidence that they ever existed? There
were no pictures of them around the house, no possessions that they had passed
on, no graves to visit, no anniversaries to mark. I knew my grandfather's name
was Adolf, just like Hitler, and that I was named for him. For some reason I
found this very funny. "They wanted to call me Adolf but the name had gone
out of fashion among Jews," I would tell people. I did not know my
grandmother's name.

Later, I was too busy growing up, going to college, establishing myself in my
career, to be bothered with the dead and distant past. That was, I now believe,
how my father wanted it to be. Then came the years of getting married and
having my own children. It was only in the summer of 1992, when my father and
I were on vacation together, that he opened up. In his mid-seventies,

comfortably retired, he suddenly felt a need to speak. Stories poured out, wartime adventures that I had never heard before, stories of childhood, stories of his parents. There emerged a picture of a past I had not imagined existed. I decided we ought to travel together to Russia and Poland to try to revisit some of the places he had passed through during the war. That is how this book was born.

So in the summer of 1993 we found ourselves meeting in the Frankfurt airport concourse and boarding a plane for St. Petersburg. It was not feasible to re-create the entire journey, which would have taken us through several newly independent republics and areas of unrest. But we hoped we would be able to at least see the region of the labor camps in Karelia and the Cossack village of Nezlobnaya.

In Karelia, we discovered that little remains of the gulag. We did locate the transit prison in Medvezh'yegorsk where the boys were held for a few days before being sent off to the camps. It was still a prison, with machine-gun nests at the corners of the compound. When we attempted to take photographs, uniformed men quickly came out of the prison and warned us not to. There are no playful bear cubs outside the houses, although there are still bears roaming the surrounding forests, we were told.

As for the camps themselves, they were dismantled in the 1970s and left to decay. Once the authorities decided to close a camp, they removed the incriminating evidence and anything of value. Local residents quickly scavenged the rest. While we were in the area, the local newspaper, *Severny Kourier* (The Northern Courier) reported that the remains of one camp had been found deep in the forest. "A month ago, *Severny Kourier* told readers that in the area of the White Sea—Baltic Canal, by a miracle a preserved camp from the era of Stalinist repression was found. Within days, an expedition arrived there to preserve all available remains for museums," the newspaper reported. The expedition flew in by seaplane but was unable to land at the site because of the thick covering of birch trees. But they eventually managed to land on the shore of a nearby lake and fight their way through the vegetation to the site, where decaying watchtowers and a few wooden structures still stood. "In a few years," the reporter noted, "there will be no trace left." The team collected a few items and brought them back to Medvezh'yegorsk, where residents were trying to create a small museum display. But, the reporter wrote, "There most probably will not be any money available to mount the exhibits."

At the time of our return, many who survived the Soviet labor camps and other eyewitnesses were still too frightened to speak out. In the village of Povenietz, where the White Sea canal flows into Lake Onega, we met Fedosia Ivanova, a feisty women in her seventies who was an active Communist party official during the Stalinist period. She had visited the Volozero camp and was able to provide many details that confirmed Gene's and Mark's recollections. "Thousands of prisoners died," she told us. "We all knew about it but we kept quiet. For years I was eating the dirty bread of the Party, and I knew it wasn't right, even though at Party meetings they said it was for the good of the Motherland." She had begun trying to draw attention to the period, writing regular letters to newspapers about her recollections, but none of them were interested in publishing her work. Ivanova directed us to some nearby mass graves, which she said held the remains of prisoners who died while working on the White Sea canal. Brushing aside swarms of mosquitoes, we stumbled through the thick forest looking for them. Eventually a farmer led us to a long row of unmarked mounds. He thought they contained the bodies of German prisoners of war who were sent there after the battle of Stalingrad to repair war damage to the canal. No one will ever know the names of those buried or what happened to them. How many bodies were buried in each mound? The farmer did not know.

In the Caucasus, my father and I stayed with an Armenian family in Georgievsk. The town had grown, but some things were still much the same. The railroad station, where the Germans dumped the bodies of people they executed, had not changed. The old Gestapo headquarters in the town center remained, although it was scheduled for demolition. But the once sleepy village of Nezlobnaya had changed beyond recognition. Its population had grown to 12,000, many of whom lived in ugly, Soviet-style apartment blocks on the outskirts of the village. However, the flourmill remained largely unchanged. The little cottage where Gene and Mark lived, its red roof almost overgrown by vegetation, was one of the few original dwellings that still stood. No one lived there. Thick bushes obscured the view from the window where Gene first spied Galia's shapely legs. But we could still see the slope Gene and Mark used to escape from the Germans.

Gene found his visit to Nezlobnaya depressing. Much of its beauty had been destroyed. Trucks rumbled incessantly down the main road belching exhaust fumes. No one in the village remembered Gene. Andrei Sonim, his old neighbor, had died several years before. We asked about Galia and her mother, but nobody remembered them. Our spirits only recovered when we drove out of the village into the steppe. It was a clear morning. There in the distance, soaring above us with almost unbelievable clarity, were the twin peaks of Mount Elbrus. Gleaming white and magnificent, towering over the green plain, it was a heart-stopping sight.

We spoke to one old woman, Tatiana Ivanova Tarentsova, who told of hiding a Jewish family in her kitchen when the Germans arrived. Someone denounced them. The family was taken away and all were shot, except one son who somehow survived. Several years later, he returned to the village, searching vainly for the rest of his family. Tatiana clearly remembered the police chief who collaborated with the Germans. His name was Nikolai Kalamitsov, she said.

Nezlobnaya's Cossacks have retained their pride, although little survives of traditional Cossack life. Tatiana's son told us, "When a Cossack takes a job in a factory, he ceases to be a Cossack. He loses his voice and becomes a shadow of a Cossack. That's what most of us have been reduced to." As we were on the way out of the house he took us aside. "The Germans treated us very well when they were here, and don't let anyone tell you different," he whispered. We offered him some money for his troubles but he refused to accept it, impatiently pushing our hands aside.

From Russia we flew to Poland. Gene was visibly moved as we drove through the hills around Nowy Sącz. The scenery was splendid, the hills lined with tall haystacks just as he remembered. But the town itself was upsetting. There were no Jews in Nowy Sącz and few signs of their former presence. Jews had lived there since the fourteenth century, but they were not missed. The old Jewish quarter had been completely demolished and replaced by soulless apartment blocks. The town's main synagogue was the only building in the quarter to have survived. It served as a gallery of landscape paintings. A tiny sign noted that the building was a former synagogue, but all Jewish symbols had been removed.

My father's old house still stood. Seeing it brought a flood of memories. Gene posed enthusiastically for pictures and rushed around excitedly to view the building from different angles. "On this side there used to be an orchard and here there were open fields," he said, pointing to some crumbling apartments. We also visited his old school, saw the river where he swam, and stopped at the homes of various friends killed in the Holocaust. I found the experience intensely unsettling. My father described life in the now-dingy building where he had grown up, but I felt a strong desire to leave. I found it deeply disturbing to be surrounded by ghosts of people who had once lived there and now were no more.

From Nowy Sącz we followed the route Gene had taken on Nunek's bicycle when he traveled to Lwów. We passed Jasło and eventually reached Sanok, where we found the bridge Gene crossed to enter the Soviet zone. We paced out the distance across it. On the other side of the bridge was an open-air museum with old wooden buildings and churches collected from various villages in the area.

Our final stop was Bełżec, the death camp where my grandparents were murdered. Before setting out that morning, I bought two bunches of flowers from a gypsy woman in Przemyśl. We drove north on an empty road, occasionally overtaking farmers driving horses and carts, rarely seeing other cars. As we drew closer to Bełżec, the cornfields began giving way to thick forests. Our conversation turned to generalities—we both seemed to be avoiding the subject that had brought us on this part of the journey. When we reached Bełżec, a relatively small town, we looked for a sign pointing the way to the death site. There was none. We stopped a local man, and my father asked him in Polish where the museum was. He shook his head. "Then where is the memorial?" my father persisted. The man shrugged blankly. He was an elderly man, and it crossed my mind that he could well have been there when the daily transports of Jews were arriving. "The place they killed the Jews?" my father finally asked.

Comprehension dawned on the man's face. "Go to the crossroads and turn right. It's two kilometers down, next to the railway line," he said. As we turned, we saw a rusty sign, half-hidden by trees, next to a larger sign advertising agricultural vehicles. There was no parking lot. We pulled up next to the gate, outside a private house from which pop music was blaring on the radio. A kid was puttering around in the backyard. We were the only visitors. Small signs in

English and Polish said a monument to commemorate Jewish children killed in Poland from 1939 to 1945 would be built on the site and gave a bank account number for contributions. As we got out of the car, a woman came out of the house to talk to us. "It's not true that they killed children here," she told us. "They just put up that sign to get people to give money." So—a Holocaust denier who lived by the gate of an extermination camp! But when she saw the flowers in our hands, she went into the house and brought back two vases filled with water.

In researching this book, I began reading about Bełżec, a place I had previously known nothing about. Suddenly it became important to find out more about where my grandparents had died and to learn more about how they died. No longer did I think of them as two blank statistics among the six million. Many of the Holocaust sites in Poland were neglected and decaying, but Bełżec was in a worse state than most. Everything about the town and the campsite was dirty, dingy, dilapidated. The area was silent, isolated, and wild. There was little evidence that anyone cared for it. Even to call Bełżec a camp was a misnomer; it was a death factory for Jews, pure and simple.

I discovered that Bełżec had a prominent place in the catalog of evil. It was the first purpose-built death camp, the first place where gas chambers were erected. They were installed in the winter of 1941-42, and the camp received its first shipment of Jews on March 17, 1942. Within several weeks, it was handling thousands of victims a day.

Although reports of Auschwitz-Birkenau have given us the impression of the efficiency of the Nazi extermination effort, Bełżec was chaotic, ill planned, and messy. Like the other camps, it was also almost unbelievably sadistic. The few eyewitness accounts available describe the frenzy that prevailed with the arrival of several thousand people a day to die in its primitive carbon monoxide chambers. The camp was operated by Ukrainian guards working under German supervision. This place was erected solely for the purpose of killing Jews. With a handful of exceptions, all those who died were Jews—500,000 of them in less than a year. The major Jewish communities of Lublin and Lwów were destroyed in Bełżec, as were those from scores of smaller towns and villages in Galicia— six centuries of learning and scholarship extinguished in less than a year!

On the day we visited, a powerful aura of evil hung over Bełżec, a sense of the forgotten and unhonored dead. A block of granite near the entrance, engraved in Polish, noted that 600,000 Jews and 1,500 Poles who helped Jews died horrible deaths here. I placed one bunch of flowers there. A few meters behind was another memorial, a statue of an emaciated figure supporting another skeletal figure. The Polish inscription here read: "In memory of the victims of Hitler's terror murdered from 1942 to 1943." Here I placed the second bunch.

All the monuments were decaying, crumbling away. The overwhelming effect was of neglect. There was not a single Jewish emblem—not a Hebrew word, not a Star of David—although there was a small statuette of the Virgin Mary among the trees. The whole area was overgrown with weeds and there were remains of campfires, as if people came here to picnic. I saw two women with shopping bags taking a shortcut home through the site.

For my father, the experience was clearly overwhelming. As soon as we entered he was overcome with great, shuddering sobs that went on and on. For the first time I saw my father cry. "My mother, my poor dear mother," he kept saying. He moved around the site, stopping to lean against the trees and cry. "Those poor, poor people, they must have been so terrified," he sobbed. "My God, how they must have suffered."

I had never seen my father cry and I did not quite know how to react. At first I left him alone. Then, I went up to him and hugged him. He leaned heavily on me and I felt his body shuddering with a grief I could scarcely comprehend. Trembling myself, I told my father that I loved him. "I love you too," he told me. We stood there, locked together for a few more minutes. Then, I slowly led him away. At the gate, the woman in the house asked for a tip for lending us the vases.

Later, Gene thanked me for bringing him there. He said he had never cried for his parents and that it had been a tremendous emotional relief for him to visit their graveside, horrible as the place was. But there was no such release for me. What I felt was anger. Finally I had a sense of my grandparents as people. They were real. They were not phantoms. And their deaths were real. Their last years must have been full of horror and humiliation, but their final days and hours, I now realized, had been more cruel than hell itself. It was their human right to grow old and know their grandchildren, bring them birthday presents, tell them stories, spoil them outrageously. Instead, they died because they were Jews.

When I returned home, I began writing articles about what I had seen at Bełżec. There was an immediate response. I received letters from people all over the United States, from Canada, from South Africa, and a telephone call from Australia. These were the children and grandchildren of victims of Bełżec, demanding that their loved ones be commemorated with respect. Jewish institutions also responded and slowly a plan was formed to build a new memorial. Over the next few years, the dream began to take shape. With the hard and patient work of many people in the United States and Poland, the new memorial was constructed.

In June 2004, the new memorial was inaugurated. The President of Poland and much of the Polish government were there. The U.S. ambassador and the ambassadors of Germany, Austria and Israel were there. An honor guard from the Israel Defense Forces also attended. The Pope sent a message, so did President Bush. Thousands of local people waited patiently to tour the brand new museum that had been erected. One of the first images they saw as the entered was a large photograph of my grandfather, Adolf Elsner. My wife and I were also there, sitting alongside my mother and father. Truly, it was a closing of the circle.

I hope my father's life and that of my uncle and of Henek will inspire future generations of our family and many others as well. Its message is clear: that with courage, determination, an indomitable spirit, and a love of life and of each other, we can win against even the most fearsome odds. Hitler is gone, Stalin is no more, but we are still here!

A NOTE ON SOURCES

This book was based first and foremost on many hours of taped interviews with my father and uncle. Sometimes I would meet with them individually, sometimes together. Most of the time, their accounts were remarkably similar, although sometimes they had varying perspectives or differed on slight particulars. When there were discrepancies, I sometimes consulted other sources to try to resolve them. Often, when one of them remembered something, it would jog the memory of the other and he would come up with new details. Seeing them re-create the days of their youth together was a real privilege. The wealth and depth of their memories astounded me. More than fifty years later, their experiences were still indelibly printed in their minds. They remembered dates, names, places, conversations, descriptions, what they were wearing, what they ate, what they felt, thought, and said.

All the incidents recounted in this book really happened. None are invented. But occasionally, the brothers could not recall the names of some of the people with whom they interacted. When this happened, for example in the case of the port official who played chess with my father in chapter 12, I have invented names.

In Poland, my father was known as Genek and my uncle as Mundek. I have anglicized their names for an English-reading audience and also to avoid the confusion of dealing with three leading characters called Genek, Henek, and Mundek.

Obviously, it is impossible exactly to re-create dialogue so long after the fact. I have tried to reconstruct conversations based on the brothers' general recollections of what was said, but I do not pretend to have recaptured the exact words used. Still, I have tried hard to be true to the spirit.

I was also helped by a surprising wealth of written material, primarily letters, which survived the war. Additionally, I interviewed my father's first girlfriend, Nusia Chanales, and a cousin, Isaac Dorenter, who were able to shed additional light on the story. Both have since died.

To help add historical context to the book, I consulted other memoirs, historical texts, and documents, some of which are listed in the bibliography. The memorial books of the Jewish communities of Nowy Sącz and Jasło in the Library of Congress, written in Yiddish and Hebrew, were invaluable. Books written by gulag survivors were also helpful in confirming details about camp life.

Finally, my trip with my father to Russia and Poland allowed me to see some of the places he passed through with my own eyes.

I have to thank many people for this book. The support of my family has been tremendous. My father has been the most thorough and meticulous editor any writer could wish for. I wish to acknowledge Menachem Rosensaft for his support and help. Finally, my most heartfelt thanks go to my wife, Shulamit, who makes every day a new adventure.

BIBLIOGRAPHY

Anders, Wladislaw. *An Army in Exile*. London: MacMillan and Co., 1949.

Begin, Menachem. *White Nights*. New York: Harper Row, 1957.

Clark, Alan. *Barbarossa: The Russian-German Conflict*. New York: Quill, 1965.

Craig, William. *Enemy at the Gates: The Battle for Stalingrad*. New York: E.P. Dutton and Co., 1973.

Conquest, Robert. *The Great Terror*. Oxford: Oxford University Press, 1990.

Farson, Negley. *Caucasian Journey*. London: Penguin Books, 1988.

Feig, Konnilyn G. *Hitler's Death Camps*. New York: Holmes & Meier, 1981.

Garlinski, Jozef. *Poland in the Second World War*. New York: Hipprocrene Books, 1985.

Gilbert, Martin. *The Second World War*. New York: Henry Holt and Co., 1989.

Herling, Gustav. *A World Apart*. New York: Arbor House, 1986.

Hertzig, Ya'acov. *Nidodai B'milchama v'Jaslo Iri (My Wanderings during the War and My City Jasło*, Hebrew). Tel Aviv: Ha-Menorah, 1964.

Karol, K.S. *Between Two Worlds*. New York: Henry Holt and Co., 1983.

Longworth, Philip. *The Cossacks*. New York: Holt, Rinehart, and Winston, 1970.

Lucas, Richard C. *Forgotten Holocaust: The Poles Under German Occupation*. Lexington: University Press of Kentucky, 1986.

Maclean, Fitzroy. *Eastern Approaches*. New York: Time-Life Books, 1950.

Mahler, Raphael ed., *Sefer Sanz* (in Hebrew and Yiddish). New York: [n.p.], 1970.

Marshall, Robert. *In the Sewers of Lwów*. New York: Charles Scribner's Sons, 1991.

Paul, Allen. *Katyn: The Untold Story of Stalin's Polish Massacre*. New York: Charles Scribner's Sons, 1991.

Rawivz, Slavomir. *The Long Walk*. London: Harper and Brothers, 1956.

Rossi, Jacques. *The Gulag Handbook*. New York: Paragon House, 1989.

Read, Anthony, and David Fisher. *The Deadly Embrace: Hitler, Stalin and the Nazi-Soviet Pact of 1939–41*. New York: W.W. Norton and Co., 1988.

Rywkin, Michael. *Russia in Central Asia*. New York: Collier Books, 1963.

Solzhenitsyn, Alexandr. *The Gulag Archipelago*. New York: Harper Perennial, 2002.

Tolstoy, Leo. *The Cossacks*. New York: Everyman's Library, 1994.

Werth, Alexander. *Russia at War, 1941–45*. New York: E.P. Dutton and Co., 1964.

Wittlin, Tadeusz. *A Reluctant Traveler in Russia*. New York: Rinehart and Company Inc., 1952.